Lisa Ruby Basara, RPh, MBA
Michael Montagne, RPh, PhD

Searching for Magic Bullets: Orphan Drugs, Consumer Activism, and Pharmaceutical Development

Pre-publication
REVIEWS,
COMMENTARIES,
EVALUATIONS . . .

"**T**his book broadens one's knowledge of the avenues drugs take to become commercially available pharmaceuticals. By using a three-pronged approach–historical development of the U.S.A.'s drug approval process, orphan drugs as controversial consumer-demanded pharmaceuticals, and non-traditional channels of consumer influence on approval of pharmaceuticals–the consumer's role in drug development is articulated. AN ACCESSIBLE INTRODUCTION TO A COMPLEX SYSTEM."

Bernard Sorofman, RPh, PhD
Associate Professor, College of Pharmacy, University of Iowa

Searching
for Magic Bullets
Orphan Drugs, Consumer Activism, and Pharmaceutical Development

PHARMACEUTICAL PRODUCTS PRESS
Pharmaceutical Sciences
Mickey C. Smith, PhD
Executive Editor

New, Recent, and Forthcoming Titles:

Principles of Pharmaceutical Marketing edited by Mickey C. Smith

Pharmacy Ethics edited by Mickey C. Smith, Steven Strauss, John Baldwin, and Kelly T. Alberts

Drug-Related Problems in Geriatric Nursing Home Patients by James W. Cooper

Pharmacy and the U.S. Health Care System edited by Jack E. Fincham and Albert I. Wertheimer

Pharmaceutical Marketing: Strategy and Cases by Mickey C. Smith

International Pharmaceutical Services: The Drug Industry and Pharmacy Practice in Twenty-Three Major Countries of the World edited by Richard N. Spivey, Albert I. Wertheimer, and T. Donald Rucker

A Social History of the Minor Tranquilizers: The Quest for Small Comfort in the Age of Anxiety by Mickey C. Smith

Marketing Pharmaceutical Services: Patron Loyalty, Satisfaction, and Preferences edited by Harry A. Smith and Stephen Joel Coons

Nicotine Replacement: A Critical Evaluation edited by Ovide F. Pomerleau and Cynthia S. Pomerleau

The Honest Herbal: A Sensible Guide to the Use of Herbs and Related Remedies, Third Edition by Varro E. Tyler

Herbs of Choice: The Therapeutic Use of Phytomedicinals by Varro E. Tyler

Searching for Magic Bullets: Orphan Drugs, Consumer Activism, and Pharmaceutical Development by Lisa Ruby Basara and Michael Montagne

Searching
for Magic Bullets
Orphan Drugs, Consumer Activism, and Pharmaceutical Development

Lisa Ruby Basara, RPh, MBA
Michael Montagne, RPh, PhD

Pharmaceutical Products Press
An Imprint of the Haworth Press, Inc.
New York • London • Norwood (Australia)

Published by

Pharmaceutical Products Press, an imprint of The Haworth Press, Inc., 10 Alice Street, Binghamton, NY 13904-1580

Library of Congress Cataloging-in-Publication Data

Basara, Lisa R.
    Searching for magic bullets : orphan drugs, consumer activism, and pharmaceutical development / Lisa R. Basara, Michael Montagne.
        p.   cm.
    Includes bibliographical references and index.
    ISBN 1-56024-859-9 (acid free paper).
    1. Orphan drugs–United States. 2. Pharmaceutical industry–United States. 3. Consumer protection–United States. I. Montagne, Michael. II. Title.
RM263.B37   1994
362.1′782–dc20   93-35534
                                                                                                            CIP

Dedicated to our parents
John and Bernice Ruby
and
Roland and Margaret Montagne
with love

ABOUT THE AUTHORS

Lisa R. Basara, PhD (cand.), RPh, MBA, is Research Assistant in the Department of Pharmacy Administration at the University of Mississippi. Her research and publications have concentrated on the evaluation of consumer-oriented marketing strategies, such as the direct advertising of prescription drugs, and the impact of such practices on both the pharmaceutical industry and the patient. She is also interested in patients' roles in health care decision making and their ability to influence and improve overall quality of life. Through her involvement with the Office of Professional Programs, Ms. Basara has developed, implemented, and evaluated a number of educational initiatives for health care professionals, including pharmacists, nurses, physicians, and patients, using both traditional and innovative methods. She is a member of the American Pharmaceutical Association and the American Marketing Association.

Michael Montagne, RPh, PhD, is Associate Professor at Massachusetts College of Pharmacy. His research efforts have focused on the social, cultural, and historical aspects of drug use, the pharmacoepidemiology of drug use problems, images of drugs and drug use in mass media, the occurrence of drug epidemics in society, and the development and testing of drug education programming. Dr. Montagne's teaching activities include the social and behavioral considerations of medical and non-medical drug-taking behaviors. He has published extensively on drug development and drug use, the occurrence of drug use problems, and consumer involvement in health care. Dr. Montagne belongs to several professional associations, including the American Association of Colleges of Pharmacy, the American Public Health Association, and the Federation International Pharmaceutique.

CONTENTS

Foreword

Today, more than any time in history, we have a health-care system that is complex and costly. As we make progress in controlling health problems, new diseases appear that challenge us to discover new ways to control them. With each change, innovation, or total transformation in the process comes an array of new problems, issues, and concerns. Our sophisticated scientific processes, despite these challenges, are flexible enough to find new ways to make progress. An understanding of the history of drug discovery helps us appreciate the progress that has been made in a relatively short time. Most everything that we know about drug discovery has happened in the past few decades.

A scientist can spend a lifetime in a laboratory without experiencing the joy of the discovery of a potentially useful drug. The development process is a long, but necessary, one to ensure that a new medication is both safe and effective in disease treatment. In the first five chapters of this book, the authors outline the steps of drug discovery and development in a clear fashion. Most readers will be surprised by the complexity of these processes, but will also realize why these steps are in place.

The evolving fusion of scientific knowledge and the desire to provide safe and effective drugs is key to affordable health care for society. While patients will continue to play an expanding role in health care, the effectiveness of this contribution will depend on the patient's understanding of the drug-development and approval processes. For example, the media introduces us to happenings involving medications every day. Unfortunately, with an insufficient understanding of drug discovery, development, and distribution, patients are unable to evaluate the importance of the issues being presented. The authors, through this book, present medication consumers with a tool that can help them become better decision makers.

How many times have you been introduced to a new drug and not really understood what it was all about? Why did it take ten years and millions of dollars to gain approval for use in treating your condition? The authors present answers to these questions and more. For the individual interested in more detail, suggested readings, reference notes, and an information directory are also included in the book.

Through the selection of orphan drugs as an example of the discovery and development process, the reader is introduced to rare diseases. The percentage of our population, including health-care professionals, who have more than just an awareness of rare diseases is extremely low. The Department of Health and Human Services has defined an orphan drug or product as one used to prevent or treat a rare disease or condition–usually a condition that affects less than 200,000 persons in the United States. A drug, device, food, or biologic agent–any product that is not widely researched or available due to limited commercial interest or that has a limited market because of the rarity of the disease–may qualify for "orphan" status.[1]

> Suppose you wish to purchase cans of tunafish packed in corn syrup, but all the tuna on the supermarket shelf is packed in water or vegetable oil. Suppose you are able to locate another hundred or so devotees who like their tuna packed in corn syrup and band together to form an association to contact tuna canners. The canners would inevitably respond by stating that the market for tuna in corn syrup is so small that there is no economic incentive to create such a product. Now, let's change the scenario slightly and assume that, due to some genetic metabolic abnormality, you require tuna in corn syrup to survive. This situation closely parallels the plight of the rare disease victim whose drug is not available because the product demand and profitability are too low to develop and manufacture the drug.[2]

The serious attention given to the search for orphan drugs is only about a decade old. Although the intent is to find effective drugs for the treatment of diseases affecting 200,000 persons or less, the understanding and treatment of common diseases have also improved. Biotechnology, which is used to discover more and more about the human body in the search for mechanisms to control both common and rare diseases, is one strategy used for drug development. However, biotechnology is faced with significant problems in protecting their products. Discoveries often cannot be protected through the use of patents or the exclusivity provisions of the Orphan Drug Act. This lack of security could have disastrous effects on the future discovery of new drugs that treat orphan diseases.

Perhaps the most important section of this book addresses the problems that affect outcomes of drug usage. You, the reader, need to fully understand the rewards and risks involved when you depart from the traditional health-care system. What do you do when there is no drug of proven value to treat your disease? What are the risks in using drugs from nontraditional sources? What is involved to participate in a clinical trial? What are the opportunities for deception? Should you use drugs for unapproved purposes? Millions of dollars are spent annually on such things as unproven drugs, smart drugs, and counterfeit drugs. Some involvements can be illegal and subject involved persons to criminal action. How about the friend or neighbor who has a drug that will improve your memory, treat your multiple sclerosis, prevent colds, etc.? This is the real world! The authors address and identify the alternatives. Many persons can benefit from the information provided.

This book is not to be read and laid aside. It is a reference to return to as we see changes in the health-care system.

Lawrence C. Weaver
Minneapolis, MN

NOTES

1. L.C. Weaver and T. Cooper, "The discovery and development of orphan drugs in the U.S.A.," *Journal of Social and Administrative Pharmacy* 6 (Number 3, 1989):160.

2. E.J. Remmers, "Rare diseases and orphan drugs," *ASCH News and Views* 6 (Number 5, 1985).

Preface

Consumers and consumer advocates are demanding changes in the traditional approach to drug development. Information resources, educational programs, and cooperative buying groups are just a few examples of the ways in which consumers are "getting around the system." Why is it that patients and their families are seeking their own drug supplies, organizing clinical drug trials, manufacturing and distributing drug products, and importing pharmaceuticals from outside the country? Activities like these, many of which are illegal, are evidence of a great deal of dissatisfaction, mistrust, and confusion regarding the health-care and drug-development systems in the United States.

Health consumers need to know much more about the discovery and development of medicines, while health-care professionals and students need to understand patients' medication needs and beliefs, including their reasons for considering alternative methods to develop and acquire drugs. The goal of this book is to inform consumers and both current and future health-care professionals about each other's views on drug use. To do this, we will explore the current drug-development process, its strengths and weaknesses, and the mechanisms by which individuals and organizations are evading this process. Specific examples will be provided for the reader to highlight AIDS medications and orphan drugs, as well as consumer importation of drugs from foreign countries.

This book is divided into three parts: the first five chapters explore drug development in the U.S.–what it is, how it has evolved, and what people consider right and wrong about it. A history of the drug-development process, the current concerns with this process, and the steps associated with drug development, approval, and marketing are some of the major topics in this section of the book.

Chapters 6 through 8 examine drug development in the context of a specific example: orphan drugs. The issues surrounding rare diseases and the drugs that are used to treat them provide a relevant case study. There are many benefits and obstacles when developing and marketing drugs for patients afflicted with rare diseases. Problems and potential solutions to orphan drug controversies are presented and evaluated in the final chapter of this series.

Topics such as prescription drug importation, underground drug evaluation and distribution, and consumer-directed buying groups, including those specifically organized for persons with AIDS, are described in Chapters 9 and 10. These risky and often illegal ways of evading the U.S. drug-development and marketing systems are presented to enhance readers' awareness and understanding of the dangers associated with these initiatives.

The final chapter summarizes safe and rational techniques that empower consumers in their search for beneficial drug therapies. The cornerstone of this approach is accessible, objective health-care and drug information. Resources and strategies for obtaining and using this information are provided as a reference for readers. Additionally, a glossary of terms, acronyms, and a directory of supplementary information sources are provided in the appendices of the book. All terms that are typed in **boldface** in the text are included in the glossary in Appendix A for easy reference.

Whether we believe that the current way of developing and marketing drugs is good or bad, a valid basis for this system does exist. At the same time, however, many significant problems remain. Patients often do not have access to the medications they need. The time lapse between drug discovery and marketing can be so long that those with fatal diseases might never benefit. Finally, medication costs are often prohibitively high. This book provides a springboard from which consumers, patients, physicians, nurses, pharmacists, and students can discuss, debate, evaluate, and resolve these issues.

ACKNOWLEDGEMENTS

Many people assisted us in the evolution of this publication. Lawrence Weaver of the University of Minnesota, with his expertise in the area of orphan drugs and related legislation, and Abbey Meyers, executive director of the National Organization for Rare Disorders, provided much of the background material for Chapters 6 and 7, as well as useful comments and suggestions as we developed this information.

Mickey Smith, John Juergens, and the faculty of the University of Mississippi's Department of Pharmacy Administration provided valuable suggestions on the basis of their health-care knowledge. Margaret, Roland, and Mary Montagne; Shirley Stallings; John and Bernice Ruby; and Scott Basara also read early drafts and enhanced the consumer perspective of the book. Stuart Nightingale of the Office of Health Affairs, provided valuable insight regarding the Food and Drug Administration. Maureen Crossmaker and the staff of the Ohio Legal Rights Services provided extensive comments and recommendations from their consumer-advocate perspective. In fact, a group seminar presented by one of us (MM) at their annual conference regarding patients' rights supplied the idea and impetus for this book. Sharon Brudnicki, then a student at the Philadelphia College of Pharmacy and Science, conducted much of the library research on the U.S. drug-development and approval systems, while the staff of the Office of Professional Programs of PCPS supported and facilitated our efforts through reviews and recommendations. We are grateful to all of our reviewers for their time, input, experience, and suggestions.

Finally, we would like to thank Bernice Ruby for thoroughly proofreading and indexing the book, and Joan Francy of Ad Med, Inc. for designing several of the complex figures.

Although we have incorporated our reviewers' ideas and advice, we remind the reader that any oversights or inaccuracies are our responsibility. Readers who have additional information, comments, or suggestions to improve this publication are invited to send them, as well as relevant anecdotes and experiences, to Lisa Basara at the University of Mississippi. We would like to thank you for your use of this book and wish you success with upcoming health-care challenges. May this book provide you with practical guidance and information to make intelligent health-care decisions.

Lisa R. Basara
Oxford, Mississippi

Michael Montagne
Whispering Oaks
Martha's Vineyard, Massachusetts

Chapter 1

History of Drug Discovery and the Pharmaceutical Industry in the United States

> People of the western world, especially Americans, have come
> to expect that all medical problems can and will be solved
> through the development of new pharmaceutical agents.[1]

Drug-discovery and development processes have changed dramatically over the past 200 years. The ways that we look for potentially useful substances, test those substances for therapeutic benefits, produce and market them, and appropriately prescribe and use them is completely different from that of our ancestors just a century ago. In this chapter we will look briefly at the various ways that drugs have been discovered, and how these different approaches have evolved into the current drug-development system.

Before the dawn of the twentieth century, substances that were found useful in healing came exclusively from nature: plants, animals, and from the earth itself. To determine whether the substances were effective, the "trial and error" method was used–the substances were simply used by any person willing to try them! As the twenty-first century draws near, new drugs are discovered in a very logical and scientific manner, usually with the assistance of powerful computers and analytical equipment. Potential therapeutic compounds are tested using an extremely structured medical research process to determine the drug's safety and effectiveness. Instead of distributing a drug to anyone willing to try it, a drug is tested in animals and healthy people. Then, if the drug seems to be safe, it is tested in patients with the disease for which it has been developed.

DISCOVERING MEDICINES: FROM CRUDE DRUGS TO COMPUTER-GENERATED MOLECULES

Over the past century there have been several different approaches to the discovery and development of drugs. New drugs were typically screened, or individually tested, for a desirable therapeutic benefit. Figures 1.1 and 1.2 show a scientist screening jungle plants and extracting active substances for testing. By the latter half of the twentieth century, the approach to drug discovery had changed completely. Drug compounds were, and continue to be, systematically manipulated or "fine-tuned."[1] These slight modifications in chemical structure can improve the safety and effectiveness of a drug. (Figure 1.3 demonstrates the use of a reflux distillation procedure to purify a chemical substance for testing.)

In the 1990s, the newest strategies for drug development and evaluation are biotechnology- and computer-assisted molecular modeling and genetic engineering. Molecular modeling techniques allow testing and refining of potentially beneficial substances *before* laboratory testing occurs. Using modeling, a molecule of known structure and with known beneficial activity is altered (or manipulated) to enhance its activity. Figure 1.4 shows how computer-generated molecules are designed and compares the computer image with traditional molecular structures.

The Beginnings of Scientific Drug Discovery

During the early part of the 1900s, there was a major shift in therapeutics–the way in which symptoms and diseases were treated with drugs. This was due primarily to the scientific discoveries of Louis Pasteur and Paul Ehrlich in the 1880s and 1890s. These two scientists were trying to find ways to cure people of infectious diseases by killing the *bacteria* causing the disease without killing the *patient* at the same time. In a 1906 speech Ehrlich said, "Substances able to exert their final action exclusively on the parasite harbored within the organism would represent ***magic bullets***, which seek their target of their own accord."[2] By 1910, the search for magic bullets to treat all types of diseases had begun.

At the beginning of the twentieth century, the American pharmaceutical industry was in the business of preparing different dosage

FIGURE 1.1. Screening Jungle Plants for Beneficial Drugs. Credit: Robert F. Raffauf collection, Ramu River, New Guinea, 1965

forms–such as tablets and elixirs–of traditional medicines and remedies for physicians, pharmacists, and dentists. By using or combining these substances, physicians and pharmacists discovered whether a particular drug had therapeutic value on the basis of experience with real patients. It was not until the 1930s that the

FIGURE 1.2. Extracting Active Substances from Plant Material. Credit: Robert F. Raffauf collection, photographed by Shirley Stallings

FIGURE 1.3. Synthesizing New Compounds in the Laboratory. Credit: Robert F. Raffauf collection, photographed by Shirley Stallings

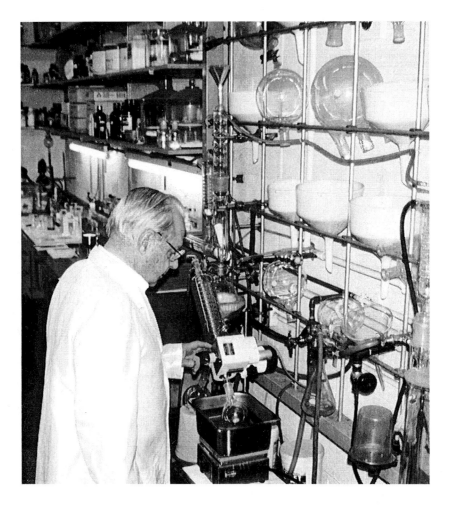

continuously expanding pharmaceutical industry became involved in drug discovery and development. The traditional approach of determining the medical uses and value of specific drugs through individual experience with patients was no longer considered adequate or safe. In addition, the drug industry was being called on to

FIGURE 1.4. Creating New Molecules Using a Computer. Credit: University of Mississippi, Research Institute for Pharmaceutical Sciences

provide something more than just an assurance of quality. The people who were discovering and developing new drug products were also the experts on how to use drugs in a safe and effective manner. This important knowledge needed to be transferred to health practitioners.

Today's Drug Discovery Process

The modern drug-development process discovers beneficial drug substances in a manner that is much different than 100 years ago (Table 1.1). A pharmaceutical scientist from the early 1900s would be very perplexed and amazed walking into today's pharmaceutical research laboratory. Not only has technology, in terms of analytical devices and equipment, been upgraded significantly, but laboratory personnel now demonstrate specialized skills and use innovative testing, evaluation, and documentation methods.

Modern drug developers use computers, molecules, genetic information, and sophisticated equipment to *create* new molecules for testing. Much of the guesswork now occurs and is verified long before a chemical molecule is synthesized. A chemical molecule that produces an effect that is not quite strong enough is altered to enhance its effectiveness and minimize adverse effects. This process of slightly altering the chemical structure of a molecule to make it "better" is called **molecular manipulation**.

Using high-powered computers, scientists modify drug molecules, changing one atom here or moving another atom there, to convert original (or parent) molecules into effective drug substances. With the results of basic chemical research, scientists can predict what might happen to a molecule and how it might act physically and chemically when changed in a certain way. This new "theoretical" substance is then tested to determine if it matches the predictions.

The discovery of DNA, the genetic code, and the ensuing genetic research using plants and animals has opened new doors in the search for drugs. Genetic engineering allows scientists to design molecules and then obtain an organism (like certain "friendly" bacteria) or an animal (hamsters, for example) to produce that molecule as part of their regular function of living. Yeast cells now are making certain drugs along with the other products of their metabolism. Biological cultures and cell and tissue samples that survive and grow in the laboratory are being used to produce a variety of substances. It might seem strange, but we now have bacterial cultures that act as miniature drug factories. There is no limit to what can be done with this approach.

TABLE 1.1. Major Events in the History of Drug Discovery and Development

2000 BC	Sumerian clay tablet from Babylon provided earliest existing record of pharmaceutical products (at University of Pennsylvania museum).
1500 BC	Papyrus Ebers of Egypt detailed earliest existing record of pharmaceutical recipes.
460-380 BC	Hippocrates, a Greek physician, founded early medical school based on a naturalistic approach.
50-65 AD	Dioscorides, a Greek physician, developed materia medica, a dictionary of drugs from plant sources.
130-201 AD	Galen, a Greek physician, founded therapeutics and treated disease with chemical (natural) substances.
980-1037 AD	Avicenna, an Arabic physician, developed methods for testing chemical substances for therapeutic effects.
1225-1345	Pharmacy separated from medicine and formed guilds for practitioners; Apothecary shops (pharmacies) flourished in Europe, with first one in Cologne.
1546	*Nuremberg Pharmacopoeia* was published; the first dispensatory or list of drugs in the world.
1656	Wren demonstrated intravenous injection of substances into the human body.
1667	Denis administered first blood transfusion in humans.
1698	First medicinal patent granted in England for Epsom Salts.
1731	First drug advertised in U.S., a reprinted British promotional pamphlet for Dr. Bateman's Pectoral Drops.
1752	First hospital pharmacy founded in U.S. at the Pennsylvania Hospital in Philadelphia.
1753	James Lind conducted first "clinical trial" when he studied the effects of various treatments on scurvy in different groups of sailors.
1778	First manufacturing pharmacy and dispensatory, founded for U.S. Revolutionary forces by Apothecary-General Andrew Craigie at Carlisle, Pennsylvania; First American formulary (a list of drugs and recipes to standardize formulation and production) developed at Lititz, Pennsylvania.
1785	William Withering published his study of foxglove (digitalis) for heart conditions, which he tested in 163 patients.
1796	First U.S. medicinal patent was granted.

1798	Jenner discovered and tested vaccination method to prevent smallpox.
1800-20s	Early drug mills were established and the pharmaceutical industry grew in the Philadelphia area.
1805	Serturner, a German pharmacist, extracted morphine from opium.
1808	*Massachusetts Pharmacopeia* was published; the first in the U.S.
1820	*U.S. Pharmacopeia* published, mostly based on the pharmacopeia of Massachusetts.
1820s	Joseph Pelletier, a French pharmacist, isolated several alkaloid substances from plants, including quinine and caffeine.
1821	Francoise Magendie founded the discipline of pharmacology.
1834	Pierre Louis developed a numerical approach to conducting clinical experiments.
1844	Wells discovered inhalation anesthesia using nitrous oxide.
1848	First drug import law enacted by U.S. Congress to limit adulteration of foreign products.
1853	Wood and Pravaz invented and perfected the hypodermic syringe.
1860-85	Louis Pasteur and Robert Koch, French bacteriologists, developed the "germ" theory of infectious disease.
1885	Joseph Remington published the first edition of *The Practice of Pharmacy*, which has become *Remington's Pharmaceutical Sciences*; Halstead discovered conduction anesthesia ("nerve blocks") using cocaine by injection.
1890s	Self-experimentation by scientists and clinicians became a popular way to test effects of new drugs before using them in patients; Vaccines, anti-toxins, and anti-sera therapies were discovered and used in patients.
1893	Aspirin was discovered.
1906	U.S. Pure Food and Drug Act was passed.
1906-10	Paul Ehrlich developed his theory of "magic bullets."
1920s	Hormones, such as insulin, and many vitamins were isolated and extracted.

TABLE 1.1 (continued)

1928	Alexander Fleming discovered penicillin mold; clinical testing of penicillin did not occur for another ten years.
1935	Gerhard Domagk, a German physician, discovered antibiotic activity of sulfonamides.
1938	Federal Food, Drug, and Cosmetic Act was passed; Safety of drug products had to be assured before marketing.
1940-50s	Many types of antibiotics were discovered.
1943	Albert Hofmann of Switzerland discovered the effects of lysergic acid diethylamide (LSD) and many other hallucinogenic substances over the following years.
1950s	Clinical trials became a standard method for testing new drugs; Cortisone and other steroids were discovered and developed.
1951	Humphrey-Durham amendments to Federal Food, Drug, and Cosmetic Act of 1938 were passed; The amendments created two categories of drugs: nonprescription and prescription; Psychotherapeutic drugs, such as thorazine and diazepam, were discovered.
1960	First oral contraceptive was marketed.
1962	Kefauver-Harris amendments to Federal Food, Drug, and Cosmetic Act of 1938 were passed; Effectiveness of new drugs had to be shown prior to marketing.
1960s	Molecular manipulation of old drugs to discover new drugs became a popular approach.
1983	Orphan Drug Act was passed.
1984	Drug Price Competition and Patent Term Restoration Act (Waxman-Hatch Act) was passed. The first part of the act established a procedure to extend patent terms for pharmaceutical products meeting specified criteria. This was done to compensate companies for the patent time lost during the drug approval process. The second part of the act authorized procedures for FDA to review and approve generic versions of post-1962 prescription drugs, which introduced "multi-source" products to prescribers and consumers.
1990s	Computer-generated models of potentially beneficial drug molecules became the primary approach to new drug development; Genetically-engineered drug products were created and produced; Amendments to the U.S. drug approval process and the Orphan Drug Act are debated in Congress.

THE PHARMACEUTICAL INDUSTRY IN EARLY AMERICA

Philadelphia Foundation

U.S. pharmaceutical manufacturing was born in and around Philadelphia in the early nineteenth century. The first drug mills operated there from 1800 to 1820. In 1826, Samuel P. Wetherill and Company announced their ability to manufacture crude drug extracts and mineral compounds for medicinal purposes. The first drug product to be produced in a large-scale fashion in the United States was quinine sulfate, which was manufactured by Rosengarten and Sons in Philadelphia in 1822. This drug was used to prevent and treat malaria, a disease that, along with yellow fever, killed thousands of people in the U.S. during the early 1800s. Throughout the 1820s and 1830s, a variety of other companies had begun to produce morphine, codeine, strychnine, silver salts, and mercury compounds. By 1831, 30 chemical companies were in operation, producing chemicals valued at over $1 million annually.

The growth of these chemical companies, which would evolve into the pharmaceutical industry, was prompted by advances in chemical extraction and isolation processes for substances and compounds. By the middle of the 1800s, chemically-pure compounds of known composition were being tested and used in patients. Before these processes had been refined, the industry had produced crude extracts from raw plant materials. These extracts contained active ingredients, but in unknown amounts or uncertain concentrations. Thus, prior to extraction and isolation technology, it was impossible for physicians and pharmacists to know the amount of active ingredient in herbal materials. Additionally, extraction and chemical isolation techniques allowed more specific evaluation of the drug's therapeutic benefits. It was now possible to identify which particular substance was responsible for producing a medicinal effect.

After the Civil War, American manufacturers, including pharmaceutical companies, continued to improve technology, including machinery and production processes. Manufacturing was organized and streamlined to enhance profitability. Businesses also recruited technically-skilled personnel and developed a highly-specialized work force. To encourage and support these developments, the federal government enacted protective tariffs, minimized regulation, and financed specific projects. By the late 1800s, the American pharmaceutical industry, along with all other industries, was manufacturing raw materials into finished products, and the importation of foreign products declined.

Global Pharmaceutical Forces Before World War I

Primarily a result of political endorsement, German companies were the dominant global force in the pharmaceutical industry throughout the 1800s and the early 1900s. The German government supported the pharmaceutical industry through research subsidies, favorable rates on government-owned transportation networks and production facilities, special tax privileges, and preferential treatment in economic and political matters. By 1916, all important members of the German dye industry, which was the foundation of German pharmaceutical manufacturing, were members of a single cartel. The cartel fostered the exchange of ideas and research results, patent and market information exchange, cooperative research activities, and profit sharing.

Although German pharmaceutical companies were dominant in the global pharmaceutical market, major competition for the American chemical and pharmaceutical industries came from Great Britain. British and American companies made great progress in similar technological areas. While competing with the British, however, U.S. companies continued to strengthen economic and industrial ties with Germany. This collaboration resulted in the dominance of German-owned companies and patent products in the U.S. until World War I.

The Impact of World War I

With the onset of World War I and the end of importation and collaboration with German companies, the American chemical and pharmaceutical industries underwent complete restructuring. By this time, because of drug shortages and a significant dependence on European competitors, there was an acute need for a strong domestic pharmaceutical industry. In fact, the newspapers of that day criticized the U.S. pharmaceutical industry for allowing the Germans to dominate such a crucial industry.

Until this realization, American pharmaceutical companies had been preoccupied with sales and distribution. Scientific research and technological advancements now became fundamental to the industry and to modern drug development. With the introduction of electric-powered assembly-line production factories, and technological advancements in large-scale manufacturing, drug-discovery responsibilities shifted from health-care professionals to industrial researchers and scientists.

By the 1900s, drug-discovery and development processes had not only become more industrialized, but more political in nature. During the 1800s, the pharmaceutical industry existed to supply drugs of acceptable and uniform ingredient quality. Physicians were responsible for appropriate drug use by patients. When drug discovery shifted to the pharmaceutical industry, the industry also assumed primary responsibility for the safety and effectiveness of pharmaceutical products.

Post-World War I Progress

After discovering the U.S. pharmaceutical industry's potential to become a dominant force in American business, the 1920s became a golden era for pharmaceutical manufacturers. A number of German patents (brand names or other proprietary information excluded) were seized after World War I. Many war factories with their equipment and highly-skilled workers, low federal taxes and interest rates, and new tariff laws, as well as profits from the war years, were also influential. These factors led to improved methods of drug discovery, development, production, and, ultimately, the evolution of a self-sufficient pharmaceutical industry. Certain companies even began to concentrate on specific therapeutic areas. American pharmaceutical companies became BIG BUSINESS!

The decades between the World Wars saw strong economic growth and consolidation within the U.S. pharmaceutical industry. The Pure Food and Drug Act of 1906 encouraged the creation of large groups of researchers, primarily to test drugs and ensure quality, but also to enhance basic scientific research. Simultaneously, the traditional American pharmacy was changing into the modern, commercial drugstore. Pharmacists' emphasis shifted from compounding, preparing, and producing medicinal agents to storing, repackaging, and distributing drug products in a variety of dosage forms.

THE EVOLUTION OF MODERN METHODS OF DRUG DISCOVERY AND DEVELOPMENT

Sulfonamides–A Breakthrough Discovery

By the mid-1930s, considerable progress had been made in the production of **antisera** (substances containing antibodies that fight specific organisms) for the treatment of infections. After the successes of many years of research, American companies invested heavily in factories and equipment for the commercial production of these biological products. With the discovery of sulfonamides, however, these companies became obsolete.

Sulfanilamide, a red dye compound, was the first sulfonamide and the first antibiotic. (Imagine a time when people could *not* take an antibiotic to cure an infection!) Because sulfanilamide was used as a dye, scientists did not consider testing it for medicinal properties. One researcher luckily discovered that the dye exhibited antibacterial action in mice. The sudden and dramatic recovery of infected humans after receiving sulfonamides further reinforced the idea of magic bullets. Over 6,000 different types of sulfonamides were synthesized and tested for possible effects against all kinds of organisms. Interestingly, because most of the early sulfonamides were originally synthesized for use as dyes, patients who took them experienced skin color changes to hues of red and orange!

Sulfonamides completely changed pharmaceutical technology. Until this time, production had focused on making massive amounts of antisera by inoculating large animals with the infective organism and collecting serum from their blood. Now, scientists and industrial engineers could synthesize drugs from natural sources. However, they had to find ways to make the drug-synthesis process more efficient. Strategies to shorten the number of steps and reduce the time of drug synthesis were needed. Methods for extracting, refining, and compounding the substance into a finished dosage form were designed, perfected, and then expanded to large-scale manufacturing for industrial output.

With the discovery of antibiotics, the pharmaceutical industry learned that drug-therapy innovations had immediate consequences. Not only would innovations influence the use and profitability of older drug products, but the new substances required different testing methods and production systems. Of course, these important therapeutic innovations had the greatest impact on patients. Antibiotics greatly reduced the incidence of infectious diseases and the number of people who died from them. Innovation in the drug industry was no longer necessary just for leadership–it became essential for mere survival.

Post-World War II Growth

After World War II, pharmaceutical manufacturers experienced rapid and prosperous expansion. This industrial growth, sustained by the introduction of novel drug products–including new therapeutic drug classes–enabled manufacturers to increase production, raise wages, finance extensive research and development programs, and modernize and expand industrial facilities. Financial holdings, such as stocks and bonds, in pharmaceutical companies stood apart from other businesses. Earnings averaged as much as 20% higher profits in some years, compared with other industries. Following a positive cycle, the ability to invest in research and development led to more drug discoveries, which led to more profits and further research and development. The introduction of new drugs into the market steadily continued. It was not only transistors, televisions, automobiles, and nuclear energy that propelled the industrial growth of the post-World War II era–at the forefront was a vast array of pharmaceuticals.

TODAY'S DRUG RESEARCH
AND DEVELOPMENT PROCESS:
FROM MANUFACTURING TO MARKETING

In the decades after World War II, big businesses, including the pharmaceutical industry, realized that new products and processes were instrumental to a company's economic growth, as well as to the nation's strength. Systematically-designed research procedures permitted the continuous discovery and development of innovative products for an expanding marketplace. To facilitate standardized and effective discovery and marketing of new pharmaceuticals, research and development evolved into four stages, which are listed in Table 1.2.

With innovation as the key to growth, the pharmaceutical industry created a research and development process that would ensure continual drug discovery. Using this approach, a **new drug**–either a more effective modification of a drug or an entirely new compound–could be discovered and produced at any time. This process focused investment in research personnel, laboratory experimentation, and technological processes, with the ultimate goal of recovering the company's costs of research, as well as a reasonable profit.

As described earlier, prior to World War I, manufacturing costs were the pharmaceutical industry's principal expenditures. The industry's major ambition was to satisfy primary customers–govern-

TABLE 1.2. Drug Research and Development Stages in the Twentieth Century

STAGE	DESCRIPTION
1	Basic experimental research and development, in which the promise of results are unidentified and uncertain.
2	Applied research and advanced development, in which basic testing identifies compounds with potential benefits, but the compounds' therapeutic value and economic potential are uncertain.
3	Product development and pilot production, in which product testing continues to identify and establish specific dosage forms that might be effective, in addition to manufacturing methods.
4	Product application research and evaluation, in which new applications, or uses, are sought for existing drugs.

ment agencies and hospitals. Because little effort had been made to promote drug products directly to prescribing physicians during this time, the marketing and distribution costs were minimal. However, the new orientation of industrial research and development required rapid expansion of research laboratories and scientific personnel. Because new buyers were potential revenue sources (to pay for these costs), the research and development orientation also meant the creation of large sales forces to bring drug products to the attention of medical professionals.

HISTORY OF PHARMACEUTICAL MARKETING

Cure-alls and Charisma

Prescription drug marketing has changed tremendously over the last several centuries. The marketing of drugs began with "patent" medicines in Europe in the 1700s and 1800s. These medicinal remedies were products that contained a "secret ingredient" that was protected by a patent (Figures 1.5 and 1.6). The products came with catchy names and were promoted as cure-alls for every type of ailment. Anyone with a good idea, a pill press, and an engaging sales pitch could sell drugs. However, if these products actually had an active ingredient, the ingredient rarely had any therapeutic value. The "patents" were usually obtained for a price and did not represent a truly original invention or product.

During the 1800s, the American social and political environments changed. As the patent-medicine industry grew, consumers became more skeptical about the medicinal benefits of these products. At the same time, physicians and pharmacists, who were operating their own bulk preparation laboratories for drug preparation and distribution, created what they called the *ethical* drug industry. The promotion of ethical drugs began after the Civil War and focused on drug quality, purity, reliability, and therapeutic value.

Throughout this time period, drug promotion and advertising were not regulated. Manufacturers and salespersons could make any product claims that they desired without penalty. It was difficult to refute advertising and promotion claims without knowing the

FIGURE 1.5. Patent Medicine Advertisement from the 19th Century. Credit: Michael Montagne, personal collection

FIGURE 1.6. Product Line of Patent Medicines from the 19th Century

product's active ingredients or the existence of standardized effectiveness guidelines. This situation changed after the 1906 Pure Food and Drug Act was passed (Figure 1.7). According to this legislation, medicine advertising had to include an ingredient list. After the enactment of the 1938 Food, Drug, and Cosmetic Act, all medicines had to be shown safe for human consumption. In addition, a regulatory body–the Food and Drug Administration (FDA)–was established to protect consumers from false claims and hazardous products.

The Advent of Regulation

During a period of high government regulation, the 1962 amendments to the Food, Drug, and Cosmetic Act (the Kefauver-Harris amendments) were enacted. These amendments were designed to regulate pharmaceutical industry advertising and promotion. They focused on the **misbranding** of pharmaceutical products–the development and use of misleading information on prescription drug labeling (written matter accompanying or enclosing the product, such as the bottle or box)–as well as the need to prove drug **efficacy** prior to marketing.

To understand the impact of drug advertising and promotion laws, it is important to note the simultaneous changes occurring in the business environment. The production-oriented business world had changed to a marketing-oriented one. Firms were no longer producing items in mass quantities and assuming that consumers would buy them. Instead, businesses were responding to consumer demands by producing more types of refined products. Color, style, model, and size became important. Consumers were able to influence business decisions by their buying habits, and *differentiation* became the name of the game for marketing-oriented firms.

This shift in consumer buying behavior had a major influence on pharmaceutical firms. Consumers, even though they could no longer buy prescription drugs on their own, were (and continue to be) able to influence the prescriber, their physician. Additionally, physicians were learning the same lessons and, like others, were more discriminating when choosing drugs for patients. Differenti-

FIGURE 1.7. Drug Advertisement After the 1906 Pure Food and Drug Act.
Credit: Michael Montagne, personal collection

DR. ECHOLS' HEART CURE.

39 Cents and 69 Cents per Box, According to Size.

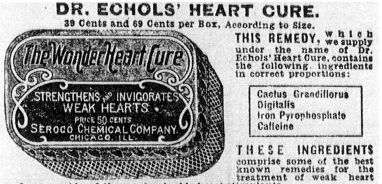

THIS REMEDY, which we supply under the name of Dr. Echols' Heart Cure, contains the following ingredients in correct proportions:

> Cactus Grandiflorus
> Digitalis
> Iron Pyrophosphate
> Caffeine

THESE INGREDIENTS comprise some of the best known remedies for the treatment of weak heart and are considered the most valuable heart stimulants.

THE HEALTH OF THE HEART IS MOST IMPORTANT. The heart is the great human pump that sends the life giving blood to every part of the body. The amount of labor it performs day and night, working incessantly year after year, is almost beyond belief. All this vast amount of work must be done and done each day. If not, your health will surely suffer in consequence of the least failure of the heart to properly perform its duties.

SYMPTOMS OF HEART TROUBLE. In order that one may determine whether the heart is affected, we call your attention to the following list of symptoms which denote heart disease. Fluttering of the pulse, palpitation of the heart, shortness of breath, tenderness and sudden sharp pains in the left side, dreaming of falling from a height, inability to sleep upon the left side, fainting or smothering spells, unconscious spells, dropsy, sudden starting in the sleep and noises in the ears. In describing these symptoms we have included the facts whereby heart trouble is recognized.

IT IS NOT CLAIMED that organic diseases of the heart can be cured. Such cases should be under the physician's care and attention, who, even if he cannot cure, can more accurately help to afford the patient at least temporary relief. There are, however, thousands of cases where the heart trouble is attributable to a reflex action upon that organ by other bodily ailments, and in such cases Dr. Echols' Heart Cure acts as a tonic stimulant, thereby affording the relief sought for by the sufferer.

IF YOU HAVE THE SLIGHTEST SUSPICION OF HEART TROUBLE, give this remedy a test. Dr. Echols' Heart Cure is a safe, scientific and carefully prepared remedy. It is based upon a prescription that has relieved hundreds of cases. It may fit your case exactly and it will afford you benefit and satisfactory results. If you are suffering from heart trouble, do not fail to take advantage of the opportunity of getting relief at a small expense and we are willing that you make a trial of Dr. Echols' Heart Cure. If you find that you have not received any benefit, simply write us to that effect and tell us that this is the first package of this remedy that you have tried and we will cheerfully refund your money. We do not want to sell our customers anything, whether it is an article of merchandise or a medical preparation, unless we know that they get value received for their money. The price of this remedy is very small indeed. If you know that you are a sufferer from heart weakness or other heart complications, we recommend to you giving a trial to Dr. Echols' Heart Cure. It has offered many a sufferer a means of relief and it may accomplish the same for you. Under our liberal terms you can ascertain whether Dr. Echols' Heart Cure is suitable for the treatment of your case without the slightest risk on your part. We are giving a list of ingredients that it contains and you will know that it cannot harm you and if it does not help you, you need only to notify us that the first box you have used of this remedy has not benefited your condition and we will return to you every cent you have paid for same.

DR. ECHOLS' HEART CURE is prepared in the form of a tablet and the remedy can be carried in the pocket without inconvenience. We furnish you a box containing forty doses for 39 cents, larger boxes containing one hundred doses for 69 cents.

THE PRICE OF THE REMEDY IS SMALL compared to its value and, if you have any heart complications, you should not be without a box of this valuable prescription.

No. 8E6   Price, per box, containing forty doses $0.39
Per dozen boxes. 3.75
No. 8E7   Price, per box, containing one hundred doses 69
Per dozen boxes. 6.40
If by mail, postage extra, per small box, 3 cents; large box, 6 cents.

ation became a key word for the pharmaceutical industry and the power of marketing flourished.

What Is Marketing?

To many unfamiliar with the discipline, "marketing" conjures images of encyclopedia salesmen and cold remedy hucksters, poor quality products and unethical sales techniques. In reality, **marketing** is a complex, multifaceted process that is integral to the success of any product or service. Almost all activities in business require the involvement of marketing: consumer research, product design, distribution, pricing, advertising, promotion, and product discontinuation.

According to the American Marketing Association, marketing is "the process of planning and executing the conception, pricing, promotion, and distribution of ideas, goods, and services to create exchanges that satisfy individual and organizational objectives."[3] Marketing can be viewed as the process of actualizing a market–it removes gaps or barriers between parties in a potential exchange relationship.[4] The goal of marketing is to organize the company's resources into a strategic plan that meets consumers' needs. Marketing activities aim at getting the right product, in the right quantity, to the right place, at the right price, and at the right time.[3]

Marketing Prescription Drugs

Pharmaceutical marketing consists of many related activities, including product development, pricing, packaging, distribution, promotion, and education. Promotion is only one facet of marketing. **Promotion** is defined as "the vehicle by which the product, its price, and methods of distribution should be described to the firm's audience coherently and persuasively."[3] It is a way to inform users about a product. Pharmaceutical promotion consists of advertising and related forms of information dissemination, such as detailing by pharmaceutical representatives, exhibits, conventions, scientific seminars, and continuing education programs.

In marketing literature, **advertising** is defined as the promotional activity that communicates information to directly or indirectly encourage the purchase of goods or services.[3] Additionally, advertising is an unofficial term in the pharmaceutical regulatory literature, and is applied to all forms of drug promotion. Advertising, in the latter context, includes descriptive printed matter, promotional materials, and all forms of labeling–including audio and visual information, exhibits, media communication, and verbal statements about a drug product and its indication. In effect, any form of communication through any type of media that calls attention to a drug product is advertising.

A SUMMARY OF THE PAST AND A LOOK TO THE FUTURE

According to the eminent philosopher, Alfred North Whitehead, "the greatest invention of the nineteenth century was the invention of the method of invention."[1] The idea that drugs could be *invented* was realized in the 1920s and gained further acceptance with continual discoveries of new antibiotics, such as sulfonamides and penicillin, in the 1930s and 1940s.

Until World War I, the American pharmaceutical industry was a "goods producer." Most products were manufactured in crude forms and sold to pharmacies and hospitals for final compounding. Throughout the 1900s, the pharmaceutical industry has evolved into a producer of highly-differentiated consumer goods for retail distribution.

The institutionalization of a formally-structured research process has been a key element in the pharmaceutical industry's growth throughout the 1900s. The early drug-discovery process of screening and testing was replaced by a broad spectrum of activities: basic laboratory work, clinical evaluation and application, industrial processes and distribution systems, marketing and promotion, and other related activities. In summarizing the drug-development process, one member of the industry stated:

> . . . a drug is not discovered, it is created. It remains a drug candidate until research has unlocked the secrets of its innermost pharmacologic soul, separating the acceptable from the unacceptable, and reassembling the parts in a manner that will enable an evaluation of the benefit-to-risk ratio.[5]

Concerns about the development, promotion, testing, and distribution of drug products are expressed on a daily basis in both the media and the health-professional literature. Many consumers insist on assurances of unconditional drug safety and effectiveness–requests that represent our society's quest for absolutes. The question often asked of scientists and managers in pharmaceutical development is whether they possess the wisdom to control the vast power of pharmaceuticals for human purposes.

In the coming chapters, a number of concerns and complaints about our modern drug-development system are described. We will present and discuss the ways in which new drug therapies are discovered and developed, and the current drug-approval process. Certain aspects of traditional drug development are currently being evaded by consumers who want new drug therapies for their illnesses immediately. There is a great deal of industrial and political activity in the areas of orphan drugs (drugs used to treat rare diseases), the initiation and organization of clinical drug trials by patient groups, prescription drug importation, and drug distribution through consumer networks.

In the end, all of us need to realize that the current system of drug discovery and development is a good one, but that it has several important shortcomings. Do we formally address these flaws and problems through legal and governmental avenues? Or should consumers develop their own plan of attack? These questions will be explored in the upcoming chapters.

NOTES

1. Stephen J. Knoop and Daniel E. Worden, "The Pharmaceutical Drug Development Process: An Overview," *Drug Information Journal* 22 (1988):259.

2. D.D. Vogt and Michael Montagne, "Historical Review," in *The Clinical Research Process in the Pharmaceutical Industry*, ed. Gary M. Matoren (New York, NY: Marcel Dekker, 1984).

3. P.D. Bennett, *Dictionary of Marketing Terms* (Chicago, IL: American Marketing Association, 1988):115.

4. Mickey C. Smith, *Pharmaceutical Marketing: Strategies and Cases* (Binghamton, NY: Pharmaceutical Products Press, 1991).

5. J.R. Knill, "The Role of Management in Successful Clinical Research," in *Factors Influencing Clinical Research Success*, ed. Marion J. Finkel (Kisco, NY: Futura, 1976): 1-6.

SUGGESTED READINGS

B. Barber, *Drugs and Society* (New York, NY: Russell Sage, 1967).

F.H. Clarke, ed., *How Modern Medicines Are Developed* (Mt. Kisco, NY: Futura, 1977).

H. Lennard, *Mystification and Drug Misuse* (San Francisco, CA: Jossey-Bass, 1971).

M. Mathieu, *New Drug Development: A Regulatory Overview* (Cambridge, MA: Parexel International, 1990).

Lloyd G. Millstein, "Advertising and Promotion of Prescription Drug Products," in *Encyclopedia of Pharmaceutical Technology*, eds. J. Swarbrick and J.C. Boylan (New York, NY: Marcel Dekker, 1988):147-187.

P. Nwangwu, *Concepts and Strategies in New Drug Development: Clinical Pharmacology & Therapeutics Series* (New York, NY: Praeger, 1984).

S.J. Reiser, *Medicine and the Reign of Technology* (Cambridge, MA: Cambridge University Press, 1978).

D.H. Spodick, "The Randomized Controlled Clinical Trial: Scientific and Ethical Bases," *American Journal of Medicine* 73 (1982):420.

D.H. Spodick, "Randomized Controlled Clinical Trials: The Behavioral Case," *Journal of the American Medical Association* 247 (1982):2258.

P. Talalay, ed., *Drugs in Our Society* (Baltimore, MD: Johns Hopkins University Press, 1964).

A.N. Whitehead, *Science and the Modern World* (New York, NY: Macmillan, 1946).

Chapter 2

Problems and Concerns with Modern Drug Development

Physicians pour drugs of which they know little, to cure diseases of which they know less, into humans of which they know nothing.

Voltaire, c. 1760

I firmly believe that if the whole materia medica, as now used, could be sunk to the bottom of the sea, it would be all the better for mankind, and all the worse for the fishes.

Oliver Wendell Holmes, 1860

The pharmaceutical revolution, while yielding significant benefits, has also generated its share of problems. The production of potent new drugs has given the physician the power not only to modify diseases processes for the benefit of his patient but also to produce new and serious side effects, as individual drugs cause unwanted toxicity or interact with other drugs or with foods to do pharmacologic mischief.

Louis Lasagna, 1969

Patients, consumers, and the general public are not the only people who think that the manner in which drugs are discovered, tested, distributed, and used is less than perfect. Many health professionals, scientists, government officials, and members of the pharmaceutical industry have objected to various aspects of modern drug development. As you can see from the opinions above, these complaints and concerns have been voiced continually for over 200 years.

Is it possible that nothing has really changed? Of course not! Our ways of discovering and developing beneficial drug products have changed radically over that same time period. But with each change, innovation, or total transformation in the process comes an array of new problems, issues, and concerns. Overall, there have been great improvements, but some relevant aspects of drug development have been sacrificed in the process of change.

Today, a variety of issues and concerns are being raised by health-care professionals, consumer advocacy groups, governmental agencies, the media, and individual health-care consumers regarding drug development, marketing, and use. What are these concerns and problems and is anything being done to address them? Because many of these concerns involve principles of ethics in health-care research and clinical practice, a brief review of biomedical ethics is necessary.

BIOMEDICAL ETHICS AND DRUG RESEARCH IN HUMANS

From the Hippocratic tradition and the Judeo-Christian religious ethic come three basic principles that guide the ethical development and use of drugs in our society (Table 2.1).[1,2] Additionally, certain ethical principles are vital in health-care and biomedical research, and are considered by health-care professionals as rules to follow in practice (Table 2.2).[2]

The Legacy of Hippocrates

The Hippocratic Oath, which was adopted by the physician Hippocrates' followers in the fifth century B.C., has been the primary code of ethics in health care. On the basis of this doctrine, the first general codes of medical ethics in the United States were developed for physicians by the American Medical Association and for pharmacists by the Philadelphia College of Pharmacy in the nineteenth

TABLE 2.1. Primary Principles of Ethics

PRINCIPLE	DEFINITION
Beneficence	Good must be done, harm must be avoided or minimized, and the benefits of therapy must justify patient injury or trauma. This is the principle inherent in health-care professionals' practice of prolonging life.
Justice or Equity	There should be an equal distribution of the burdens and benefits of therapy, except where an unequal distribution is justified by unusual merit or great need.
Autonomy	Individuals' free choice should be honored, and protection should be given to those of diminished autonomy, such as children, the mentally disabled, and prisoners. This principle defines the right of individuals to accept or to refuse treatment.

Adapted from Beauchamp and Childress, 1989.

TABLE 2.2. Additional Ethical Principles and Rules

PRINCIPLE	DEFINITION
Veracity	The patient is told the truth and not deceived.
Privacy	Confidentiality is maintained in health care.
Fidelity	Faithfulness to a covenant or social contract is provided.
Protection of Life	Death and killing are avoided.
Respect	Consideration of nature and the rights of the patient is necessary.
Conflicts of Interest	Potential conflicts in the contractual and role obligations as a health-care researcher or provider are considered.

Adapted from Beauchamp and Childress, 1989.

century. The guiding principles of these codes included a respect for human life and service to mankind.

The Hippocratic Oath was modernized by the World Medical Association in 1949 and called the Geneva Convention Code of Medical Ethics. This code directed physicians to consecrate their lives to the service of humanity and to maintain the utmost respect for human life from the time of conception, even under threat. In the same vein, during the early 1960s, the World Medical Association adopted a code of ethics for experimentation involving human subjects. The Declaration of Helsinki, adopted in 1964 and revised in 1975, incorporated the three basic ethical principles from the Nuremberg Code (see below) and more clearly defined the fundamental distinction between research that is essentially therapeutic for the patient and research that is purely scientific and without therapeutic benefit to the patient. The Declaration of Hawaii, adopted in 1977, was even more specific; it focused on psychiatry and psychiatric research and prohibited the use of psychiatry resources for nontherapeutic reasons, most especially for political or ideological ends.[3]

Nuremberg Code

In the wake of World War II, information regarding experiments conducted on humans during that war, as well as judgments made afterwards at the Nuremberg Trials, led to the drafting of the Code of Nuremberg. This ethical code was developed to regulate biomedical research and incorporated three primary ethical principles (Table 2.3).[4]

Which Code Is the Best?

To know which specific ethical principle should be followed in a given situation is much more difficult than the simple listing of these principles and rules. One approach is to order principles in some manner, giving priority to some over others. An extreme version of this approach is to follow a single, supreme principle in all decisions and actions, and ignore others. Another possibility is to consider all principles equally in a given circumstance and to at-

TABLE 2.3. Ethical Principles of the Nuremberg Code
• Obligations to the individual subject involved in a research experiment must be placed above obligations to the state or the government.
• A distinction between therapeutic and nontherapeutic research has moral implications. In other words, therapeutic needs must come before basic research needs.
• Informed consent from the subject is morally essential.
• In performing biomedical research, completely voluntary consent must be obtained from the subjects in terms of a full and enlightened understanding of all aspects of the experiment and its hazards.
• Research should seek benefits for society that are unobtainable by any other method.
• Research should be conducted using information collected from prior studies of the drug in animals.
• All unnecessary physical and mental risks should be minimized.

tempt a balance between them. In real life situations, however, laws or social norms often direct or dictate which ethical principle should be followed.

ETHICAL ISSUES IN THE CLINICAL DRUG RESEARCH PROCESS

Conflicts of Interest for Researchers

Most concerns with clinical drug research revolve around a variety of ethical issues. Clinical drug researchers can be presented with conflicts of interest between their role as healers and their role as scientists. There can also be conflicts between therapy goals and experimental goals, such that the researcher might not be able to commit totally to the sick patients' interests. Additionally, researchers try to avoid incorrect conclusions of therapeutic benefit through premature judgment of study results. However, this wish can clash with the desire to either provide the medical community with a promising new drug as quickly as possible, or to receive rewards for a breakthrough discovery.

Fraudulent Research Findings

On the basis of news reports announcing the publication of deliberately incorrect and deceptive data by medical investigators, there is a growing concern about deceit in drug trials and other scientific research. Pharmaceutical companies and investigators alike have much to gain by demonstrating that a new drug is significantly more valuable to the health-care community, both in terms of finances and prestige. Like any other industry or group, the desire for fame, glory, and financial rewards often leads to improper actions, such as falsification of information.

To counter some of the actual and potential problems associated with this unlawful activity, unbiased and objective groups, such as institutional review boards (IRBs) and advisory committees, have been created. Their goal is to evaluate and approve study designs and ensure that patients are appropriately informed about clinical research. These groups also monitor study results and inform researchers and the public of the research value, including whether a new treatment under study is significantly superior or inferior to traditional treatments.

Clinical Research as a Marketing Strategy

Unknown to many consumers and some health-care professionals, drug companies conduct or fund most drug research. Individual physicians or large institutions (i.e., hospitals, universities) are paid to organize and conduct clinical trials, sometimes before the drug has been approved by the Food and Drug Administration (FDA) and other times as a post-marketing study to determine additional benefits of the drug. Although it is feasible and common for a pharmaceutical manufacturer to be interested in learning more about the drug as a part of the drug's research and development process, the use of physicians and hospitals to conduct post-marketing studies has become a concern.

Pharmaceutical manufacturers are responsible for conducting several types of clinical trials and submitting various data for the FDA to review as it considers approval of the drug (see Chapters 3 and 4). This information is usually collected using company researchers and company-appointed physicians, universities, and investigators. Most of this research is managed in an ethical, appropriate, and efficient manner with the ultimate goal of determining the true safety and therapeutic value of the drug and facilitating its approval.

The potential for unethical activity surfaced during the 1990 Kennedy hearings. According to Sidney Wolfe, a physician and well-known consumer advocate, the prevalence of doctor-bribing and acquisition of bogus clinical data through large pay-offs is higher than most people believe. Wolfe described several cases in which physicians were paid substantial sums of money to collect data on patients using a particular drug. In one instance, physicians were offered $1,200 to record the age, diagnosis, drug dose, therapy duration, and culture and antibiotic sensitivity results for 20 hospitalized patients who were using a particular intravenous antibiotic.[5] To participate, the physician had to write a letter to the pharmaceutical company requesting this sum for the collection of the specific data. Interestingly, the individual to whom participating physicians wrote was the director of medical marketing, not a representative of the medical or clinical research department–the group that should be concerned with such data. Why would the marketing department of a pharmaceutical firm be interested in facilitating the collection of clinical research data? It is highly feasible that the goal of the initiative described above was not to collect post-marketing data on hospitalized patients using the antibiotic, but to provide an incentive for the use of the specific antibiotic by requiring that each physician collect data, and hence, use the drug, in 20 patients.

A Matter of Trust

The heart of the problem is the dangerous amount of control that the [pharmaceutical] industry has over testing. Hundreds of people have been killed and thousands injured because data have been falsified.[6]

Sidney Wolfe MD
Director, Public Citizen's Health Research Group

The negative fallout of dangerous drugs is much worse in many cases than not getting the drug approved to begin with. If a drug has to be pulled from the market, it's bad for public relations, financially, and in every possible way. It just doesn't make sense that [the pharmaceutical industry] would intentionally conceal real problems.[5]

Kenneth Kaitin, PhD
Assistant Director, Center for the Study of Drug Development,
Tufts University

Several recent scandals have increased public awareness of the nature of the FDA's research standards. Such news has begun to seriously concern consumers, patients, and health-care professionals who must address the alarm and confusion of drug users. Several questions come to mind when hearing about these abuses of the drug-approval system:

1. Why was the FDA not aware of these occurrences? Should it be their responsibility to know about such activities or occurrences?
2. Why would a drug manufacturer take the risk of marketing a product that is known to be harmful? Are financial rewards so compelling that the personal safety of drug users is ignored?
3. Can the marketing of fraudulent drugs and other dangers be circumvented in the future? How?
4. Is it possible that activities like these are simply a part of American business? Why should the pharmaceutical industry be expected to be free of unethical or illegal activities and cover-ups when certain manufacturing companies contaminate water supplies by discarding waste materials into lakes and streams, and others market faulty or dangerous products?

No one has the solutions to these questions. To help provide answers, however, the following chapters will outline and describe the responsibilities of everyone involved in the drug-development process. For example, the FDA is furiously trying to determine appropriate ways to handle current controversies and amend the FDA mode of operation. In this way, the organization can minimize the impact of such controversies on the delicate balance of trust between U.S. consumers and the government drug-approval system.

Animal Rights

The need to conduct drug research studies in animals prior to testing in humans has always been questioned by society. The debate includes issues of moral equality and the rights of animals, the actual need for animal research, and the priority of animal experimentation in the entire research process. Many people believe that basic ethical principles of biomedical research also apply to animals.[7,8,9]

The emotionally-charged issues surrounding the definition of morally-acceptable use of animals in drug research probably will not find a common ground. The real solution might be the development of alternative models and approaches to performing drug research, such as computer-aided drug evaluation and more powerful statistical analysis techniques.

Special Patient Populations

There are special concerns related to research using fetal tissue and clinical drug trials conducted in children, the mentally disabled, and prisoners. Most of these concerns involve issues of autonomy, and to some extent justice or equity, especially when individuals are stereotyped by investigators as being passive or inferior in some way. There are also practical and technical issues and problems, such as defining risks and obtaining informed consent, that arise in research with these special groups of people. On the other hand, many issues or problems become reasons for not performing research on these people, which can present an additional problem of limiting both scientific and clinical knowledge, as well as the quality and timeliness of health-care treatment for these patients.

Ethics in Clinical Drug Research

One can see why there is a need for ethical standards in conducting and reporting the results of clinical drug trials. Key factors to consider during a drug research endeavor include study design, competence of investigators, the benefit/risk balance, disclosure of the various aspects of the research study to patients, informed consent, and compensation for injury or harm that occurs as a result of participation. In addition, the inclusion of vulnerable and less advantaged persons must be addressed, and the use of placebos or deception in the disclosure process must be evaluated. The process of unethical behavior identification and discipline is also a factor. Finally, researchers must appraise the value of advisory committees and institutional review boards, consider the need for public access to research data versus professional control over the research process, and be aware of underlying goals of sponsors.

The process of modern drug development has created a variety of ethical dilemmas. The ethics of drug experimentation in prisoners and other segments of the population have been questioned and changed in recent years. However, contemporary clinical drug trials still present a number of challenges to both scientists and society. More problems will arise as endogenous substances and genetic engineering continue to play a role in drug development.

MARKETING AND PROMOTIONAL ACTIVITIES

> If you were a patient with a medical problem for which there was more than one possible medication, would you be interested in what gifts your doctor had recently accepted from the manufacturer of one of the options?
>
> *L. Frederick Fenster MD*
> *Hearings before the Senate Subcommittee*
> *on Drug Advertising and Promotion*
> *December 11, 1990*[5]

Marketing and promotional activities, although they seem relatively harmless, are serious considerations for the FDA and healthcare professionals and should be a notable concern for patients and consumers. Some of the issues in prescription-drug advertising include the use of comparative, reminder, direct-to-consumer, and multi-page print advertisements; promotion of drugs prior to FDA approval; artwork and headings in advertisements; advertising format (i.e., type, size, style, and graphics); the use of electronic media and cable television to advertise prescription drugs, including video news releases (VNRs); and the value and unique characteristics of scientific presentations (i.e., full-length seminars, symposia, teleconferences, exhibits, continuing education programs and publications).

One of the primary issues affecting the pharmaceutical industry, as well as many advertising agencies and medical communication firms, is the development of FDA guidelines that govern drug marketing and education practices. These guidelines can restrict medical knowledge by minimizing promotion of drug use for unapproved diseases or conditions. However, the pharmaceutical industry has acknowledged that some marketing practices can be harmful: drugs should be prescribed on the basis of their safety and efficacy, not in response to patients' demands or to acknowledge generous pharmaceutical industry gifts or physician perks.

DRUG PRICING AND PHARMACEUTICAL INDUSTRY PROFITABILITY

Almost everyone is aware that the pharmaceutical industry is one of the most profitable in the United States; it is recession-proof and has generated high profits compared with other industries for the last three decades. According to a recent survey article in a popular news magazine, pharmaceutical companies experienced profits equal to almost 16% of total sales while all other industries experienced profits equal to almost 7% of total sales.[10] Why is this? High drug prices, a lack of price competition, and extravagant advertising and promotion efforts might be a part of the answer. Today, however, the more important issue in the minds of consumers and lawmakers is whether or not the ability of the industry to earn these high profits should be regulated or curtailed. As health-care costs continue to spiral upward, it seems that patients and taxpayers are at a significant disadvantage and that the pharmaceutical industry is reaping the benefits of the marketplace.

The Cost of Pharmaceutical Innovation

To understand the validity of such assertions, several different issues must be examined. Is the issue of pharmaceutical costs a true concern? In 1990, U.S. consumers spent over $44 billion on pharmaceuticals, which is just 6% of the total 1990 U.S. health-care expenditure. With the increasing number of expensive biopharmaceuticals and the aging of the population, however, drug utilization and costs are destined to escalate.[11] The Pharmaceutical Research Institute for Management and Economics estimates that, barring government regulation, pharmaceutical prices will increase between 8 and 9% each year (Figure 2.1). Because the majority of drug costs are paid by individual patients, rather than Medicare or Medicaid, pharmaceutical prices have received the attention of the media and government representatives (Figure 2.2).

The industry can justify, in part, the high costs to health-care establishments (hospitals, nursing homes, medical centers) and patients because of the substantial amount of important research and drug development that occurs. Most of the research surrounding the use of pharmaceuticals to treat disease occurs in pharmaceutical companies' laboratories. Universities and government agencies are also involved, but to a much lesser extent. The development and marketing of the 30 **new molecular entities** (new and unique drugs to the marketplace) that were approved in 1991 serves as an index of the industry's ability to discover and produce truly useful medications for U.S. consumers. Additionally, it is important to consider the value of medications in terms of quality-of-life improvements, minimization of additional medical or surgical procedures, and the ability of medicines to replace costly therapeutic alternatives.

The Value of Pharmaceutical Innovation

At least one-half of all future advances in medicine will consist of new pharmaceutical products. Most of the successes in treating diseases, including Alzheimer's disease, arthritis, AIDS, and leukemia, will be due to the development of new drugs for these conditions. Dr. Louis Lasagna, director of Tufts University's Center for the Study of Drug Development, has said, "Genetic and molecular

FIGURE 2.1. Prescription Drug Inflation vs. Medical Inflation, 1980-1990

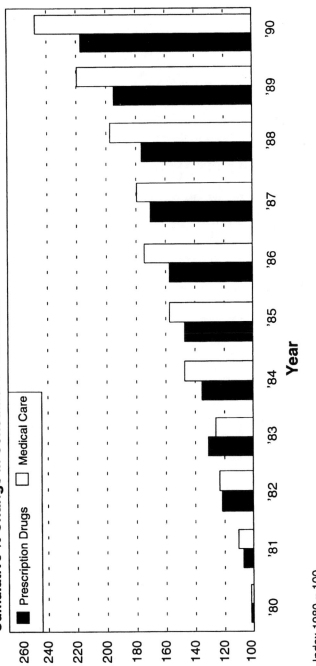

Cumulative % Change in Consumer Price Index

Index 1980 = 100

SOURCE: Senator David Pryor, Senate Special Subcommittee on Aging June 1991

39

FIGURE 2.2 The Funding of Health Care by Source, 1990

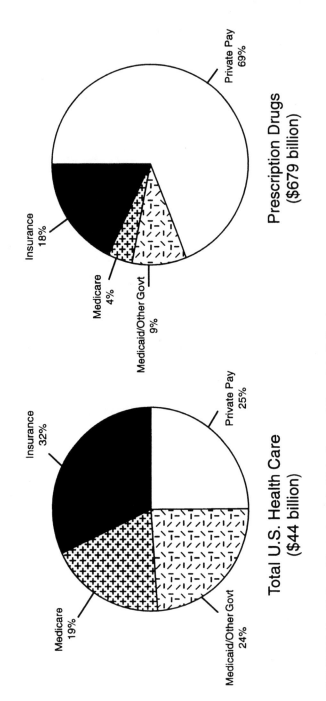

Prescription Drugs
($679 billion)

Private Pay
69%

Insurance
18%

Medicare
4%

Medicaid/Other Govt
9%

Total U.S. Health Care
($44 billion)

Insurance
32%

Private Pay
25%

Medicare
19%

Medicaid/Other Govt
24%

SOURCE: Health Care Financing Administration and Bernstein Estimates

design are bringing us closer to understanding the basic mechanism of disease, and consequently, reducing the time of developing new therapies."[12]

Additionally, it has been shown that pharmaceuticals are cost-effective. The benefits received by the use of drugs are often higher per dollar spent than other forms of health care. For example, over the past 50 years, antibiotics have helped Americans avoid between 60,000 and 90,000 deaths from tuberculosis, representing savings of approximately $10 billion in potential productivity losses. For patients with heart disease, it is estimated that with the assistance of new medications for coronary heart disease treatment, 671,000 lives were saved between 1968 and 1976, which translates to approximately $83 billion averted in indirect costs.[13]

Unfortunately, a recent Gallup poll found that only 12% of Americans understand just how much new drug discoveries have contributed to the country's health over the past 30 years. Pharmaceutical products are given the least amount of credit for medical progress when compared with lifestyle changes, diagnostic devices, and surgical techniques. The survey also found that 70% of consumers do not know that the pharmaceutical industry supports most of the pharmaceutical research and development that provides these medications.[12] In actuality, of the 100 most-prescribed drugs still under patent, 94 were patented by the pharmaceutical industry, and only 6 were patented by universities, government organizations, or individuals.[14] Medication consumers' lack of knowledge regarding pharmaceutical industry contributions to health care has prompted the Pharmaceutical Manufacturers Association (PMA) to publicize such facts through various media, including television and print advertisements.

However, as discussed earlier, the increasing amount of money spent by the industry in marketing prescription drugs is not as easily justified as research spending. Much controversy currently surrounds the marketing of drugs through reminder items to physicians, support of lavish "educational" meetings, advertising of drugs directly to consumers on prime-time television, and acquisition of "research data" through practitioners who use simple patient documentation forms and collect large honoraria.

To Regulate or Not to Regulate?

Although there are several smaller issues within the larger one surrounding the viability and value of drug-pricing regulation, it seems, given the current political and social environments, that both the federal government and consumers will not concede to continuing escalation of drug prices. In 1992, Senators David Pryor and Henry Waxman began promoting several Congressional bills that could alter drug pricing practices. Their goal is to minimize drug spending in relation to other components of the health-care system.

QUALITY OF DRUG INFORMATION

As technology and scientific information continue to grow, information overload is becoming a part of every health professional's daily existence. Maintaining an up-to-date yet working knowledge of drugs and diseases is a demanding task. This task is not alleviated by the sheer volume of information that is distributed each day. It has been estimated, for example, that physicians receive over 40 pounds of books, journals, magazines, brochures, and newsletters describing advances in medical care, new drugs, and other medical information *each week*!

For patients and consumers who want more information, direct advertising of prescription drugs and the *Physician's Desk Reference* (PDR) have become two very popular mechanisms by which to obtain drug information. Because many patients believe that they are not receiving enough information from health professionals, they are accepting guidance from nontraditional sources, including volunteer agencies, the medical literature, and volunteer or patient advocacy groups.

Prescription to nonprescription status changes will become an issue that raises new concerns for consumers. A drug product is given nonprescription status if the FDA believes that labeling (i.e., directions for use) can be written to ensure safe and proper use without medical supervision. Tavist-D® and Gyne-Lotrimin® are examples of prescription medications that are now available without a prescription. If the FDA believes that medical supervision is required, then the product is restricted to the prescription-only category. The notions of fair balance and brief summary information–including safety and effectiveness statements–do not generally apply to nonprescription drug advertising, which is regulated by the Federal Trade Commission (FTC). According to FTC regulations, labeling for nonprescription drug products must state intended uses and likely results from use of the product, adequate directions for proper use, and warnings against unsafe use, side effects, and adverse reactions. This information must be provided in terms that are readable and easily understood by the typical consumer under usual conditions of purchase and use. More information about the concerns surrounding patient self-medication is provided in the last chapter.

SOCIETAL PERCEPTIONS AND ACCEPTANCE OF NEW DRUG THERAPIES

Accepting a New Drug in Society

It appears that most drugs pass through three stages of acceptance in Western societies.[15] A newly-introduced drug product is usually over-valued and over-used in inappropriate ways. As problems arise from misuse, the drug becomes under-valued and often condemned. A balance is eventually achieved as the advantages and disadvantages are weighed in determining the therapeutic worth and rational use of the drug. For example, it has been shown that the minor tranquilizers (i.e., diazepam [Valium®, Roche]) have gone through these stages of acceptance (Table 2.4).[16] These phases of professional and public response have been noted for the acceptance of all types of tranquilizers.

Societal perceptions and acceptance of research products (e.g., nuclear power, weaponry, pharmaceuticals) vary considerably. Advances in high technology research are viewed favorably in general, especially when perceived as contributing to our national economic strength. Research on medications, however, is often viewed with suspicion. An elaborate system of social and regulatory controls has been created to protect consumers from what is viewed by many as a manipulative industry.

TABLE 2.4. Stage of Acceptance for Prescription Drugs

STAGE	DESCRIPTION
1: Euphoric Ignorance	The new drug outperforms the older drug products, and long-term problems are not yet apparent.
2: Paranoid Uncertainty	Disappointment and disillusionment increase as the drug is found to be less safe than originally imagined (i.e., adverse reactions or drug use problems are reported frequently).
3: Judicious Evaluation	The benefits and value of the drug become clearer, and it is used in a proper or more appropriate manner.

The Difference Between Drugs and Other Products

While our society passively accepts many industrial mistakes and problems, such as recall of thousands of automobiles with faulty parts and defective construction, an unpredicted adverse reaction to a new drug, which might affect only a handful of individuals, usually results in public outcry and a great deal of negative media attention. While few people in our society demand or desire absolute safety in machinery and other consumer goods, most people insist on absolute safety for medicines.

Perhaps, in the century since the industrial revolution, Americans have come to terms with machines and different forms of technology. We accept the risks inherent in using mechanical instruments and technological devices. However, we have not come to terms with those things we only vaguely understand, such as nuclear power and modern pharmaceuticals. As Rene Dubois has pointed out in discussing pharmaceuticals, "Absolute lack of toxicity is an impossibility because absolute selectivity is a chemical impossibility."[17]

Health-care professionals and the pharmaceutical industry must make consumers aware of this truth, while continuing to maintain strong and ethical mechanisms of ensuring the safety and efficacy of drug therapies. This sentiment has been echoed in a recent article in a popular news magazine, "In a culture that has long been addicted to the quick fix, a healthy respect for the power of the pill–negative as well as positive–may prove to be the best medicine of all."[5]

MEDICALIZATION OF PERSONAL AND SOCIAL PROBLEMS OF LIFE

What Is Medicalization?

Medicalization is the process of redefining or relabeling a personal or social problem as a medical condition, thus necessitating involvement in and control by the health-care delivery system. More broadly, it can be seen as the substitution of medical care for conditions that were once non-medical in nature. Many aspects of life are influenced or dominated by medicine, to the point where some people have argued that we are seeing the medicalization of everything in life during the twentieth century. Whether the medicalization process and its outcomes are positive or negative, however, is yet unclear.

The process of medicalization of social and personal concerns can occur conceptually, institutionally, or interpersonally in response to governmental policies and health-care payment mechanisms, rather than diagnostic or therapeutic reasons.[18] As a result, health-care providers assume authority in many personal and social aspects of life and health-care systems become safety nets for the failures of social services and welfare systems.

Medicalization–Positive or Negative?

On the conceptual level, medicalization is reflected in the vocabulary of health and illness, from either a patient or health professional's perspective, and in the way problems are defined. Medicalization on the institutional level occurs when health professionals are the gatekeepers of authorized products and services. It is also evidenced when health-care providers alter their mission, products, or procedures in response to external factors and pressures. Interpersonal interactions of health professionals and patients reflect medicalization through paternalistic treatment of patients and the habit of keeping the role of patients relatively passive.

One of the concerns regarding medicalization is that it prevents the balanced assessment of both medical and nonmedical therapies to prevent or treat illness. Instead of attempting interpersonal, social, or structural changes to alleviate diseases and conditions, drugs are prescribed and used for symptomatic relief. Pharmaceuticals are often a relatively inexpensive, accessible, and convenient form of health-care technology. Pharmaceuticals are also viewed as pure and potent, and their effects are detectable, which ensures efficacy in patients' minds. Even as the pharmacologic activity of a drug declines (i.e., less activity in the body due to potency, tolerance, or some other biological or pharmaceutical phenomenon), the symbolic act of taking a drug becomes important in bringing about the effects experienced by the user.[19]

The issue of promoting medications for personal or social problems involves a difficult balance between medical definitions of what constitutes a disease and consumers' perceptions of what they want or need in the way of optimal health and well-being. There are certain conditions that are poorly defined in terms of the traditional model of disease (Tables 2.5 and 2.6). Other conditions, such as child abuse, ordinary stress ("pressures of life"), small breasts, thinning hair, mental fatigue, and certain personal and social problems are often considered diseases by some–afflicted consumers and health-product manufacturers and promoters–but not by others–health professionals and health insurance companies. A major question becomes, "Who determines which conditions are diseases to be addressed by medical care systems, and which conditions are problems and concerns better addressed by the family unit, social welfare agencies, religious groups, or society in general?"

An Example–Oral Contraceptives

Oral contraceptives were the first modern pharmaceutical product developed primarily for a non-disease condition–preventing conception and pregnancy.[20] These substances have been hailed as providing reproductive autonomy to women. Oral contraceptives provide the user with freedom of choice in having or not having children, a safe and convenient treatment option, and freedom from coerced sterilization. Many physicians and other health professionals believe

TABLE 2.5. Consumer Needs and Societal Functions that Drugs Serve with Examples

CONSUMER NEEDS	SOCIETAL FUNCTIONS
achievement–memory drugs, steroids	aesthetic (artistic experiences)– mescaline, LSD
affiliation–alcohol, oral contraceptives	aphrodisiac–yohimbine
diversion–psychedelics, narcotics	ego-disruption (escape)–alcohol, marijuana
dominance–cocaine	psychological support–tranquilizers
exhibition/recognition–use of newest drug (i.e., fluoxetine [Prozac®], Lilly)	religious–psilocybin, LSD
health–antibiotics	research–memory drugs
independence–tranquilizers	social control–tranquilizers, alcohol
novelty–designer drugs (i.e., smart drugs)	therapeutic–antibiotics
security–anti-seizure medications, antidiabetic medications	war and other conflict–nerve gases
sexuality–aphrodisiacs	
stimulation–stimulants, tobacco	

Adapted from B. Barber, *Drugs and Society* (1967) and M.C. Smith, *Principles of Pharmaceutical Marketing* (1991).

that oral contraceptives should be available to women without a prescription.[21]

Educational materials, promotional campaigns, and health-care professionals provide or portray different reasons for using oral contraceptives. These drugs can prevent a specific biological state (pregnancy), now viewed by many women as a medical condition

TABLE 2.6. Personal and Social Concerns Targeted by Drug Promotion Campaigns

CONCERN	EXAMPLES
Performance enhancement	mental (memory, intellectual) physical ability (athletics, work energy, sexual ability)
Mental/emotional adjustment	stress psychiatric symptom states mood control and enhancement
Aging	senility physical signs of aging (wrinkles, hair loss)
Chemical and other dependencies	smoking/nicotine addiction alcohol and drug addiction
Lifestyle	socioeconomic status interpersonal relationships
Conception and family planning	pregnancy control
Life stressors and coping	tension reduction relaxation
Pleasure enhancement	sexual ability
Body image/appearance	height, weight, shape muscle mass skin tone, color (tanning)

Source: M. Montagne, *Journal of Drug Issues* 1992.

or disease. Oral contraceptives prevent problems associated with that state (i.e., the results of becoming pregnant and having a child), such as neglected or abused children, disrupted relationships and broken marriages, or any stigma or guilt associated with having children (i.e., as a single parent). Oral contraceptives also allow the user greater sexual freedoms and a more active sex life. The last reason is limited now by the other biological adverse effect of sexual activity–sexually-transmitted diseases, including AIDS. It is easy to imagine, however, that if cures or preventive means (vaccines) for all sexually-transmitted diseases were discovered, what is perceived by many as the only remaining health concern that deters sexual activity would cease to exist.

Making Decisions About Diseases

As shown, medicalization raises some very interesting questions. When are changes in physical and mental states interpreted as symptoms leading to illness? Are certain conditions, such as pregnancy, child abuse, ordinary stress and tension, small breasts, thinning hair, mental fatigue, and many other personal and social life problems really *diseases*? What is gained or lost by using medications to solve these problems? The answers to these questions are different depending on whom is questioned. It is for the patient to determine his or her own opinions and make decisions on the basis of sound reasoning and judgment.

NOTES

1. Robert M. Veatch, *A Theory of Medical Ethics* (New York, NY: Basic Books, 1981).

2. T.L. Beauchamp and J.F. Childress, *Principles of Biomedical Ethics*, third edition (New York, NY: Oxford University Press, 1989).

3. K. Berg and K.E. Tranoy, eds., *Research Ethics* (New York, NY: Alan R. Liss, 1983).

4. D.M. Gallant and R. Force, eds., *Legal and Ethical Issues in Human Research and Treatment* (New York, NY: S.P. Medical and Scientific Books, 1978).

5. Sidney Wolfe, testimony during Hearings before the Senate Subcommittee on Drug Advertising and Promotion, Washington, DC (December 11, 1990).

6. Andrew Purvis, "Can Drug Firms Be Trusted?" *TIME Magazine* (10 February 1992):43.

7. J.A. Sechzer, ed., *The Role of Animals in Biomedical Research* (New York, NY: New York Academy of Sciences, 1983).

8. A. Rowan, *Of Mice, Models, and Men: A Critical Evaluation of Animal Research* (Albany, NY: State University of New York Press, 1984).

9. M.A. Fox, *The Case for Animal Experimentation* (Berkeley, CA: University of California Press, 1986).

10. Anonymous, "The Top 1000 U.S. Companies Ranked by Industry," *The 1992 Business Week 1000* (April, 1992): 180, 182.

11. John Coster, "Payors, Consumers, and Price Regulations: Access, Efficiency, and Cost Containment," Presentation at the Wharton Health Care Conference, Philadelphia, Pennsylvania (21 February 1992).

12. Anonymous, "A Tale of Two Studies," *American Druggist* 205 (Number 3, March 1992):16.

13. Pharmaceutical Manufacturers Association, *Reporters Handbook for the Prescription Drug Industry* (Washington, DC: PMA, 1992).

14. Karen Dorsey, "Helping Pharmacists Correct Public Misperceptions," *Pharmacy Times* (April 1992):136-137.

15. Mickey C. Smith, *A Social History of the Minor Tranquilizers* (New York, NY: Pharmaceutical Products Press, 1991).

16. S. Cohen, "Current Attitudes about Benzodiazepines: Trial by Media," *Journal of Psychoactive Drugs* 15 (1983):109-113.

17. Rene Dubois, "On the Limitations of Drug Research," in *Drugs in Our Society*, ed. Paul Taladay (Baltimore, MD: Johns Hopkins University Press, 1964):41.

18. P. Conrad and J.W. Schneider, *Deviance and Medicalization: From Badness to Sickness* (St. Louis, MO: Mosby, 1980).

19. Michael Montagne, "The Promotion of Medications for Personal and Social Problems," *Journal of Drug Issues* 22 (1992):391-407.

20. L. McLaughlin, *The Pill, John Rock, and the Church* (Boston, MA: Little, Brown, 1982).

21. H.B. Holmes, B.B. Hoskins, and M. Gross. *Birth Control and Controlling Birth: Women-Centered Perspectives* (Clifton, NJ: Humana Press, 1980).

SUGGESTED READINGS

R.J. Apfel and S.M. Fisher, *To Do No Harm: DES and the Dilemmas of Modern Medicine* (New Haven, CT: Yale University Press, 1984).

J.B. Bakalar and L. Grinspoon, *Drug Control in a Free Society* (London, England: Cambridge University Press, 1984).

B. Barber, *Drugs and Society* (New York, NY: Russell Sage, 1967).

C. Bezold, *The Future of Pharmaceuticals* (New York, NY: John Wiley & Sons, 1981).

J. Goodfield, *Playing God: Genetic Engineering and the Manipulation of Life* (New York, NY: Random House, 1977).

R. Mapes, ed., *Prescribing Practice and Drug Usage* (London, England: Croom Helm, 1980).

Gary M. Matoren, ed., *Clinical Research Process in the Pharmaceutical Industry* (New York, NY: Marcel Dekker, 1984).

P.B. Meyer, *Drug Experiments in Prisoners* (Lexington, MA: D.C. Heath, 1976).

M. Mintz, *By Prescription Only* (Boston, MA: Beacon Press, 1967).

M. Silverman and P.R. Lee, *Pills, Profits and Politics* (Berkeley, CA: University of California Press, 1974).

Peter Temin, *Taking Your Medicines: Drug Regulation in the United States* (Cambridge, MA: Harvard University Press, 1980).

World Health Organization, *The Rational Use of Drugs* (Geneva, Switzerland: World Health Organization, 1987).

Chapter 3

Developing Medications for Consumers

The development of new drug therapies by pharmaceutical companies is a relatively recent phenomenon. As described in the first chapter, there have been many significant changes in the ways that new drugs are discovered and utilized. Before healers became a designated part of society, people used traditional remedies that had been handed down from generation to generation, or they searched throughout nature for their own cures. Societies, through their healers, accumulated information by directly observing the effectiveness of certain remedies.

It has only been in the last century, with the combination of the industrial revolution and the development of scientific medicine, that consumers are no longer actively searching for new sources of therapeutic compounds. In the past 50 years, with the growth in technology, health professionals no longer test potentially useful therapies on individual patients in everyday practice. The pharmaceutical industry has taken over as the discoverer, developer, promoter, and provider of new drugs. How did this role reversal come about?

DISCOVERING MEDICATIONS TO TREAT ILLNESS: A BRIEF HISTORY

The Empirical Approach

The act of healing (therapeutics) has traditionally been viewed as an art, not a science. The healer's ability to make a diagnosis and provide treatment had reached high standards through observation of individual patients and the cautious drawing of conclusions about the disease and the cure. Most treatments were intended to assist the patient's natural power of healing from within the body through the use of simple diets, exercise, and herbal remedies.

This process of disease treatment is known as the **empirical approach**: knowledge of afflictions and beneficial treatments was gained from firsthand experience and observation in individual patients with little regard for science or medical theory. With a heavy emphasis on cures, various mineral and herbal substances were used. If a substance worked for one patient, it was given to another with a similar condition. A great variety of substances might have been studied in a patient until one was found to work successfully. This approach was practiced, unfortunately in many cases to the extreme, for many centuries.

Testing Drugs Prior to Use in Ill Patients

In the early years of the Middle Ages, over 1,000 years ago, the famous healer Avicenna (980-1037) developed some interesting rules for testing drugs. He suggested that a potential new remedy should be tested by:

1. using it in its natural state on an uncomplicated case of a disease;
2. observing the new remedy's effects through comparison of the case with another case using a different treatment; and
3. studying the onset and duration of the remedy's effects, and whether those effects occur repeatedly when used at different times or in different patients.

Avicenna also said that "experimentation must be done with the human body, for testing a drug on a lion or a horse might not prove anything about its effect on man."[1]

In the late 1700s, the great French physician, François Magendie established the science of pharmacology, which is the study of the actions and effects of drugs in the body. He developed a rational, orderly procedure for testing chemical compounds (Table 3.1).

The contemporary approach to discovering new drugs truly began with Paul Ehrlich's notion of drugs as magic bullets. This view of how chemical substances work to produce drug effects uses the

TABLE 3.1. Magendie's Procedure for Testing Chemicals

STAGE	PROCEDURE
1	Prepare the chemical compound from raw material.
2	Determine the physical and chemical properties of that compound.
3	Identify therapeutic effects in animals.
4	Identify therapeutic effects in healthy and diseased humans.
5	Develop the compound into different dosage forms, corresponding to the ways in which the new drug can be administered into the body.

idea of a drug molecule fitting into, or connecting with, a receptor (a receiving area) in or on a cell in the body. The image that most people–including scientists and health professionals–use to understand this idea is that of a key (the drug molecule) fitting into a lock (the cellular receptor), as shown in Figure 3.1.

Testing the ability of a drug molecule to fit a receptor and determining what happens in cells and organs of the body as a result is beneficial. Not only does it help to explain the activity of known drugs–information that can be used to design new drug molecules with increased safety and effectiveness–it allows scientists to understand how the body normally functions (physiology), and what goes wrong when disease develops (pathophysiology).

TESTING DRUGS IN HUMANS: FROM INDIVIDUAL EXPERIENCE TO CLINICAL DRUG TRIALS

The first clinical drug trial, although it was not called that, took place over two centuries ago. It signaled the shift from therapeutics as an *art* to therapeutics as a *science*. In 1753, James Lind published

FIGURE 3.1. How a Drug Molecule Fits a Cellular Receptor

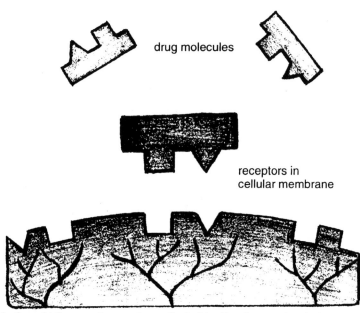

drug molecules

receptors in
cellular membrane

Only the middle receptor can be activated by the drug molecule because their
structures fit together.

his major medical study, *Treatise on the Scurvy*. Scurvy is a condition caused by a lack of vitamin C. In those days, it especially
plagued sailors and other people who could not eat fresh fruit on a
regular basis.

In his study aboard a ship at sea, Lind identified 12 sailors with
scurvy, each having symptoms and characteristics as similar as
possible. He placed them in one area and on a common diet. After a
period of time, the sailors were divided into pairs and ordered to
follow one of several treatments (Table 3.2).

According to Lind's results, "The consequence was that the most
sudden and visible good effects were perceived from the use of
oranges and lemons, one of those [patients] who had taken them
being at the end of six days fit for duty. The other [patient] was the
best recovered of any in his condition."[1]

TABLE 3.2. Lind's Scurvy Study

Two sailors were placed in six groups. Each group received one of the following treatments:

- 25 drops of elixir of vitriol 3 times a day on an empty stomach

- two spoons full of vinegar three times a day

- a quart of cider each day

- a half-pint of seawater every day

- a medicinal paste made of garlic, mustard, myrrh, and balsam of Peru

- two oranges and one lemon every day

Step-Wise Testing of Drugs

By the end of the nineteenth century, medical science had developed two different approaches to researching the therapeutic benefits of chemical compounds. The dominant approach was developed by Magendie, and focused on testing medicines for safety and potentially useful pharmacologic activity in animals. This approach was, and continues to be, a valuable way to determine the toxicologic or poisonous effects of a new drug and to identify possible physiologic effects that might be beneficial in treating disease. This approach is inadequate, of course, because it does not determine the exact curative power of the drug in sick humans. The study of drug action in animals, however, remains an important part of the contemporary drug-development process.

Statistical Evaluation of Drugs

The other approach to researching the effects of drugs emphasized statistical, or mathematical, evaluation of new compounds. This "numerical method" was espoused by Pierre Louis in his 1834 publication, *Essay on Clinical Instruction*. With regard to determining the value of different forms of treatment, he stated:

... if it is possible for us to assure ourselves of the superiority of one [treatment] or other among [patients] in any disease whatever, having regard to the different circumstances of age, sex, and temperament, of strength and weakness, it is doubtless to be done by enquiring if under these circumstances a greater number of individuals have been cured by one means than another. Here again it is necessary to count. . . [1,2]

The success of organized research efforts in the post-war period of the twentieth century was due in part to breakthroughs in experimental methods and statistical research methodology. The process of interpreting research data had become problematic, and the development of new scientific methods signaled the beginning of planned, controlled experiments. The early use of statistical methods and techniques occurred in product development, manufacturing, and quality control. The pharmaceutical industry then applied these techniques to the development and screening of new chemical compounds, production methods, and testing processes of drugs for therapeutic benefits. The full potential of these controlled and **experimental study** methods was realized in the 1950s with the adoption of clinical drug trials as the standard method for evaluating new drug products.[3,4]

The Evolution of Clinical Trials

Clinical trials attempt to replace health professionals' day-to-day observations with a structured approach to testing drugs using a large numbers of patients. Additionally, clinical trials are conducted on the basis of specific scientific theories and involve another form of treatment (or no treatment) to allow objective comparison.

Self-Experimentation by Scientists and Clinicians

Until the 1900s, clinical drug studies consisted of either self-experimentation by researchers or the direct screening of potentially beneficial compounds in patients. Self-experimentation–when the researcher serves as his or her own subject in the experiment–has a very strong, yet unappreciated, tradition in medical drug research.

In these cases, scientists experimented on themselves first when testing a new drug. While some self-experimental studies have resulted in tragedy, many led to important discoveries. A few cases resulted in major breakthroughs and the identification of totally new types of chemical substances for clinical research.[5]

Altman uncovered almost 140 separate experiments over the past four centuries in which 200 different scientists and clinicians served as their own subjects.[5] The most successful examples that had a profound impact on medicine and therapeutics were:

- Forssman, a German surgeon, first discovered the technique of cardiac catheterization (inserting a narrow tube down a vein and into the heart to administer a dye) by conducting the procedure on himself.
- Serturner, a German pharmacist, and Purkinje, a physiologist, determined the dosage range (and overdose limits) of morphine and digitalis (a heart medication) by trying different doses on themselves and noting the effects that occurred.
- The discoverers of disulfiram (an anti-alcoholic drug used in alcoholism treatment) first tested the new drug for its effectiveness in treating worm infections; they discovered that they got very sick (vomiting, headaches) when they drank even small amounts of alcoholic beverages during their experiments. Further self-experimentation disclosed that the drug was more effective in preventing alcoholic relapse than in treating infections.

There were unfortunate instances, however, in which scientists engaged in self-experimentation and the outcome was not quite as positive:

- William Halstead, a Johns Hopkins University surgeon who discovered various forms of anesthesia through self-experimentation with opiates, cocaine, chloroform, and other substances became addicted to those substances.
- Physicians who studied the causes of venereal diseases and cholera, inoculated (injected) themselves with infected pus or blood from sick patients in the hope of finding the cause of the infection, but they all died from the disease.

Chauncey Leake, the great contemporary pharmacologist, has said, "I think pharmacologists have a moral obligation to try such drugs on themselves after appropriate clearance with experimental animals before using them experimentally on any other human being."[6]

Clinical Drug Research

With the organization of drug research activities, individual clinical scientists combined efforts in large specialty research laboratories. The intensely personal spirit of self-experimentation changed to a more detached and impersonal statistical view of drug discovery. The focus of clinical research became the *process* of clinical drug research, rather than the *participants* or the sick patients who were awaiting new therapies.

By the 1930s, the pharmaceutical industry was adopting experimental methods and research designs to develop and screen new compounds, improve production outputs, and test drugs for therapeutic benefits. The full potential of experimental methods in drug research was realized in the 1940s with the growth in scientific knowledge and industrial technology that was initiated by the war effort. Clinical trials became the standard way of measuring therapeutic benefits of new drugs. In the 1960s, the controlled clinical trial, in which a group of patients receiving the experimental drug is compared with another group receiving a control drug or no treatment, had become the standard method of pharmaceutical research. By then, the double-blind strategy of drug testing (when both the patients and researcher are unaware of which treatment is being taken by whom) was adopted to limit the effect of external influences or biases on the true pharmacologic action of the drug. Drug regulations of the 1960s also reinforced the importance of controlled clinical trials by requiring proof of effectiveness of new drugs through the use of these research methods.

CONTEMPORARY CLINICAL DRUG TRIALS

Today, many different types of contemporary drug trials are conducted using a variety of methods. The fundamental purpose is to try or test a new drug in medical (or clinical) environments on sick patients. The goal of the clinical trial is to determine the therapeutic benefits of the new drug in ill humans, after proving safety in animals and safety and effectiveness in healthy humans. The design of drug trials can include various components, including the types of treatments that are being evaluated and compared, patient selection criteria, and the **blinding mechanism** (Table 3.3 and Figure 3.2).

There are several types of clinical drug trials that range considerably in scope and statistical validity. For example, **clinical inquiry**, a simple, nonexperimental method in which patients receive a new drug and massive amounts of data are collected and analyzed to determine its effect, uses no control or comparison group. The **controlled clinical trial**, in which the **control group** consists of either patients who are *not* from the original pool of potential study patients, or patients whose past cases involved receiving treatment in regular health-care or research situations, does not include the process of **randomization** or random assignment.

To determine the true therapeutic benefit of a new unknown drug therapy, the best approach is the **randomized controlled clinical trial**. Because a clinical trial is often performed at a number of hospitals, clinics, and research centers, the number and diversity of study subjects is high. The use of randomized controlled clinical trials leads to more powerful and generalizable results and can also shorten the time of the study.

PARTICIPATION IN CLINICAL DRUG TRIALS

What Are the Concerns?

The general public's attitudes toward clinical drug trials are quite positive. In a 1982 survey, only 6% of consumer respondents believed that medical research in the U.S. was *not* ethical.[7] Participation in clinical trials was seen by respondents as beneficial to both patients and society because it improves medical knowledge. Consumers and patients are still concerned, however. Many problems and issues exist, such as determining whether gains in knowledge from a slight alteration in trial design justify increased risks to

TABLE 3.3. Components of Clinical Drug Trials

Experimental Study:	A research method in which one group of subjects (experimental group) receives a new treatment (e.g., drug, device, surgery), and are compared with one or more control groups who receive different treatments. These groups are studied over the same time period using the same measurements of safety and effectiveness.
Experimental Group:	This group of patients receives the new drug that is under investigation in a clinical trial.
Control Group:	This group of patients receives a different type of treatment, either a traditional one (already approved and used in therapy) or no treatment (they receive a placebo) in a clinical trial.
Randomization:	The process of assigning individual patients to different treatment groups in such a way that each patient has an equal chance, independent of every other patient, of being selected for any particular group. The goal is to make all study groups as equal as possible at the beginning of the experiment.
Blinding:	The process of ensuring that everyone involved in the drug trial is unaware of who is receiving the experimental drug and who is receiving a traditional drug treatment, or a placebo, throughout the duration of the study. In experimental studies, a lack of knowledge about which patients are receiving the treatment being studied can be limited to just the patients (single-blind), both patients and clinicians (double-blind), or patients, clinicians, and the scientific evaluators (triple-blind).
Placebo:	An inactive form of treatment, usually an inert sugar pill, received by patients in the control group. The use of a placebo provides the rationale for the control group to receive no (beneficial) treatment so that a good comparison can be made with the results of the experimental group.

FIGURE 3.2. The Process of Clinical Trial Research

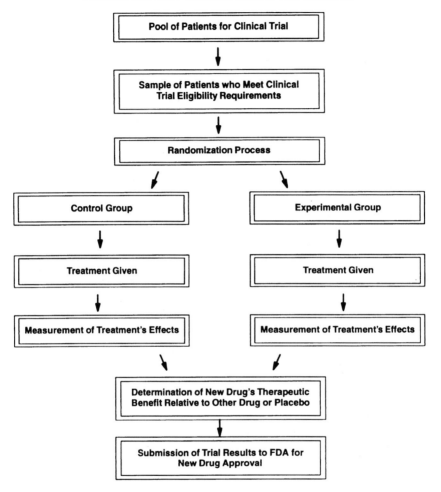

patients or when it is ethical to withhold standard treatment. These issues have become even more important with the increased incidence of certain infections (i.e., AIDS) and chronic diseases. Additionally, although supportive of clinical drug trials, consumers are beginning to question the ethics of placebo control groups in experiments, as well as the lengthy period of time normally required to transfer clinical trial results to general medical practice.

Ethics of Clinical Trials

Strong consumer support for clinical drug trials is likely to be a response to the development of informed-consent procedures. Informed consent evolved during the 1960s and 1970s from one of the key principles of the Nuremberg Code: voluntary consent to participate in a clinical trial by the human subject is morally essential. The code was written in response to the unethical activities of German researchers during World War II.

Clinical trials can be conducted in an ethical manner if they are described carefully to participants. The description of the clinical trial must clearly distinguish *therapeutic* components of the study–those that benefit the patient who is ill–from *research* components of the study–those that benefit the researcher or clinician who is looking for a new treatment approach.

Several issues have become serious concerns for patients considering participation in clinical trials. One example is the randomization process. Randomization, a key part of clinical trial design, might not be justified in all circumstances. This issue has arisen in the quest for drugs to treat AIDS. For example, patients with AIDS believe that all patients should be allowed to participate in clinical trials; no one should be denied treatment because they were randomly placed in the control or placebo group. But if a researcher truly wants to know, scientifically, if a new chemical substance is effective, he or she must employ this experimental technique. Regardless of the existence or type of randomization process used, patients should always be informed of the trial design and whether a randomization procedure will be used.

In response to concerns about the ethics of randomization procedures in clinical research, a new design for randomized clinical trials has been proposed that is well-suited to comparisons of traditional treatment with an experimental treatment. In this design, patients are randomized into one of two groups, similar to the current approach. Patients in the first group receive the traditional (or control) treatment. The second group consists of patients who, prior to the enrollment in the trial, were asked if they would accept the experimental treatment. If a patient in the second group declines experimental treatment, he or she receives the traditional therapy. In analyzing the data at the end of the trial, all patients in the second group, which is considered the experimental group regardless of whether the treatment they actually received was traditional or experimental, are compared with those in the first group, all of whom received the traditional drug. Any loss of statistical efficiency caused by the addition of patients who refused the experimental drug to the experimental group, can be overcome by increasing the total number of patients in the experimental group.

The presumed advantage of this new clinical trial design is that before providing informed consent, patients will know if they are to receive an experimental procedure. Additionally, because it removes the patient from unnecessary participation in the randomization process and allows some patients to choose between traditional and experimental treatments, it is acknowledged as ethical and reasonable. This proposed design, however, has received much commentary and criticism: disadvantages include elimination of blinding, reduced statistical efficiency, and the existence of several different ethical issues.

Because alternative clinical trial methods are acceptable, many questions arise regarding the conventional design, including why the randomization process and the use of a control group is necessary to determine new drug effectiveness.[1] The answers to these questions are determined on the basis of mathematics and probability principles, as well as the influence of the **placebo phenomenon**.

The Placebo Phenomenon in Drug Research

The primary goal of an experimental drug study is to determine whether a new drug is more effective and safer than an existing drug, or than no treatment at all. However, the placebo phenomenon can complicate research and skew results.[8] It is well known that many people experience what they believe are drug effects after taking an inert (inactive) sugar pill. If the placebo phenomenon occurs during new drug testing, researchers do not have definite proof that effects described by patients are due to the drug itself, the placebo phenomenon, or a combination of the two influences. In other words, a comparison of therapies is needed to validate research results.

Recall the experiment conducted by James Lind. How could he

be certain that citrus fruit would help alleviate scurvy? Just because two sailors who ate fruit felt better, does that mean that everyone who eats citrus fruit could be cured of scurvy?

The following modern example might help to illustrate the importance of the placebo phenomenon in a drug study:

> A company's scientists have just discovered a new drug that they hope will be effective in relieving pain. To determine the drug's activity in humans, the company has designed a clinical trial. Fifty patients were identified and recruited, all of whom suffer from arthritis pain. Patients were given the new drug for six weeks, and at the end of that time, 60% of the patients claimed that they felt less pain.

What does this statistic mean? Did the drug actually relieve pain in 30 patients? What are possible reasons for this result?

OPTION 1:   The drug does have pharmacological activity and is effective for relieving pain in most patients.

OPTION 2:   Most of the patients were so excited and hopeful that this new drug would relieve their pain that it *seemed* as if they were in less pain after six weeks of therapy. This could be due to:

(a)   Slight but real therapeutic activity, such that the effect that most patients experienced, a reduction in pain, was imagined to be much greater than it really would be for most people.

(b)   Most of the patients experienced a regression or temporary reduction in their pain because their arthritic condition was going into remission during the time in which they participated in the drug study. (This remission can be caused by changes in season or temperature, reduced stress in the patient's life, reduced exposure to toxic chemicals at home or at work, and other illnesses that the patient is experiencing, just to name a few possibilities.)

OPTION 3:   Patients could have been using many other types of therapies during the drug study, and did not tell their doctor/researchers about them. Patients might have been experimenting with, or already taking, other prescription or nonprescription drugs, herbal medicines, home remedies, or using non-drug treatments (e.g., hot packs, massage, medical devices). As such, it cannot be known which of the therapies used during the study actually produced the pain relief; it could have been any one or any combination.

As you can see, it would be difficult for the company to prove that the new drug is effective in relieving pain. How could efficacy be determined with greater certainty? The researchers need a group of patients with the same condition who are *not* taking the new drug (a control group), for comparison during the study. The company must ensure that patients in both the control and experimental groups, clinicians who treat them, and the primary researchers who observe the drug's effects are not biased by knowing which patients are receiving the drug and which patients are not (double blinding).

With a double-blind study design and randomization, most people involved in the study will not know who is receiving the experimental and the control treatment, allowing a more objective assessment of the new therapy. Of course the blinding process can "break down" in studies where some patients are not receiving any treatment, and other patients are taking a potent drug with intensely noticeable and specific effects. In this instance, it will only be a short time before participants and researchers know who is getting which treatment on the basis of significant effects that some of the patients are experiencing.

Mathematics and laws of probability also influence how clinical trials are conducted, as well as the need for the randomization process. Every patient in the original patient pool (or group) must have a chance, equal to every other patient, of being assigned to a particular treatment group. If that does not happen, then the "equivalence" of the treatment groups cannot be known.

If we continue with the example of the study of a new pain medication:

The researchers have decided to include the first 25 patients who are interested in the study and assign them to the experimental group. The other 25 patients are assigned to the control group. What do the study results mean now?

It is possible that the first 25 patients were those with greater baseline pain. Patients were informed of the clinical trial, and those who were "hurting" most enrolled sooner than those patients with less pain. Thus, there is a difference between the two groups at the start of the study, before anyone begins receiving any type of treatment; the group receiving the new drug is sicker than the control group. Consequently, the new drug could seem more or less effective than it truly is when the comparison is made.

There are other variations in clinical trial methodology that have an impact on patient participation. Some of these involve very unique or innovative approaches, including the organization and direction of clinical trial studies predominantly by patient groups, rather than physicians or clinical researchers. These consumer-directed studies will be discussed in Chapters 9 and 10. For a traditional, uncomplicated clinical drug trial, however, there are some basic steps that occur, and the rules surrounding a participant's role in such a study are quite similar.

Participation in a Clinical Drug Trial: What Happens?

The first step in becoming involved in a clinical drug trial is to identify where trials are taking place. Most clinical trials are conducted by universities, usually at a medical school's teaching hospital, at large research-based hospitals, or in pharmaceutical company laboratories. Potential clinical trial subjects are usually notified and recruited through private practitioners (especially specialists who might be involved as investigators in the study), newspaper advertisements, and other announcements of planned or ongoing research studies (especially in college and alternative newspapers), or through private medical and health-care clinics that engage in contracted research projects. These advertisements and notices provide basic information regarding the nature of the study and the types of patients that are needed.

Patients who wish to participate in a clinical trial must contact the study team to become enrolled in the trial. Basic information on the patient's medical history and prior drug use is collected to ascertain eligibility for enrollment. Selection criteria identify other diseases, drug use, and associated problems that could confuse, disrupt, or present problems in the study process. If the investigational drug has the potential to produce adverse reactions for patients with certain concurrent conditions, or if it is contraindicated with other medications that the patient is taking, the patient will be excluded from the study. All selection criteria lists are designed to protect the research subjects and to limit the incidence of problems in the study process.

Although there is a great deal of paperwork during clinical trial enrollment, the most important item is the **informed-consent process**. Informed consent has become the cornerstone of policies and procedures related to the ethical design and clinical drug trial conduct. Informed consent refers to the disclosure and understanding of information about the experiment to the patient and the voluntary consent of that patient. Unfortunately, a patient's signature on an informed-consent form does not guarantee that the subject has truly given *fully-informed consent*. A recent study of the readability of informed-consent forms has shown that the reading grade level of these forms was substantially higher than the eighth-grade standard. Furthermore, upon review and modification of the forms, the reading-grade level had not changed significantly.[9] What this means for researchers is that trial participants might be confused by the form and misinterpret its contents. Special efforts to ensure that patients understand and agree with clinical trial requirements should be made.

There are a number of basic elements in informed-consent agreements. The essential aspects of the clinical drug trial process that must be understood by potential participants are listed in Table 3.4, as well as other pertinent information that is included on the informed-consent form or offered to clinical trial participants.

In most cases, the inclusion of informed-consent items depends greatly on the guidelines of individual institutions and their research review boards. The inclusion of these elements can also result from changes in governmental policies regarding the use of human sub-

---

TABLE 3.4. Information Included in Informed-Consent Forms

- An invitation, not a request or a demand, to participate.

- A description of the research project, including title, purpose, study design, location, patient selection criteria, duration, and scheduling of participation.

- A description of foreseeable risks and discomforts to the patient.

- A listing of appropriate alternative treatments and procedures that can benefit and that are available to the patient.

- A description of the benefits of the study to the individual patient, to other patients, and to society.

- A statement regarding confidentiality of patient records, or in some instances (such as in some survey research), a description of how the participant's anonymity will be assured and maintained.

- An explanation of compensation or medical treatment provided to the patient in case of injury or harm.

- A description of procedures used in storing and destroying all materials and samples at the conclusion of the study.

- A listing of the names and phone numbers of the principal investigator, contact persons, and/or other personnel connected with the study, in case the participant has questions, concerns, problems, or wishes to withdraw.

- A statement making it clear to the potential participant that participation is voluntary, that a choice not to participate will involve no penalty or change in current or future treatment, and that the patient can withdraw at any time without penalty or loss.

---

jects in biomedical research. Health-care researchers should always refer to the specific policies and procedures of their institutions and inquire into any policy changes at the professional organization and governmental agency levels.

Every clinical drug trial must protect the patient. The informed-consent process allows prospective participants to review all aspects of the study, determine their own benefits and risks, outline what will be done, and establish what will happen if something goes wrong. This step will also include many rounds of tests and examinations to collect baseline data on each patient who will receive treatment.

Next, the clinical trial begins and treatments are started. It is feasible that changes will be made in the study plans. However, patients must be notified of these changes if they significantly affect them or the treatment they are receiving. More rounds of examinations and tests will be conducted, and preliminary reports on how well the treatments are working will be provided. An important issue for patients is their compliance with the treatment regimen and the study's guidelines. A major problem in many clinical trials is that patients are noncompliant; they do not take the medication exactly as directed. As you can imagine, patients taking an experimental drug in a manner different from the protocol (study plan) can confuse the results.

Finally, the clinical trial ends. This date, called the endpoint, is stated at the beginning of the study in the informed-consent form. For instance, when a patient receives information about the clinical trial, he or she will know that the treatments will be taken for a specified period of time. The endpoint of a clinical trial can change; usually it is moved up and the trial ends sooner. The best example of this is when the experimental treatment is found to be significantly more effective than the control treatment. If the investigational drug is shown through the clinical trial process to save patients' lives or prevent their disease from causing irreversible damage, then patients receiving the placebo drug or control treatment cannot be denied the new treatment.

Patients participating in a clinical trial should ask questions throughout the process, whenever they are confused or want to know what is happening. Participants should always feel comfortable with the trial and should feel free to drop out at any time. Additionally, patients should be aware of quackery disguised as real clinical research. Asking questions, reading the informed-consent form, and meeting the trial's investigators will reduce problems of this type. A release form or other document that waives patients' rights if they are harmed during the course of the study should not be signed. Finally, patients should be very suspicious if they are asked to pay any amount of money for the investigational drug, examinations, or tests that are given, or for additional treatment of problems that result from participation in the study. Appendix B of this book provides several sources of information for patients interested in participating in clinical drug trials.

To review clinical trial research plans and protect participants, **institutional review boards** (IRBs)–groups of health-care professionals and researchers–are organized (Table 3.5). As study of the informed-consent process has shown, some patients and researchers use the research process for their personal benefit.[10] The development and implementation of IRBs is vital to ensure integrity in conducting clinical drug trials. The ability of these boards to monitor research and their effectiveness in assuring informed consent, however, can be limited by the board's ability to constantly evaluate the trial's progress.[11]

CONCLUSION

It should be obvious that clinical drug trials, especially those that are randomized and controlled, are an excellent approach for deter-

---

TABLE 3.5. Purpose of IRB Review of Clinical Drug Trial Plans

The goal of institutional review boards is to ensure that:

- Selection of subjects is fair and equitable, and there are safeguards to protect subjects, especially those of diminished autonomy.

- Informed consent is obtained and documented for each patient.

- Risks to subjects are minimized; research procedures used are consistent with good scientific design and do not expose subjects to unnecessary risks; if the subject is a patient, procedures that are already being performed on the patient for diagnostic or therapeutic reasons are continued.

- Risks to subjects are reasonable in terms of the expected benefits and the knowledge gained.

- The research plan (protocol) includes monitoring of all information to ensure continual safety for the subjects.

- Provisions are made to protect the privacy of subjects and to maintain the confidentiality of the information collected.

mining the actual beneficial effects of new drug compounds. In fact, one clinical trial expert has stated that the clinical trial method has become the most desirable and most conclusive way to gain knowledge on drug efficacy. It has been stated that clinical trials have become as indispensable to medical science as are autopsies.[12] Even though there has been much progress in the design and conduct of clinical trials, they still are far from being a perfect method of ensuring drug safety and effectiveness.

The clinical drug trial can be thought of as a large-scale, standardized alternative to the process through which individual clinicians gradually accumulate knowledge using "bedside" clinical experience with a particular therapy. In essence, clinical medicine becomes scientific through the use of a clinical trial. In a drug trial, clinical observations tend to be made in a systematic manner, while in personal clinical experience, they tend to be anecdotal in nature. Personal experience is usually more subjective and less quantitative, or numerical, than observations made on the basis of a randomized and controlled experimental design. On the other hand, clinical trials only answer those questions that have been specifically asked. Personal experience can address factors that have not yet been examined in the trial process. One argument concerning the usefulness of clinical trials is that the experimental conditions of the trial often differ so much from the conditions encountered in clinical practice (real life), that the trial results might not be applicable to everyday patient situations.

The quality of clinical trials has been another concern expressed over the past ten years. In a review of previous clinical trials, it was found that the majority were uncontrolled, poorly controlled, or were poorly designed. The percentage of adequately controlled trials to all research studies has actually declined over the past three decades.[13]

A recent development has been the use of multi-center clinical trials, which are experiments that involve two or more clinical facilities, each of which is responsible for recruitment, treatment, and follow-up of patients under a commonly-accepted plan. Data from all centers are then combined in the research-analysis stage. Multi-center trials have a number of advantages, especially in terms of the number of patients that can be enrolled and evaluated. The majority of single-center trials that are performed have too few patients. Additionally, the range of different people involved usually leads to a better research design and more careful execution of the study. The larger number of clinics and the different patient populations can also provide a more realistic test of the treatment in question. Multi-center trials, however, can be more complex and more expensive to organize and operate.

NOTES

1. D.D. Vogt and Michael Montagne, "Historical Review," in *The Clinical Research Process in the Pharmaceutical Industry*, ed. Gary M. Matoren (New York, NY: Marcel Dekker, 1984).

2. Claude Bernard, *An Introduction to the Study of Experimental Medicine* (New York, NY: MacMillan, 1927).

3. L.M. Friedman, C.D. Furberg, and D.L. DeMets, *Fundamentals of Clinical Trials* (Littleton, MA: John Wright, 1981).

4. S.H. Shapiro and T.A. Louis, eds., *Clinical Trials, Issues, and Approaches* (New York, NY: Marcel Dekker, 1983).

5. L.K. Altman, *Who Goes First? The Story of Self-Experimentation in Medicine* (New York, NY: Random House, 1987).

6. Chauncey D. Leake, *An Historical Account of Pharmacology to the Twentieth Century* (Springfield, IL: Charles C. Thomas, 1975).

7. R.B. Casselith, E.J. Luck, D.S. Miller, and S. Jurwitz, "Attitudes Toward Clinical Trials Among Patients and the Public," *Journal of the American Medical Association* 248 (1982):968.

8. H. Brody, *Placebos and the Philosophy of Medicine: Clinical, Conceptual, and Ethical Issues* (Chicago, IL: University of Chicago Press, 1977).

9. Rebecca J. Murgatroyd and Rhonda M. Cooper, "Readability of Informed Consent Forms," *American Journal of Hospital Pharmacy* 48 (1991):2651-2652.

10. B. Barber, J.J. Lally, J.L. Makarushka, and D. Sullivan, *Research on Human Subjects* (New York, NY: Russell Sage, 1973).

11. B.H. Gray, *Human Subjects in Medical Experimentation* (New York, NY: John Wiley & Sons, 1975).

12. K.K. Uberla, "Randomized Clinical Trials: Why Not?" *Controlled Clinical Trials* 1 (1981):295.

13. E. Hemminki, "Quality of Clinical Trials–A Concern for Three Decades," *Methods of Information in Medicine* 21 (1982):81.

SUGGESTED READINGS

T.L. Beauchamp and J.F. Childress, *Principles of Biomedical Ethics* (New York, NY: Oxford University Press, 1983).

K. Berg and K.E. Tranoy, eds., *Research Ethics* (New York, NY: Alan R. Liss, 1983).

R.E. Cranford and A.E. Doudera, *Institutional Ethics Committees and Health Care Decision Making* (Ann Arbor, MI: Health Administration Press, 1984).

R. DerSimonian, L.J. Charette, B. McPeek, and F. Mosteller, "Reporting on Methods in Clinical Trials," *New England Journal of Medicine* 306 (1982):1332.

D.M. Gallant and R. Force, eds., *Legal and Ethical Issues in Human Research and Treatment* (New York, NY: SP Medical and Scientific, 1978).

E.L. Kinney, "Underrepresentation of Women in New Drug Trials," *Annals of Internal Medicine* 95 (1981):495.

R.J. Levine, *Ethics and Regulation of Clinical Research* (Baltimore, MD: Urban and Schwarzenberg, 1981).

A.A. Rubin, ed., *New Drugs, Discovery and Development* (New York, NY: Marcel Dekker, 1978).

A. Shafer, "The Ethics of the Randomized Clinical Trial," *New England Journal of Medicine* 307 (1982):719.

U.S. Food and Drug Administration, "From Test Tube to Patient: New Drug Development in the United States," *FDA Consumer* 1 (1988):1-59.

Chapter 4

The Food and Drug Administration and Drug Approval

Before the 1900s, consumers of drug products were exposed to considerable risks. Product ingredients and claims of drug manufacturers were not verified or regulated. Because some medications can be toxic or addictive if inadequately tested or inappropriately used, the United States government has assumed primary responsibility for protecting consumers. By instituting procedures that ensure drug safety and effectiveness, the government is able to regulate the pharmaceutical industry and minimize hazardous situations for patients.

HISTORY OF DRUG REGULATION IN THE UNITED STATES

The Laws: Safety and Effectiveness

A serious concern in the late 1800s was a rise in the number of itinerant pill peddlers and traveling medicine shows that sold bottled elixirs and other patent medicines as cure-alls for dreaded illnesses. These "life-saving" products were often colored and flavored water or inert tablets. Additionally, an increase in drug poisonings and publications like Upton Sinclair's *The Jungle* in 1906, forced Congress to bring fraudulent practices under control. One individual, Harvey Washington Wiley, Head Chemist for the Department of Agriculture's Bureau of Chemistry, provided the impetus to develop a plan to make food and drug protection a responsibility of the federal government.[1] The Pure Food and Drug Act (or Wiley Act) of 1906 was passed to prevent, or locate and remove, **adulterated** (contaminated) or misbranded (inaccurately or incompletely labeled) food products from the marketplace.

In the early 1900s, medications were not considered a problem, except for the inclusion of alcohol or various psychoactive drugs, such as heroin, cocaine, and marijuana, in some patent medicines. The 1906 drug law did not require product testing for safety or therapeutic effectiveness, or product registration before marketing. It did require active ingredients to be listed on the product's labeling, including the alcohol content of patent medicines (Figure 4.1). Later amendments prohibited false labeling of drug products and fraudulent claims of treatment. Unfortunately, the responsibility of demonstrating that the product's labeling was false or fraudulent was on the *federal government*.

In 1937, over 100 people–mostly children–died after ingesting an elixir of sulfanilamide that was improperly prepared. This product contained one of the first sulfa drugs and was quite popular because it was one of the first oral anti-bacterial preparations available to the general public. The product was prepared by dispersing the active drug in a liquid suspension using diethylene glycol (antifreeze), instead of the usual solvent, propylene glycol. The deaths that occurred after use of this product demonstrated a profound need for safety-testing methods to ensure product safety prior to marketing.

As a result of this tragedy, the Federal Food, Drug, and Cosmetic Act was passed in 1938. This legislation contained measures that required assurances of drug-product safety, strengthened provisions of earlier laws governing drug labeling and therapeutic claims, and enhanced the power and responsibilities of the U.S. Food and Drug Administration (FDA). (To facilitate generation of needed revenues and increase their visibility, the Bureau of Chemistry had become the Food, Drug, and Insecticide Administration in 1927. In 1931, the name was changed to the Food and Drug Administration.)[1] The Food, Drug, and Cosmetic Act also required premarketing clearance of drug products, not only for purity, but also for safety when taken as labeled. The regulation placed the burden of proof on the *manufacturer* to demonstrate product safety *before* marketing. Ad-

FIGURE 4.1. Herbal Medicine with Ingredient List. Credit: Michael Montagne, personal collection

HAVE YOU CATARRH ?

CATARRH OF THE THROAT? NASAL CATARRH OR CATARRH AFFECTIONS?

Do you suffer from catarrh of any kind, in any of its stages or from any of its effects? If so, try Dr. Hammond's Internal Catarrh Remedy.

Retail price...$1.00
Our price, per bottle.. .5 I
Our price, per dozen bottles... 5.00

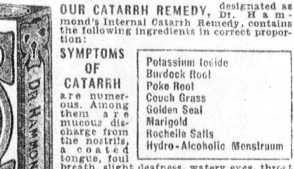

OUR CATARRH REMEDY, designated as Dr. Hammond's Internal Catarrh Remedy, contains the following ingredients in correct proportion:

SYMPTOMS OF CATARRH are numerous. Among them are mucous discharge from the nostrils, a coated

| Potassium Iodide |
| Burdock Root |
| Poke Root |
| Couch Grass |
| Golden Seal |
| Marigold |
| Rochelle Salts |
| Hydro-Alcoholic Menstruum |

tongue, foul breath, slight deafness, watery eyes, throat troubles, indigestion, and in fact, catarrh has been mistaken in throat troubles for tonsilitis and other complications. Its effects are quite similar in these instances and often deceive those so afflicted. If you have any one or more of these symptoms, you are invited to give Dr. Hammond's Internal Catarrh Remedy a trial. It is designed to go straight to the root of the malady and enables the tissues affected to throw off poisons and perform their functions perfectly.

DR. HAMMOND'S INTERNAL CATARRH

REMEDY is a preparation which has met with decided success in the treatment of this disease. It is a highly efficient preparation and composed of ingredients known for their beneficial action upon catarrhal diseases.

IF YOU KNOW THAT YOU ARE A SUF-

FERER FROM CATARRH, send for a bottle of Dr. Hammond's Internal Catarrh Remedy and give it a thorough trial, according to directions. Your experience, no doubt, will be the same as that of thousands of other customers who have received benefit by the use of this remedy right from the start and obtained final relief and cure by continuing the treatment a reasonable length of time.

ditionally, the emphasis of these laws and regulations shifted from foods to drug products.

The Humphrey-Durham Amendments to the Food, Drug, and Cosmetic Act, which were enacted in 1951, created two separate categories of drug products: prescription and nonprescription. Until this law, there was no requirement for a particular drug product to be labeled as "prescription only." **Prescription drugs** are viewed as unsafe for self-medication and require physician direction and supervision. Patients must visit and discuss health problems with a licensed prescriber (i.e., physician, dentist, osteopath, and a few other health professionals in certain states) to obtain a prescription drug. A **nonprescription**, or over-the-counter, **drug** does not require a prescription from a licensed prescriber.

Another important legislative change occurred as a result of the 1984 Price Competition/Patent Term Restoration Act. This law extended the period of patent protection for products, and enabled pharmaceutical manufacturers to be compensated for years of patent life lost during research, development, and product approval by the FDA. **Generic drug** approval was also addressed by this legislation. Provisions for **abbreviated new drug application** (ANDA) submission for all drug products were also described.[1]

The Laws: Drug Pricing and Advertising

A variety of congressional hearings, lurid journalistic accounts, and other events in the 1950s and 1960s identified irregularities in the activities of pharmaceutical companies. These hearings emphasized prescription-drug pricing, especially administrative pricing–prices determined not by forces of supply and demand but by administrators within the pharmaceutical industry. This decision-making process was examined to determine just how price structures were established and maintained within the industry. By the hearing's conclusion, the industry was viewed as ignoring public interest and subverting science for monetary gain. The highly-publicized drug disaster of the early 1960s–the use of thalidomide, a drug that produced birth defects in children–seemed to confirm the public's suspicion that the pharmaceutical industry was more concerned with profitability than the public's welfare.

Congressional hearings on the pricing of prescription drugs also uncovered many abuses in the realm of advertising. Questionable promotional practices at that time included the following:

- emphasis of a drug's beneficial effects and de-emphasis of adverse effects and limitations of use,
- claims of beneficial effects outside the drug's actual pharmacological activity,
- claims made on the basis of testimonials or other accounts and statements that were not supported by well-controlled studies,
- an overemphasis of trade names and exclusion of common or generic names,
- the use of superlatives (i.e., unique, superior, best, fastest) to describe a drug's effectiveness, especially in cases where the drug possessed no outstanding qualities beyond similar products on the market.[2]

To add to the problematic situation, it was assumed that physicians had sufficient expertise regarding the appropriate use of drug therapies and that they would not fall prey to false or misleading advertising. As such, prescription-drug advertising was not included in legislation for misleading advertising. Consequently, the responsibility of verifying the information, claims, data, references, and testimonials in drug advertisements and promotions was the exclusive responsibility of readers: the physicians!

Vocal concern over the hearing's findings quickly resulted in legislative action: the Kefauver-Harris amendments to the Federal Food, Drug, and Cosmetic Act were passed in 1962. These amendments enabled the regulatory body–the FDA–to force the withdrawal of a drug from the marketplace if it was deemed to be unsafe or if there was lack of substantial evidence that it was effective. The statute placed the burden of proving both safety, and now *effectiveness*, on the pharmaceutical manufacturer seeking product marketing approval.

In the Kefauver-Harris amendments, the FDA also provided guidelines for drug testing that would generate acceptable data for the drug-approval process. Mandatory proof of *effectiveness* was added to the previous requirement of safety testing for a new drug product. Because of the increased costs of drug testing and the large amount of information needed for the FDA's approval process, these amendments resulted in a reduction of the number of new and different drug products brought to the U.S. market.

Before the 1962 amendments, responsibility for the regulation of drug advertising belonged to the Federal Trade Commission (FTC) of the U.S. government. The 1962 amendments shifted the responsibility for *prescription* medication marketing to the Secretary of Health, Education, and Welfare, a position now known as the Secretary of Health and Human Services. Thus, FDA regulates and enforces prescription-drug advertising under a delegation of authority. Responsibility for regulating *nonprescription* drug marketing (i.e., over-the-counter drugs, herbal remedies, nutritional supplements, and health commodities), especially advertising in media intended for viewing by consumers, such as television and magazines, was retained by the FTC.

TODAY'S DRUG APPROVAL

> How many times have you heard or read a new story about a scientific "breakthrough" in the development of a promising new drug, only to find out later that marketing of the product is still years away? . . . Any one of us, at some time, may be in need of a new therapy to cure an ailment or improve the quality of our lives. . . . If you understand the process, you will be less vulnerable to false hopes and better able to realistically gauge the true value of so-called "breakthroughs."[3]
>
> *Frank E. Young, MD, PhD*
> *former Commissioner of the Food and Drug Administration*

Why Is the U.S. Drug-Approval System Important?

Although it is a somewhat tedious process to an outside observer, the drug-approval system in the United States is actually very dynamic and controversial. It is quite a challenge for the FDA to respond quickly and effectively to the constantly-changing healthcare environment. Debates regarding decisions to alter the methods of drug approval and implement changes can be intense. And, to make the situation more urgent, patients' lives often lie in the balance.

Many groups are stakeholders in the activities of the FDA, including the pharmaceutical industry, health-care professionals, and patients. The drug-approval process has seen major shifts in priorities and several crises over the past decade (i.e., the generic-drug scandal). Additionally, substantial changes have been made in the types and nature of the information that can be presented or recommended by the industry and by health-care professionals. For example, recent guidelines that redefine the pharmaceutical industry's responsibilities in the education of health-care professionals about prescription products have significantly affected related marketing practices.[4]

Patient access to drugs is also influenced by laws and regulations affecting the drug-approval process. For example, critically important drug therapies and vaccines for life-threatening conditions, such as AIDS, are now made available more quickly. Thus, an awareness of the drug-approval process and potential changes in related regulations can help patients learn about and obtain new drugs sooner, become enrolled in a clinical trial of a life-saving investigational agent, or receive a vaccine to prevent life-threatening illness if potentially at risk.

With passage of the Pure Food and Drug Act of 1906, the American pharmaceutical industry was restricted by regulations that defined drug labeling. Because the way in which the contents were to be *used* was not affected or restricted by law, a lack of jurisdiction remained regarding patent medicines, and curative claims went uncontested. Producers did not need to prove claims for their products, no matter how deceptive. Today, the introduction of a new drug requires manufacturers to submit the results of safety and efficacy testing to demonstrate that use, under the conditions described on the label, is indeed safe for humans.

What Is the Food and Drug Administration?

While regulation of health-care practice and health professionals occurs mostly at the individual state level, the federal government is the primary regulator of drug *products*. The FDA is an agency of the federal government that has several responsibilities (Table 4.1).

TABLE 4.1. Responsibilities of the Food and Drug Administration Related to Human Drugs

- premarketing clearance of all new drug products on the basis of purity, safety, and effectiveness

- regulation of all labeling, including advertising, of prescription-drug products

- regulation of manufacturing by using "good manufacturing practices" and by instituting recalls of unacceptable products

- regulation of bioequivalence standards for generic drugs

- postmarketing surveillance (after a drug is on the market) to detect unanticipated adverse reactions and other problems associated with a drug's use

It is not the FDA's job to conduct the clinical or animal testing of drugs, nor does the FDA develop new drugs. The agency's functions include review of drug-approval applications, which are submitted by industry researchers (or sponsors), and protection of consumers after products are approved through a wide range of surveillance activities.[2]

Although they are not specifically addressed in this book, food products, cosmetics, and medical devices, such as diagnostic equipment, are the domain of the FDA as well. Overall, the 7,000 employees of the FDA regulate over 90,000 businesses and monitor the sale of over $570 billion worth of products each year–all at a cost of about $2 per taxpayer.[5] It is also important to recall that while the FDA approves new drug products for safe and effective use, including substances that will be made available as nonprescription or over-the-counter drugs, the advertising of nonprescription drug products is regulated by the FTC. Both the FDA and the FTC, however, have little control over the prescribing behaviors of health professionals. Once a drug product has been approved for the market, there is little that the FDA can do to regulate *how* it is used. Thus, a drug *can* be used in daily practice to treat symptoms or diseases for which it has not been formally approved by the FDA. The FDA will act if products are promoted for unapproved uses, or if approved products result in personal injury after they are marketed.

Although inability to regulate drug use might seem to contradict the goals of the FDA, physicians' ability to prescribe drugs outside of official labeling is an important factor in ensuring optimal and unrestricted medical care. Such drug use helps expand medical knowledge and identify more effective therapies for particular conditions. Often, the bureaucratic wheels of the FDA turn too slowly for medical professionals and patients, and perceived benefits associated with unapproved drug use appear to outweigh potential risks. Usually, the FDA and pharmaceutical manufacturers will request or file for formal approval of the drug's use in a condition that has been treated outside of official labeling.

THE BASIC DRUG-APPROVAL PROCESS

The Center for Drug Evaluation and Research (CDER) of the FDA is responsible for regulating the review and approval of drug products, including both nonprescription (over-the-counter [OTC]) and prescription drugs. There are eight offices of the CDER: the Office of the Director, the Office of Management, the Office of Epidemiology and Biostatistics, the Office of Compliance, the Office of Drug Standards, the Office of Pharmaceutical Research Resources, and two offices dealing with Drug Evaluation (the first dealing with cardio-renal, neuro-pharmacological, chemotherapeutic and radiopharmaceutical, surgical-dental, coagulation, and gastrointestinal drug products; the second dealing with anti-infective, endocrine, and anti-viral drug products).[6] Biologics are reviewed and approved by the Center for Biologics Evaluation and Research (CBER) of the FDA.

For the purposes of this discussion, **drugs** are defined as natural or synthetic substances that are effective in the prevention, treatment, or cure of disease. They include such products as aspirin, aluminum-magnesium antacid, and propranolol. **Biologics** are any virus, therapeutic serum, toxin, antitoxin, vaccine, blood, blood component or derivative, allergenic product, or similar product applicable to the prevention, treatment, or cure of diseases or injuries of humans. Specific biologics include albumin and packed red blood cells–two products that are used for volume replacement in patients experiencing significant blood loss and shock–and oral poliovirus vaccine–which has served to virtually eliminate polio in the United States.

There are four major steps in the drug-approval process.

Step 1: Preclinical Research

Initial discovery and synthesis of a new drug substance are the first steps toward the marketing of a prescription drug. Discovery of an effective and safe drug has been likened to finding the proverbial needle in a haystack–hundreds of chemical structures and molecular formulas are considered before one becomes a truly useful prescription drug. According to the Pharmaceutical Manufacturers Association (PMA), which represents research-based pharmaceutical firms, a drug requires 12 years and over $200 million to undergo study, testing, and evaluation before it can be marketed to the public (Figure 4.2).[7] As one can see, the costs of producing a successful drug, as well as the money lost to drugs that failed, are substantial.[2]

Drug discovery and synthesis are unique processes–there is no standard mechanism for finding a safe and effective pharmaceutical agent. Sometimes nature provides a substance that is proven effective. Other times researchers work backwards from the disease to the drug, looking for ways to combat a particular infection or target a specific cancer cell. In the latter case, a drug molecule is modeled to fit a particular need, using computer technology, biotechnology, or study of the body's biochemistry. For example, lovastatin (Mevacor®, Merck Sharp and Dohme), a popular drug used to treat high cholesterol, was discovered after intense research of the chemical reactions that occur in the body to make, use, and metabolize cholesterol.

Evaluation of a potential new drug begins in the laboratories of pharmaceutical manufacturers and occurs in animals. Both short-term (one to three years) and long-term (two to ten years) research is conducted to determine safety and effectiveness of a new entity. Until it is believed that the compound might be effective in humans, it remains in a researcher's laboratory, and the FDA remains unaware of its existence. Hundreds of compounds are synthesized, developed, and researched in this manner each year, compared with the 20 to 30 new drugs that are approved annually by the FDA. The

FIGURE 4.2. Drugs Development Cost

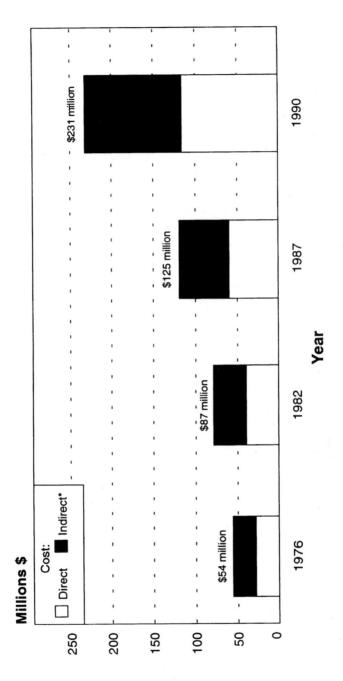

Millions $

Cost:
☐ Direct
■ Indirect*

$54 million — 1976
$87 million — 1982
$125 million — 1987
$231 million — 1990

Year

*Cost of money invested over time (opportunity cost)

SOURCE: PMA

failures–those that were not safe or effective–are abandoned for other possibilities.

Step 2: Filing an Investigational New Drug Application or a New Drug Application

After successfully conducting laboratory and animal tests with a new drug, the second step toward achieving marketing approval for the manufacturer is the submission of an investigational new drug (IND) application to the FDA. An **investigational new drug** is a new pharmaceutical product that has not yet been shown to be safe and effective in humans, but that does seem to be safe and effective in the management of a disease or condition on the basis of animal tests.

An IND is submitted by a pharmaceutical manufacturer or **sponsor** to request permission to conduct **clinical trials** (human testing) of the drug. After a 30-day IND-review period, the sponsor is allowed to investigate the value of the drug in human subjects. If there are any concerns regarding the drug's safety, the FDA places the IND on clinical hold and the sponsor may not begin testing until changes are made to eliminate safety concerns. (See Figure 4.3 for an elementary overview of the U.S. drug-approval process.) Because the Food, Drug, and Cosmetic Act allows investigational new drugs to be shipped from state to state within the U.S., researchers around the country can evaluate the drug in a variety of patients, and consumers have the opportunity to acquire the drug prior to U.S. marketing approval.[8] Other specific components of an IND are listed in Table 4.2.

Step 3: Clinical Testing of the New Drug

Unless the FDA puts an IND on clinical hold during the review period, clinical testing of the drug can begin. The overall goal is to collect and review data to determine whether the possibility of dangerous adverse events outweighs the expected utility of the drug.[9] Clinical testing is conducted in three phases:

Phase I: Clinical Pharmacology and Toxicology

The first phase of clinical testing is directed at determining the drug's safe dosage range, the preferred administration route, the

FIGURE 4.3. The U.S. Drug-Approval Process

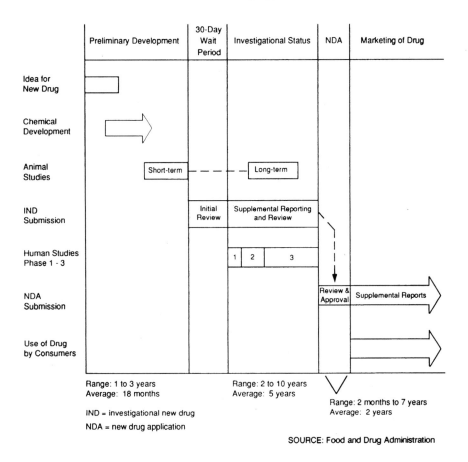

Range: 1 to 3 years
Average: 18 months

Range: 2 to 10 years
Average: 5 years

Range: 2 months to 7 years
Average: 2 years

IND = investigational new drug
NDA = new drug application

SOURCE: Food and Drug Administration

mechanisms by which the drug is absorbed into the body, target organs, and possible levels of toxicity. These tests are usually conducted in 20 to 80 normal healthy volunteers and require less than 12 months. Fifty to 70% of the drugs tested in Phase I are abandoned by their sponsors due to problems with either safety or efficacy–often adverse effects of the drug become evident at doses too small for clinical benefit to occur.

TABLE 4.2. Components of an Investigational New Drug Application

- descriptive name of the drug
- the drug's administration route
- complete list of both active and inactive ingredients
- quantitative composition of the drug
- source of the new drug
- chemical and manufacturing information
- preclinical test results (any clinical studies or experience)
- clinical study protocol
- scientific training and experience of investigators
- statements that the sponsor will notify the FDA when and why studies have been discontinued
- a notice that an institutional review board will be responsible for continuing review of the proposed study
- a description of plans to ensure that procedures are followed to protect human subjects

---

Phase II: Initial Clinical Effectiveness and Tolerability

The purpose of this clinical testing phase is to learn more about the drug's safety and efficacy, or effectiveness, in treating a certain disease or symptom. The number of patients included in these studies is usually 50 to 200, and they are volunteers who have the disease or symptom for which the drug seems to be effective. Additional animal testing can also be included in Phase II to gain further information about the drug's long-term safety. Phase II trials usually require up to two years. If the studies show that the drug is useful in a particular disease and animal data show no unwarranted harm, the sponsor can proceed to Phase III. To facilitate the transition in the scope of the clinical trials, a meeting is usually held between the sponsor and the reviewing division of the FDA to discuss the sponsor's plans for Phase III study. According to the FDA, approximately one-third of the drugs that are in Phase II testing continue on to Phase III (Figure 4.4).[2]

Phase III: Treatment Effectiveness

This phase of clinical research involves the most extensive drug testing. Phase III studies assess safety, effectiveness, and the ap-

FIGURE 4.4. Profile of Pharmaceutical Research and Development

Percent of INDs Completing Each Phase

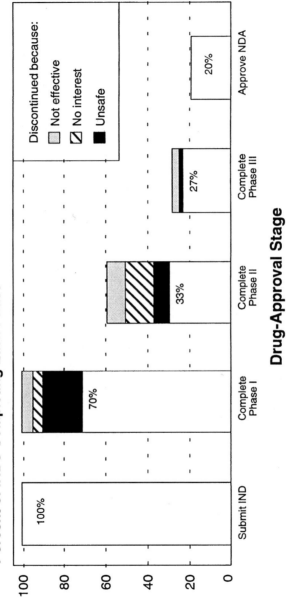

Drug-Approval Stage

INDs submitted from 1976 to 1978

SOURCE: U.S. Food and Drug Administration

propriate dosage range for the drug in treating a specific disease in a large group of patients in clinics and hospitals around the world. The number of patients involved ranges from several hundred to several thousand, depending on the drug. During Phase III studies, the drug is used by practicing physicians in the manner similar to the way in which it would be used when marketed. Additional testing to more specifically characterize the adverse effects of the drug are also conducted in Phase III. On average, only 25% of the drugs from Phase II successfully complete Phase III testing. In other words, of 100 investigational new drugs (INDs), about 25 will ultimately be approved for marketing. The costs and time associated with the 75 failures is lost.

Step 4: Review and Approval of the New Drug Application

After clinical testing of the new pharmaceutical agent, the manufacturer is required to submit a **new drug application** or NDA. (For biologics, the sponsor is required to submit a Product License Application or PLA.) NDA submission marks the beginning of the final sequence of events that can lead to new drug approval and marketing. The NDA is divided into six sections: chemistry, pharmacology, pharmacokinetics (drug absorption, distribution, metabolism, and elimination data), microbiology, clinical (results of testing, dosage studies, a copy of the proposed product labeling, etc.), and statistics (mathematical calculations to determine the validity and significance of the clinical trial results).

NDA Review

Upon receipt at the FDA, each NDA is assigned an application number and checked for completeness. Specific data are entered into the FDA's computerized information system for tracking, and the application is assigned and distributed to one of six drug-reviewing divisions. The six divisions are responsible for specific classes of drugs and consist of clinical reviewers, pharmacologists, and chemists. Consultants with expertise in biochemistry and statistics are also involved. Finally, outside reviewers, known as FDA Advisory Committees, are identified and recruited to complement the FDA staff.

The FDA review staff is required to process the NDA within 180 days. This time period, called the **regulatory review period**, begins on the day the application is received at the agency and lasts until a final decision is made. During the review process, the FDA can request additional information of the sponsor, which can extend the time period necessary for approval. The NDA review and drug-approval process usually requires two to three years.

Drug Classification System

Early in the drug-approval process, a new drug is classified by chemical type and therapeutic potential. This classification system provides a rating for each drug on the basis of its comparability to currently-marketed products, as well as a priority rating for review. *Chemical type* can range from "1" to "7," where "1" is an original molecular entity, and "7" is a drug that is marketed in the U.S. but does not have an approved NDA. (See Table 4.3 for a complete description of each type of chemical.)

Until January 1992, *therapeutic potential* ratings described the importance of the therapeutic gain provided by the new product using a system ranging from "A" to "C." The "A" designation was given to a drug that might provide effective therapy for a disease that is not adequately treated with current drugs, while "C" referred to a drug with little or no therapeutic gain–a "me-too" product or one that is comparable to an existing drug (Table 4.4). "AA" was reserved for AIDS drugs, whose NDAs were given highest priority review. In 1992, however, the system was changed from "A" through "C" to either "P"–priority review–or "S"–standard review (Table 4.5). The "AA" rating for AIDS drugs was abandoned in the hope that approval of breakthrough drugs for all diseases would occur more quickly.[10] Some commonly known and recently approved drugs with their respective classifications (designated prior to the implementation of the amended system) are listed in Table 4.6.

Approvable Letters

To signal that the NDA review and drug-approval processes are almost complete, the FDA sends the drug's sponsor an **approvable**

TABLE 4.3. Food and Drug Administration Chemical Rating System

TYPE	DEFINITION
1	**New Molecular Entity:** the active portion or moiety has not been marketed (either as a parent compound or a salt, ester, or derivative) in the U.S. for use as a single or combination drug product.
2	**New Salt:** the active moiety is marketed in the U.S. by the same or another manufacturer, but the particular salt, ester, or derivative is not yet marketed in the U.S. either as a single or combination product.
3	**New Formulation:** the compound is marketed in the U.S. by the same or another manufacturer, but the particular dosage form or formulation is not.
4	**New Combination:** the product contains two or more compounds that have not previously been marketed together in a drug product in the U.S. by any manufacturer.
5	**Already Marketed Product:** the product duplicates a drug product (same active moiety, same salt, same formulation, or same combination) already marketed in the U.S. by another firm.
6	**New Indication:** the product adds a new indication for a drug product already marketed in the U.S. by the same firm.
7	**Marketed without an NDA:** drug is on the U.S. market, but does not have an approved NDA.

NOTE: These chemical types are not mutually exclusive; a new formulation (Type 3) or a new combination (Type 4) can contain a new molecular entity (Type 1) or a new salt (Type 2). In such cases, both numbers are used in the overall classification number of the drug.

TABLE 4.4. Food and Drug Administration Therapeutic Rating System–
Pre-1992

THERAPEUTIC RATING	DEFINITION
AA	**AIDS Drug:** any drug that might be effective in treating acquired immunodeficiency syndrome (highest-priority review).
A	**Important Therapeutic Gain:** the drug might provide effective therapy or diagnosis for a disease that is not adequately treated or diagnosed by any marketed drug, or provide improved treatment of a disease through enhanced effectiveness or safety (including decreased abuse potential).
B	**Modest Therapeutic Gain:** the drug has a modest, but real, potential advantage over other marketed drugs (i.e., greater patient convenience, elimination of an annoying but not dangerous side effect, potential for large cost reduction, less frequent dosage schedule, or usefulness in specific subpopulations of those with the disease).
C	**Little or No Therapeutic Gain:** the drug essentially duplicates one or more already marketed drugs in medical importance and therapeutic usage (lowest-priority review).
H	**Orphan Drug Candidate:** the drug might meet criteria for orphan drug designation.
V	**Designated Orphan Drug:** the drug has received orphan drug designation, entitling the manufacturer to tax credits and exclusive marketing rights.

NOTE: These ratings are mutually exclusive. Only one of these letters is included in a drug's overall classification.

TABLE 4.5. Food and Drug Administration Therapeutic Rating System–
Post-1992

THERAPEUTIC RATING	DEFINITION
P	**Priority Review:** a drug that might be valuable in the treatment of AIDS, cancer, or other life-threatening illnesses or conditions. These drugs receive high priority in order to facilitate testing and approval.
S	**Standard Review:** a product that is not an AIDS drug, breakthrough cancer agent, or orphan drug. In other words, a drug that was rated "B" or "C" using the old system.
H	**Orphan Drug Candidate:** see Table 4.4.
V	**Designated Orphan Drug:** see Table 4.4.

letter. This letter is sent if the FDA believes that the NDA will be approved, but only if specific additional information or material is submitted or specific conditions (i.e., changes in labeling) are agreed to by the sponsor. The sponsor has ten days to respond to the FDA, and the response is usually one of the following:

1. The sponsor can file an amendment to the NDA (or notify the FDA that the company intends to file an amendment).
2. The NDA can be withdrawn from consideration.
3. The sponsor can ask the FDA to provide an opportunity for a hearing to question the existence of grounds for denial of the NDA.
4. The sponsor can notify the FDA that they agree to an extension of the review period.

Most sponsors respond by amending the NDA to include requested information.

Marketing Approval

Upon review of all components of the NDA, a review package consisting of a draft action letter, the reviews, and possibly a **sum–**

TABLE 4.6. Prescription Drugs, Indications, and NDA Classifications

DRUG	INDICATION	CLASSIFICATION
didanosine (Videx®, Bristol-Myers Squibb)	treatment of the symptoms and minimization of the morbidity of AIDS	1AA
nicotine patch (Habitrol®, Ciba-Geigy, others)	aid for smoking cessation by reduction of nicotine craving	3C
pravastatin (Pravachol®, Bristol-Myers Squibb)	control of elevated cholesterol levels	1C
clarithromycin (Biaxin®, Abbott Laboratories)	antibiotic for mild to moderate respiratory tract infections and skin infections	1B
fentanyl patch (Duragesic®, Janssen)	management of chronic pain in patients who require narcotic analgesia	2B

mary basis of approval is prepared by the FDA. The summary basis of approval reiterates the key findings and characteristics of the new drug, including safety and efficacy data, pharmacokinetic parameters, and product labeling. The review package is circulated to the review staff, including supervisors and the division director, for concurrence and sign-off. Final clearance is provided by the director of the specific CDER Office.

Phase IV: Post-Marketing Surveillance

After a drug is approved for marketing, the sponsor must continue to submit information to the FDA on a regular basis. On occasion, additional information is required as a condition for approval. Such data requirements are considered Phase IV clinical trials, and are a part of **post-marketing surveillance** of the drug product. Since the early 1970s, the FDA has been responsible for monitoring the safety and quality of drugs. Additionally, physicians, pharmacists, nurses, and other health-care professionals are asked to report **adverse drug reaction**s to the FDA using a standard form, or a telephone call if the reaction is life-threatening or dangerous. Also in Phase IV, clinical trials of the drug in various segments of patients, such as children or women, are conducted to better define the drug's efficacy and safety in these special populations.

REPORTING PROBLEM PRODUCTS

To facilitate the identification and updating of product literature and FDA files, the FDA and the United States Pharmacopeial Convention (USP) coordinate drug-problem reporting services. The FDA's Drug Quality Reporting System (DQRS) and the USP's Drug Product Problem Reporting Program serve as mechanisms for physicians, pharmacists, nurses, and patients to report defective drug products (Figures 4.5 and 4.6). Incorrect labeling information, damaged products, container defects, and discoloration are just a few examples of commonly-reported drug quality concerns that these agencies receive from health-care professionals. Reports like these usually result in forwarding of the information to the drug product's manufacturer, evaluations of other products in the same manufacturing lot, and, if the problem is potentially dangerous for drug users, recall of the product from pharmacy shelves. Consumers and patients can also report drug-product defects and problems to the FDA by calling the FDA's 24-hour emergency number 301-443-1240 and to the USP by calling 1-800-638-6725 (Table 4.7).[11]

Adverse drug reactions should also be documented and forwarded to the FDA and USP for review. Physicians, pharmacists, nurses, and other health-care professionals can record such occurrences using Form 1639 of the FDA or the USP's Medication Error Report Form. This information is collected, verified, and evaluated to help the FDA monitor drug safety. As a result of these reports, product-labeling revision can be requested by the FDA of the drug manufacturer.

PRODUCTIVITY OF THE U.S. DRUG-APPROVAL PROCESS

Although 20 to 30 new drugs are approved each year, many new chemical entities are not. Estimates indicate that, in general, only one in 2,000 new chemicals are found sufficiently safe and effective by the FDA. Additionally, only one-quarter of new chemical entities that are given IND status receive marketing approval. In the 1970s, twice as many investigational new drugs were approved for the marketplace. Unfortunately, it seems as if legal and economic reasons (i.e., liability) have become more influential in preventing a new drug's approval than scientific or therapeutic ones (i.e., lack of effectiveness). Additional reasons for chemical substance rejection are listed in Table 4.8.

An additional rationale for the decrease in new drug approvals might be decreased pharmaceutical research and development productivity (Table 4.9). The industry has learned that less time and resources are needed to offer old drugs in new dosage forms or delivery systems (i.e., nicotine skin patches instead of chewing gum). Additionally, a successful new drug must not only generate revenues for its research and development costs, these revenues also cover the lost financial resources that accompanied drug failures. This need for high revenues can inhibit the drug-development process and innovation occurs less often. Thus, companies become involved in the creation of new dosage forms for existing products and the development of nonpatented (generic) and nonprescription drugs to minimize financial risk. Some strategies to enhance new drug discovery and innovation are listed in Table 4.10.

FACILITATING DRUG APPROVAL

The Supplemental NDA

The **supplemental new drug application** (supplemental NDA) is submitted when a drug's sponsor requests approval to promote an existing drug with either a new **indication** or new labeling, or when manufacturing procedures have changed. Because the same regulations and requirements do not apply for review and approval of a

FIGURE 4.5. Drug Product Problem Reporting Form

USP® DRUG PRODUCT PROBLEM REPORTING PROGRAM

File Access Number

PRODUCT NAME (brand name and generic name)

DOSAGE FORM (tablet, capsule, injectable, etc.)	SIZE/TYPE OF CONTAINER	STRENGTH	NDC NUMBER

LOT NUMBER(S) | EXPIRATION DATE(S)

NAME AND ADDRESS OF THE MANUFACTURER | NAME AND ADDRESS OF LABELER (if different from manufacturer)

YOUR NAME & TITLE (please type or print)

YOUR PRACTICE LOCATION (include establishment name, address and zip code)

PHONE NUMBER AT PRACTICE LOCATION (include area code) | If requested, will the actual product involved be available for examination by the manufacturer or FDA? (Do not send samples to USP) ☐ Yes ☐ No

PLEASE INDICATE TO WHOM USP MAY VOLUNTARILY DISCLOSE YOUR IDENTITY (check boxes that apply)

You may release my identity to:
☐ The manufacturer and/or labeler as listed above
☐ The Food and Drug Administration
☐ Other persons requesting a copy of this report

SIGNATURE OF REPORTER | DATE

PROBLEMS NOTED OR SUSPECTED (If more space is needed, please attach seperate page) Date problem occurred or observed:

Call Toll Free Anytime

1-800-638-6725

In Maryland, call collect
1-301-881-0256 between 9:00 AM
and 4:30 PM Eastern Time
FAX 1-301-881-5021

BUSINESS REPLY MAIL
FIRST CLASS PERMIT NO. 39, ROCKVILLE, MD.

Postage will be paid by addressee:

Joseph G. Valentino
USP Drug Product Problem Reporting Program
12601 Twinbrook Parkway
Rockville, Maryland 20852

FIGURE 4.6. Medication Errors Reporting Form

MEDICATION ERRORS REPORTING PROGRAM
Coordinated by the United States Pharmacopeial Convention, Inc. for
the Institute for Safe Medication Practices, Inc.
Huntingdon Valley, PA

1. For errors relating to drug labeling, packaging or the naming of drug products, please complete the following:

DRUG #1	DRUG #2
Brand Name _____	Brand Name _____
Generic Name _____	Generic Name _____
Manufacturer _____	Manufacturer _____
Labeler (if different from mfr.) _____	Labeler (if different from mfr.) _____
Dosage Form _____	Dosage Form _____
Strength/Concentration _____	Strength/Concentration _____
Type and Size of Container _____	Type and Size of Container _____

2. Please describe the medication error or potential error (if more space is needed, please attach separate page)
Please note the type of personnel involved (R.Ph., R.N., M.D., student, etc.)

3. Please include any pertinent patient information that may be
relevant including patient age, sex, diagnosis, etc.
(patient identification not necessary)

4. Did injury or mortality occur? (if injury, please be specific)

5. Date and time incident occurred.

6. When and how was the error discovered?

7. Reports are most useful when materials such as product label, physician's order copy, graphics, etc., can be reviewed by the Institute. Do you have such materials available? ☐ Yes ☐ No
If yes, please specify _____
Please retain these materials/samples if possible for 60 days.

This Section Is Optional

The Institute on occasion needs to conduct follow-up analysis on reports. Kindly provide the contact information below. You may use your home address and telephone number should you prefer. The USP and the Institute will not voluntarily disclose your identity in processing this report without your permission.

Name _____
Title _____
May we contact you by mail? ☐ Yes ☐ No
Address to be used: _____

May we contact you by telephone? ☐ Yes ☐ No
Phone number: ( ) _____

8. This incident has been reported to: *(check all boxes that apply)*
☐ Institution *(via incident report)*
☐ Peers
☐ Supervisor
☐ Manufacturer
☐ State regulatory board/department of health
☐ Coroner
☐ Not reported to anyone else
☐ Other _____

9. Do you have any recommendations to prevent recurrence of this error?

RETURN TO:
The Medication Errors Reporting Program
c/o The United States Pharmacopeia!
Convention, Inc.
12601 Twinbrook Parkway
Rockville, MD 20852

or call toll free anytime
1-800-23-ERROR
FAX 1-301-816-8247

File Access Number

Date Received by USP

TABLE 4.7. Questions to Ask When Considering a Drug-Problem Report[10]

Before reporting a product that might have caused injury or illness, ask the following questions:

• Did you use the product for other than its intended purpose?

• Did you fail to follow carefully the instructions for the product?

• Was the product old or outdated?

• Do you have an allergy or other medical condition that might have something to do with the suspected harmful effect?

If the answer is YES to any of these questions, it is unlikely that reporting the incident will be of benefit. You should, however, obtain medical treatment, if necessary, for the illness or injury.

supplemental NDA as for a standard NDA, the request does not undergo the same scope of review and is usually approved relatively quickly. An example of a drug for which a supplemental NDA has been filed and approved is aspirin, when clinicians and researchers realized that aspirin has benefits in patients who have experienced a heart attack or stroke.

Accelerated NDAs

When a promising new drug is found to be effective in the treatment of a life-threatening condition, such as cancer or AIDS, but has not yet been approved for U.S. marketing, the FDA permits its use outside of controlled clinical trials under certain conditions. If the disease is "serious" or "life-threatening" and there is no alternative treatment, physicians can request the drug for a particular patient. However, if you recall some of the concerns regarding clinical trials of breakthrough drugs in Chapter 3, patient enrollment in necessary clinical trials might be decreased. Many patients do not want to participate in these trials because of the risk of receiving placebo or traditional therapy rather than the investigational product.

TABLE 4.8. Reasons Why New Chemical Entities are Not Approved by the FDA

- problems in the synthesis or production of the drug on a large-scale basis
- problems with drug stability or general quality
- the drug is not effective
- the drug has too many adverse effects and is not safe
- the drug has too many side effects (those that are annoying rather than unsafe)
- the drug is too expensive to manufacture
- the drug's patent status is unclear (refer to Chapter 8)

TABLE 4.9. Possible Reasons for the Decline in Research Productivity

- deficiencies in knowledge of the causes of diseases
- patent infringement from identical competitor products, especially in biotechnology
- chemical research focuses too much on me-too drugs (i.e., simple molecular manipulation)
- totally new therapeutic compounds and approaches are difficult to identify and develop

In 1987, the FDA issued Interim Regulatory Procedures for patients with AIDS and other serious diseases. Among other provisions, these procedures codified and expanded the acceptance by the FDA of **accelerated new drug applications**. An accelerated NDA is submitted for drugs that might be effective in the treatment of life-threatening diseases, such as AIDS, cancer, and rare diseases. The major objective of the Interim Regulatory Procedures was to facilitate approval of drugs that have been shown to be safe and effective in such conditions. By applying modified review criteria to the processing steps of accelerated-NDA review, FDA officers are able to evaluate new drugs that possess breakthrough medical benefits more quickly than traditional NDAs. (See Chapter 5.)

TABLE 4.10. Improving the Drug-Development Process
• accelerate drug-development and approval processes • look for innovations from new, small companies, and not from diffuse, institutionalized companies • change drug laws and regulations • reduce potential drug-product liability • standardize drug-development and approval processes internationally • encourage research and development, especially interdisciplinary collaborative activities • eliminate trade barriers

In 1992, the FDA implemented regulations that were designed by the Council on Competitiveness, a congressional committee then headed by Vice President Quayle. The Council's goal was to ease unnecessary regulatory burdens and strengthen U.S. competitiveness in world markets. Four initiatives were approved:

1. Accelerated approval: According to this provision, breakthrough drugs can be granted approval early if they appear to be effective in the initial stages of the review process. Studies to confirm efficacy are then conducted after marketing approval. This process was used in the approval of didanosine (ddI) for AIDS in 1992.

2. Parallel tracks: Similar to the treatment IND regulations, this initiative permits AIDS patients to receive experimental therapies as early as possible in the drug-development process. To do this, the FDA and the National Institutes of Health cooperate to provide the drug to particular patients. While this policy is currently intended only for AIDS patients, it will be evaluated for consideration in other patient populations in the future.

3. Safety testing harmonization: This provision allows the use of safety data from foreign countries, including Japan and the European Community, and eliminates the need to duplicate valid animal testing. Because of this provision, the long-term testing that was previously required can be reduced by approximately six months.

4. Outside expert reviews: To facilitate routine drug approval, qualified experts from organizations outside the government are compensated to evaluate drug-approval applications. While the FDA retains final approval authority, the expert reviewers are responsible for the tedious tasks associated with information review. Computer-assisted NDA review (CANDAR) was also suggested to minimize documentation and facilitate data retrieval and statistical review of research findings.

According to Quayle, "These actions will save both lives and money, reduce human suffering, [and] substantially improve FDA's ability to respond vigorously to the nation's health needs by allowing important new drugs to be approved months or even years earlier than was previously possible."[12,13]

NOTES

1. Satya D. Dubey, "The FDA and the IND/NDA Statistical Review Process," *Clinical Research and Regulatory Affairs* 9 (Number 3,1992):139.

2. Michael Montagne, "Drug Advertising and Promotion: An Introduction," *Journal of Drug Issues* 22 (1992):195-202.

3. Frank E. Young, "The Reality Behind the Headlines," *From Test Tube to Patient: New Drug Development in the United States* (supplement to *FDA Consumer*) (January 1988):4.

4. Lisa R. Basara and Susanne L. Dudash, "FDA Guidelines: Some Practical Help in Times of Uncertainty," *Product Management Today* 2 (1992):6-8.

5. Anonymous, "The Food and Drug Administration: An Overview," *FDA Backgrounder* 91-1.0 (1991):1.

6. Richard A. Nicklas, "The Investigative Process for New Drugs," *Annals of Allergy* 63 (Part II, December 1989):598.

7. C. Vance Gordon and Dale E. Wierenga, "The Drug Development and Approval Process," *Orphan Drugs in Development* (Washington, DC: Pharmaceutical Manufacturers Association, 1991):19.

8. Ann Myers and Steven R. Moore, "The Drug Approval Process and the Information it Provides," *Drug Intelligence and Clinical Pharmacy* 21 (October 1987):822.

9. Robert P. Paone, "FDA Approval Process and Your Patients: A Primer," *Massachusetts State Pharmaceutical Association* 8 (1992):8-9.

10. Anonymous, "FDA Changes Rating System for Drugs," *FDC Reports* (13 January 1992):9.

11. Anonymous, "Reporting Problems to the FDA," *FDA Backgrounder* 91-9.1 (November 1991):1.

12. Richard L. Vernaci, "FDA is Speeding Up Approval Process for Some New Drugs," *Boston Globe* (10 April 1992):85.

13. Anonymous, "FDA Plan Will Speed Drug Approvals," *Pharmacy Today* 31 (Number 9, 27 April 1992):1.

SUGGESTED READINGS

Upton Sinclair, *The Jungle* (New York, NY: New American Library, 1906).

Paul Starr, *The Social Transformation of American Medicine* (New York, NY: Basic Books, 1982).

Peter Temkin, *Taking Your Medicines: Drug Regulation in the United States* (Cambridge, MA: Harvard University Press, 1980).

Chapter 5

Changing the Drug-Approval Process

A new era in drug research seems to have dawned, largely as a result of the pressing need to treat AIDS. The Food and Drug Administration is changing the way it approves new drugs for persons with AIDS, both to speed up the process and to increase access to experimental drugs.[1]

THE AIDS CRISIS

With increasing prevalence of AIDS, consumers and health-care professionals are vehemently asserting the need for agents to treat and prevent the spread of the human immunodeficiency virus (HIV). The Food and Drug Administration (FDA) is taking new steps to improve the drug-approval system for such medications in response to this critical need.[2]

Interestingly, a drug that was discovered in 1964 and then abandoned because of lack of efficacy in treating cancer, later turned out to be one of the most important drugs in today's medical arsenal against AIDS. This drug is zidovudine (Retrovir®, Burroughs Wellcome Co.), formerly known as azidothymidine or AZT, an antiviral drug used to treat patients with AIDS. After shelving the drug for 20 years, zidovudine was reconsidered as a potential antiviral agent to treat AIDS. Upon submission of the investigational new drug (IND) application in May 1985, and testing of the drug in both Phase I and II trials, it was realized that zidovudine had the potential to significantly prolong the life of AIDS patients–19 of the AIDS patients receiving a placebo died within the six-month trial period, compared with one patient in the zidovudine group.[1] Because of this overwhelming success, Phase III trials were never conducted. In October 1986, the new drug application (NDA) was filed for zidovudine, and the drug was given to over 4,000 patients with AIDS. Marketing approval was granted in March 1987, a record of only five months between NDA filing and FDA approval.

FACILITATING APPROVAL–
THE TREATMENT INVESTIGATIONAL NEW DRUG

Stimulated by a desire to increase patients' access to promising experimental drugs, the FDA revised its rules in the spring of 1987 to make IND approvals shorter and more efficient. The ability to submit a **treatment investigational new drug** (IND) application was granted for two primary reasons: (1) to facilitate the availability of promising new drugs to desperately ill patients as early in the drug's development as possible, and (2) to define conditions under which drug manufacturers can charge a fee for investigational new drug products. The repercussions of the treatment IND regulations included more freedom in clinical trial design, improved adverse reaction reporting systems, increased consultation between the FDA and drug sponsors, and streamlined procedures for proposing and conducting clinical studies.

Additionally, a treatment IND allows patients to be treated outside of the formal clinical trial. This occurs under the following conditions:

1. the drug is intended to treat a "serious" or "immediately life-threatening" disease;
2. no comparable or satisfactory alternative drug or other therapy is available to treat that stage of the disease in the intended patient population;
3. the drug is under investigation in a controlled clinical trial using an IND in effect for the trial, or all clinical trials have been completed; and
4. the sponsor of the controlled clinical trial is actively pursuing marketing approval of the drug with due diligence.[3]

Orphan drugs, or medications that treat diseases that affect less than 200,000 people in the U.S., are almost always given treatment IND status because of the nature of the diseases for which they have been developed. Chapters 6 through 8 discuss this subject in more detail.

ACCELERATED NDA REVIEW

The treatment IND process that was initiated in 1987 was an important step toward hastening the drug-approval process for life-saving drugs. The procedure allows the use of investigational drugs to treat patients with a "serious or immediately life-threatening disease." It is important to realize that treatment IND regulations do not alter the stages of the drug-approval process; they only allow the use of the drug in patients other than those enrolled in a clinical trial. Unfortunately, several important pharmaceutical agents, such as investigational AIDS vaccines (of which there are several in varying stages of research), do not meet treatment IND criteria because they are used to *prevent* disease in healthy individuals, rather than *treat* a life-threatening illness.[4] Thus, they cannot be used in patients at risk of contracting HIV prior to FDA approval under the treatment IND procedure.

Realizing the need to implement a system for such agents, the FDA took the second major step to help patients with AIDS, as well as other serious diseases: the accelerated drug review process. The accelerated review process, which was proposed and adopted in 1988, permits the FDA to review and approve a new drug *before* all three phases of clinical trials are completed (Figure 5.1). Thus, if it is clear that a drug is effective and beneficial to patients, as zidovudine was, it can be approved before clinical trials are complete. As the first AIDS therapy to be approved by the FDA, zidovudine served as the model for this accelerated review system. This legislation has also facilitated the approval of several drugs, including didanosine (ddI, Videx®) and zalcitabine (Hivid®), two antiviral agents that minimize the symptoms and prolong the lives of patients with AIDS (approved in six and two months, respectively) and alglucerase, a treatment for a rare disorder known as Gaucher's disease (approved in 11 months).[5,6] Interestingly, zalcitabine is the first drug to be conditionally approved. That is, if ongoing clinical

FIGURE 5.1. Accelerated Drug Development Process

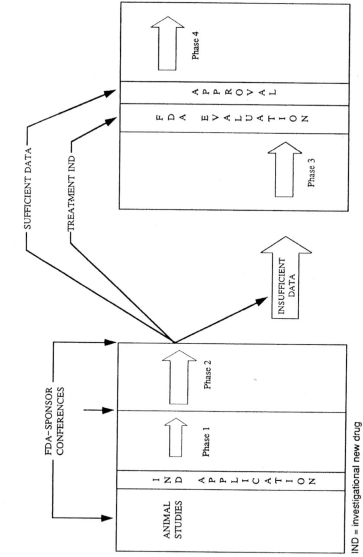

IND = investigational new drug

SOURCE: Food and Drug Administration

trials demonstrate that zalcitabine is not effective or has serious adverse effects, it will be withdrawn from the U.S. market.[7]

PENDING FDA DRUG-APPROVAL CHANGES

Amendments to the drug-approval system were proposed in late 1991 by FDA Commissioner David Kessler, who claimed at a press conference ". . . It is no longer enough to keep unsafe products off the market. The FDA must also place a high priority on the process of bringing safe and innovative products to the market."[8] According to proposed plans, drugs that can potentially treat life-threatening or serious diseases, or diseases for which there are no existing therapies (such as orphan diseases) are considered priorities and will receive accelerated approval. The FDA ensures that the process of drug review and approval for all other drugs will also be more timely and cost-efficient.

These changes have significant implications for patients and their families, especially those with cancer, Alzheimer's disease, rare diseases, and AIDS. Because patients' ability to benefit from breakthrough drugs can be substantially enhanced by these changes, it is important for patients and health-care professionals to understand the proposed changes and their potential implications.

Accelerated Drug Approval: According to the 1992 President's Council on Competitiveness, the sponsor of the conference at which proposed drug-approval amendments were introduced, the average length of NDA review for drugs is 30 months. If the accelerated approval system is implemented for specific drugs, it was estimated that the NDA review process will be reduced to six months. In addition, the number and complexity of clinical trials required for drug approval will be reduced. Thus, the total time to bring a drug through preclinical and clinical research, as well as review and approval, will be compressed from 117 to 66 months, a 56% decrease (Figure 5.2).

Surrogate Endpoints: Instead of waiting for conclusive evidence that an investigational drug is effective in prolonging the lives of patients with life-threatening illnesses, the FDA now ac-

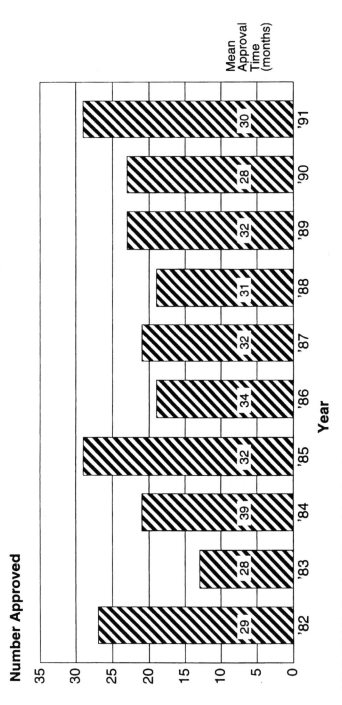

FIGURE 5.2. Mean Approval Times for New Drugs, 1982-1991

SOURCE: U.S. Food and Drug Administration

cepts other, more short-term, evidence that a drug is effective. In some cases, this evidence could allow new drugs to be made available months earlier. For example, demonstration of tumor shrinkage will be acceptable efficacy data for a breakthrough cancer therapy. Thus, on the basis of limited data, a new drug will be approved for marketing. However, after approval, the drug will continue to undergo study to confirm that the surrogate endpoint (reduction in the size of the tumor) was in fact a valid indicator of the drug's efficacy.

External Reviewers: To facilitate reduction of the current paperwork backlog at the FDA, portions of the NDA review process will be assigned to outside organizations, such as medical institutions, universities, and statistical research companies. Expanding the drug review process using nongovernment scientific experts will expedite FDA review and approval of new drugs.

International Harmonization: By harmonizing or standardizing FDA drug review standards with those of other industrialized nations, the United States, as well as other countries, can benefit from other countries' medical information and clinical data. Currently, new drug studies are duplicated for each country in which a drug is marketed. By working with other countries, the U.S. and other nations can move toward common testing procedures, which will reduce duplication and speed approvals world-wide. If the FDA is able to recognize other countries' approved drugs without conducting the rigorous testing associated with the current drug-approval process, patient access to drugs that are not currently available in the U.S. can be increased. This is an important change for patients with AIDS, cancers, and other diseases who have attempted to obtain such drugs illegally. (See Chapters 9 and 10.)

Computerized Information: The FDA will allow computerized drug-application reviews by 1995 so that reviewers can scan databases rather than reams of paper. There are several advantages to this shift: (1) researchers, who use computers to hold and analyze data, will not need to reproduce this information on paper, saving both time and resources, (2) data and information can be retrieved by reviewers much more efficiently, (3) if desired, reviewers will be able to evaluate data themselves using statistical programs, (4) computerized information can be transferred electronically, updated easier than traditional documents, and stored in compact files.

All of these proposed changes are representative of the process used to approve the AIDS drug, didanosine. Didanosine (ddI) was approved on the basis of information collected by U.S. researchers in close cooperation with Canadian investigators who were working on the same project. In this unique situation, the decision to approve didanosine (in both the U.S. and Canada) was reached using surrogate endpoints and without waiting for the completion of clinical trials. The total time required for the FDA to approve the drug's application was approximately five months.

Some Repercussions of Drug-Approval Reform

Although all of the proposed reformations of the drug-approval process have not yet been implemented, the reactions by interested groups have been both emotional and diverse. Pharmaceutical manufacturers are pleased with the prospect of minimizing both the costs and time associated with bringing a new drug to market, where research and development costs can be recouped. According to the Pharmaceutical Manufacturers Association, the plan is "one of the most important developments in many years in addressing the inefficiencies of the U.S. drug-approval process. The reforms have the clear potential for getting badly needed new medicines to patients sooner."[8] Others, including several members of Congress, are concerned about the use of external reviewers. Because the FDA will not have strict control over the actions and conclusions of external review committees, it is believed that decisions made on the basis of such reviews might not be the most judicious. The influence of a pharmaceutical manufacturer on a particular external agency or research team, or the effects of vested interests of reviewers and committee members can have a significant impact on decision-making and recommendations. This concern is, indeed, a valid one–the generic drug scandal experienced by the FDA in the 1980s showed the negative impact that influential organizations can have on drug reviewers.

For patients, the proposed drug-approval reforms are a major advantage. The ability to obtain and use a new drug can mean the difference between pain and relief, or death and life. Patients with AIDS, incurable cancers, and rare diseases might be able to receive more effective therapies sooner, rather than waiting for approvals or taking the risk of obtaining drugs illegally through foreign countries. The risks associated with the proposed changes are also worth considering. Because drugs are approved with less information about safety and effectiveness, it is possible that a harmful drug could be approved for use. In patients with life-threatening diseases, this risk might not be a concern. However, if the drug is used by physicians for unapproved uses, the potential for the emergence of long-term adverse effects is higher. Prudent use of drugs approved in an accelerated fashion will be necessary, as well as strict adverse event reporting procedures and additional long-term safety and efficacy testing. Reports of serious adverse events or lack of efficacy will force the drug's removal from the marketplace.

OVERSEEING CONTEMPORARY PHARMACEUTICAL MARKETING

In addition to monitoring the drug research and development process and ensuring the timely approval of safe and effective medicines, the FDA is responsible for the regulation of prescription-drug advertising. The scope of this task is monumental, especially when one considers the breadth of the audiences and media approaches that a pharmaceutical marketer can use to advertise prescription drugs. For example, drug products can be advertised only for their specific pharmacological activity and FDA-approved therapeutic use, not for an array of disease states. Current advertising requirements are listed in Table 5.1.

Advertising is an unofficial term in the regulatory literature that is generally applied to *all* forms of drug marketing, including printed matter, promotional advertisements, all forms of labeling (which encompasses audio and visual information, exhibits, and communications through all forms of media), and verbal statements. In essence, any form of communication through any type media that calls the attention of health professionals and consumers to a drug is considered pharmaceutical advertising.

TABLE 5.1. Food and Drug Administration Prescription-Drug Advertising Requirements

- A fair summary of the effectiveness of the drug in the conditions for which it is being promoted.

- A listing, with fair balance in the presentation, of adverse effects and cautionary information.

- A reasonably close association of information on safety with information on effectiveness in similar degrees of prominence in both the text and artwork of the advertisement.

- The use of only those promotional claims that are supported by substantial evidence, which is generated by adequate and well-controlled clinical investigation.

As demonstrated by FDA requirements, one of the most important considerations during FDA evaluation of promotional materials and advertisements is the existence of **fair balance**. According to this principle, a promotional piece or advertisement must present an objective account of all relevant information–both the risks and benefits of the drug–affecting the decision to prescribe and use the drug product.

Violations of advertising regulations can be penalized by the FDA in one of the following ways:

1. simple notation and a letter seeking either a specific response or reflection on the matter;
2. a request that the advertisement be corrected, modified, or discontinued;
3. the mailing of correction or regulatory letters ("Dear Doctor" letters) to physicians and other key health professionals; or
4. criminal prosecution.

While the true effects of drug advertising on prescribing behavior are not well known, neither are the effects of corrective measures and regulatory efforts. Corrective activities by the FDA against a particular manufacturer or advertiser can actually have a positive impact on other groups. While the pharmaceutical company's reputation with the FDA is harmed, the financial community and the company's stockholders can benefit from media attention to a particular drug. For example, the negative publicity that surrounded the antidepressant fluoxetine (Prozac®, Eli Lilly) in 1991 did not cause a decrease in its use. The drug was ranked 19th in a list of the top 200 prescription drugs dispensed most often in the United States in 1990. In 1991, after claims that it increased suicidal thoughts, Prozac's rank was 18th.[9]

The FDA is not interested in regulating free speech, or in limiting commercial speech, as long as fair balance exists and no misleading information is presented. Additionally, because the FDA cannot engage in battles with marketing or advertising agencies over every type of promotional approach, restraint and responsibility on the part of pharmaceutical manufacturers and marketers is inherent. In other words, the pharmaceutical industry is responsible for its own action and self-regulates drug advertising to a great extent. To help the reader understand the scope and goals of the FDA in regard to pharmaceutical advertising, a simple quiz is provided below. Consider each question carefully and answer either "true" or "false."

The FDA and Prescription Drug Advertising– A Quiz

A prescription-drug advertisement that appears in a peer-reviewed medical journal has most likely been reviewed and precleared by the editorial staff of the journal prior to its publication.   T   F

A prescription-drug advertisement that appears in a peer-reviewed medical journal has most likely been reviewed and precleared by the FDA prior to its publication.   T   F

A prescription-drug advertisement that appears in a general or lay-press magazine or newspaper has most likely been reviewed by the editorial staff of the magazine or newspaper prior to its publication.
     T   F

A prescription-drug advertisement that appears in a general or lay-press magazine or newspaper has

most likely been reviewed by the FDA prior to its
publication.   T   F

A prescription-drug advertisement that appears on a
network television channel has most likely been reviewed by the editorial staff of the television station
prior to its broadcast.   T   F

A prescription-drug advertisement that appears on a
network television channel has most likely been reviewed by the FDA prior to its broadcast.   T   F

SOURCE: *Marvin Z. Schrieber, MD, JD, FDA Division of
Marketing and Information, Northeastern University Sym-
posium (29 April 1992); with permission.*

The correct answer for all of the above questions is *false*. Neither
editors nor FDA reviewers evaluate or preapprove medical journal
articles, lay-press information, or television broadcasts. While the
FDA *requests* pre-approval of consumer-directed advertisements, it
does not have the authority to proactively assess and authorize such
activities. This is important for consumers and health-care professionals to remember when evaluating information from these
sources.

The FDA "Watchdog" Role

Pharmaceutical companies are spending larger sums on questionable tactics that subvert basic standards of medical standards, tempting doctors with lavish vacations, gifts, and cash
payments. The industry is greatly enriched but hardly re-
formed. . . . Prescription drugs offer unique benefits, but they
also pose unique risks. Patients have the right to expect that
the prescription drug they are taking is medically appropriate
for their illness–not part of their doctor's "Frequent Prescriber
Vacation Plan."[10]

Senator Edward Kennedy

Although existing FDA regulations address some of the concerns
associated with prescription-drug advertising, many individuals and

groups are troubled about the long-term repercussions of current marketing practices, including the advertising of prescription drugs directly to consumers and advertising strategies disguised as educational activities. Because the industry's advertising and promotional activities have once again become the subject of significant debate within the Senate's Labor and Human Resources Committee, FDA commissioner, David Kessler, has targeted advertising and promotion regulations as a priority.

To determine the extent of the violations of marketing and advertising regulations by the pharmaceutical industry, Senator Edward Kennedy (D–Mass.) chaired hearings conducted by the Senate Committee on Labor and Human Resources in December 1990. These hearings shed light on the numerous indiscretions of certain companies within the pharmaceutical industry, such as week-long trips to well-known physicians for "educational" symposia and meetings and the use of inappropriate spokespersons to provide testimonials regarding the efficacy of a particular drug. Repercussions of such activities on the prices of drugs were discussed, as well as the potential for biased decision-making on the part of health-care professionals and patients.

In response to the concern regarding prescription drugs, the American Medical Association (AMA), the Pharmaceutical Manufacturers Association (PMA), and the FDA proposed ethical standards or guidelines to which pharmaceutical companies and physicians must adhere. The guidelines provided direction for pharmaceutical promotion (i.e., advertising) and educational activities (i.e., continuing education symposia and publications). Although the activities of pharmaceutical marketers and advertising agencies have changed, accomplishment of the guidelines' goal–to ensure that activities like those described in the Kennedy hearings do not continue–is yet to be fully realized.

SUMMARY

The Food and Drug Administration is a very powerful organization within the federal government. It is responsible for ensuring the availability of safe and effective drugs, the approval of life-saving medications for patients, and accurate and objective presentation of information in educational materials, advertisements, and promotions of prescription drugs. Because of this large scope of activity, and the desire for immediate modification of major problem areas by several groups (patients, consumers, health professionals, the pharmaceutical industry, and other stakeholders), the FDA has reached several critical points in its regulatory evaluation.

Long drug-approval periods and the use of inappropriate advertising methods are just two of the serious issues that require immediate attention. To illustrate some of the real concerns that surround drug approval, the next three chapters discuss orphan drugs–drugs that are used to treat rare diseases–to show the impact of legislation that included financial incentives for orphan drug development, and the controversies that resulted from government regulation of such activities. The specific roles that patients, consumers, and health-care professionals can play to influence the amendment and improvement of issues like orphan drugs are also highlighted for the reader.

NOTES

1. Wendy K. Mariner, "New FDA Drug Approval Policies and HIV Vaccine Development," *American Journal of Public Health* 80 (March 1990):336.

2. Harry Schwartz, "Radical Reforms at FDA Long Overdue," *Pharmaceutical Executive* (August 1990):12,14.

3. Henry I. Miller and Frank E. Young, "The Drug Approval Process at the Food and Drug Administration," *Archives of Internal Medicine* 149 (March 1989):656.

4. David A. Kessler and Wayne L. Pines, "The Federal Regulation of Prescription Drug Advertising and Promotion," *Journal of the American Medical Association* 246 (Number 19, 1990):2413.

5. Anonymous, "FDA's New Molecular Entity Approvals in 1991 Match Its 1985 Record; Average Approval Time was 30 Months Overall, 15 Months for "1A" Drugs," *FDC Reports* (6 January 1992):12-14.

6. Anonymous, "FDA Approves AIDS Drugs," *American Pharmacy* NS32 (Number 9, 1992):13.

7. Anonymous, "Roche's Hivid Approved June 19 as Combination Therapy with Retrovir for Second-Line Use; Company Agrees to Submit Data from at least Two Additional Studies," *FDA Reports* (22 June 1992):5.

8. Ann Allen, "Regulatory Reforms: A Shot in the Arm for R&D," *Medical Advertising News* (January 1992):28.

9. Anonymous, "The Top 200 Rx Drugs of 1990," *American Druggist* (February 1991):56.

10. Opening statement by Senator Edward Kennedy. Senate Labor and Human Resources Committee Hearing on Advertising, Marketing, and Promotional Practices of the Pharmaceutical Industry (December 11, 1990).

Chapter 6

Rare Diseases and Orphan Drugs

If a friend was ill, would you try to help him or her get well? What if a friend needed significant amounts of time, energy, and money from you–would you help then? What if your friend had absolutely no way to repay you for your time and efforts, potentially leaving you in debt for years to come?

Although it seems difficult to identify and deal with this scenario, it was faced on a daily basis by pharmaceutical manufacturers and researchers in the 1970s and early 1980s. This "friend" is real, representing the over 20 million people who are afflicted with specific conditions known as rare diseases. The "significant amounts of time, energy, and money" are the costs associated with the research, development, and marketing of a useful drug, usually called an "orphan" drug. Your friend is unable to repay these costs because the price tag on most orphan drugs is more than even his or her insurance company can pay.

For our friends–this small proportion of the population afflicted with rare diseases–treatment options and medical information is almost as rare as the diseases with which they are afflicted. People with rare conditions are often unable to go to a physician or hospital for treatment because the drugs they need are unavailable. Most patients do not face obstacles like these. Needed drugs are readily accessible and relatively affordable, and most common disorders are usually easy to diagnose and manage. We all know people with high blood pressure, arthritis, and diabetes who take diuretics (water pills), analgesics, and insulin to manage their diseases. However, most people do not know someone with a rare disease, and those who do probably watch this person suffer without treatment, or pay considerable amounts of money for effective drug therapy.

This unfortunate situation occurs primarily because the ability of pharmaceutical companies and the medical community to develop and provide effective treatments is limited by costs, legislation, and sparse knowledge of these understudied diseases. Making the situation worse for people with rare diseases is the fact that many health-care professionals (physicians, nurses, and pharmacists) do not recognize the symptoms of rare diseases or know how to obtain treatments.

What can we do to help our "friends?" What has been done since the 1970s? Why does this issue remain in our society, one that is among the most advanced in terms of health care? The following three chapters will offer people with orphan diseases, family members, health-care professionals, and lawmakers a better understanding of the answers to these questions.

ORPHAN DISEASES

In 1976, I read an article in a newspaper about Tourette's syndrome. My oldest son, who was seven at the time, had been blinking his eyes, twitching his face, shrugging his shoulders, and flapping his arms for two long harrowing years. He grunted repeatedly, stuttered, and cleared his throat constantly despite our begging, pleading, and even punishing him for symptoms, which we had been told were "nervous habits." When I read that newspaper article, I knew instantly that my son was not nervous, that we had wrongly accused him of purposeful attention-getting behaviors and, most of all, that the advice we had been offered by every professional we had come in contact with in previous years had been wrong. . . . Our son had been misdiagnosed for more than two years.[1]

Abbey S. Meyers, Executive Director,
National Organization for Rare Disorders (NORD)

This story is typical of patients and families faced with rare diseases. Autism, narcolepsy, Gilles de la Tourette's syndrome, Lyme disease, Crohn's disease, and amyotrophic lateral sclerosis (Lou Gehrig's disease) are just a few examples of the rare disorders that affect approximately 20 million Americans.

What is a rare disease? How are these diseases treated? And why are accurate diagnoses so difficult? Federal agencies, lawmakers, health-care professionals, and patients have worked together to improve the future for those afflicted rare diseases. This chapter will help the reader understand the patient's perspective–actions that have been successful and actions that are still necessary.

Although the names of the diseases listed above are familiar to most people because of news reports and television shows, these conditions are rare diseases. **Rare diseases** are those that affect less than 200,000 patients in the United States. They are often characterized by painful and disfiguring symptoms, embarrassing manifestations, disability, and loss of control, both physical and emotional. Many of them can be fatal. **Orphan diseases** are special rare diseases because they traditionally have not had funding, a supporting investigator, or agency dedicated to researching their prevention, diagnosis, and treatment. Investigation of the cause of these diseases or their treatment is pursued by few scientists, leaving patients with orphan diseases little hope.

How Many People Are Affected?

Unlike the United States Census, which is conducted every ten years to determine the number and characteristics of Americans, and the Morbidity and Mortality Weekly Report, which lists the incidence, prevalence, and deaths due to common conditions and diseases, there is no survey to determine the prevalence of rare diseases. Until the passage of the Orphan Drug Act in 1983, most rare diseases were identified through case reports and tracked privately by interested physicians, researchers, volunteer agencies, and epidemiologists (people who study patient populations to determine the cause of a disease as well as common features of those afflicted). National information sources were not available to help physicians and patients recognize a rare disease or learn of others with the same condition.

Although the need for a single orphan drug is confined to a small number of patients, the proportion of the population affected by orphan diseases is considerable. Approximately 20 million Americans suffer from one of the over 5,000 known rare diseases, and this patient population continues to grow.[2] To help the reader under-

stand the proportion of people this number signifies, approximately
ten million people live in the states of New York and Pennsylvania,
and over 60 million Americans suffer from high blood pressure
(hypertension), one of the most common afflictions in our country.

A selection of rare diseases is listed in Table 6.1. It is important
to note that this list of rare diseases can only increase. Under current
federal law, if a rare disease is identified and the number of patients
affected grows to over 200,000, the disease remains a rare disease
and any drugs approved for its treatment remain orphan drugs.

A timely example of a growing rare disease is AIDS. When first
characterized in 1984, the number of persons afflicted was quite
small. Drugs like zidovudine (Retrovir®, Burroughs Wellcome),
aerosolized pentamidine (NebuPent®, Lyphomed), and didanosine
(Videx®, Bristol-Myers Squibb)–three medications that help to
minimize the symptoms of AIDS and AIDS-related conditions–received orphan drug status. In the future, although it is estimated that
the number of Americans with AIDS will increase to over one
million by the turn of the century, the disease will remain a rare
disease (unless the federal Orphan Drug Act is changed).

ORPHAN DRUGS

The term "orphan drug" has been mentioned several times–what
does it mean? A drug that appears or is proven effective in the
treatment of a rare or orphan disease, but that is not profitable to its
manufacturer, is termed an **orphan drug**. These drugs have low
commercial value because very few people need them; their ability
to recoup research and manufacturing costs is minimal, and their
ability to generate substantial profits is virtually nil. Prior to the
Orphan Drug Act, medications like these were orphans in the traditional sense–drugs that no one wanted to "adopt" or manufacture
on a large-scale basis. Even if a chemical compound could cure a
painful or life-threatening rare disease, it was not available for
human use and remained on a laboratory shelf. Imagine the impact
of knowledge of such a drug on a patient suffering from the disease
that the compound has been shown to cure or relieve!

TABLE 6.1. Selected Rare Diseases	
ABO incompatibility	hyperbilirubinemia
acquired immune deficiency	hypercholesterolemia,
syndrome (AIDS)	homozygous familial
amenorrhea	lactic acidosis, congenital
anemia	infant botulism
anorexia	multiple sclerosis
antithrombin III deficiency	muscular dystrophy
apnea	myelodysplastic syndromes
asthma (severe steroid requiring)	myoclonus
bacteremia	Paget's disease
blepharospasm	panencephalitis
burns, hydrofluoric acid	*Pneumocystis Carinii* pneumonia (PCP)
cachexia	polycythemia vera
cancers	Raynaud's disease
carnitine deficiency	respiratory distress syndrome, neonatal
chemotherapy complications	sickle cell anemia
corneal disease	Sjogren's syndrome
cryptosporidiosis	spasmodic torticollis
Cushing's syndrome	spasticity, intractable
cystic fibrosis	thrombocytopenia
cystinosis	tissue/organ transplantation
cystitis, interstitial	toxoplasmosis
cytomegalovirus (CMV)	trigeminal neuralgia
factor XIII deficiency	tuberculosis
Gaucher's disease	Turner's syndrome
glycoside intoxication	uremic osteodystrophy
graft versus host disease	Von Willebrand's disease
growth hormone deficiency	Wilson's disease
hemophelia	

Why Do We Need Orphan Drugs?

An example of a life-saving orphan drug is trientine, one of two drugs available to treat Wilson's disease.

Wilson's Disease

Katie, an 18-year-old high school student, watched her grades plummet from A's to a C average. "I was depressed and lethargic. I found it hard to go to class and hard to concentrate," Katie recalls. . . . Friends noticed that Katie, whom they had known as a slim, attractive, outgoing overachiever, had become overweight, withdrawn, and frumpy. She seemed to have a strange odor about her. Neither family nor friends could understand what was causing these dramatic changes. After trying psychologic counseling, it was discovered that Katie needed surgery for an enlarged spleen; her white blood cell count had been abnormally high. While removing her spleen, surgeons noticed that her liver was also diseased. After putting the pieces of the puzzle together, her physicians realized that Katie had Wilson's disease; a disease that affects less than 8,000 people in the United States.[3]

Wilson's disease is a genetic disorder that causes the body to accumulate copper. Copper is necessary in very small amounts in the body. When amounts of copper accumulate in people like Katie who cannot eliminate it, it tends to build up to toxic levels. Left untreated, Wilson's disease damages the kidneys, liver, brain, and eyes, leading to suffering and ultimately death, usually by the age of 30.

Fortunately for patients with Wilson's disease, Merck Sharp and Dohme, one of the world's largest pharmaceutical manufacturers, had developed penicillamine (Cupramine®). This drug controls the progression of the disease by binding to copper and facilitating its elimination through the kidneys. However, penicillamine can have severe side effects, including kidney failure.

In the early 1980s, another drug for Wilson's disease, trientine, which also serves to facilitate the body's elimination of copper, was being developed in England. In 1982, the FDA realized the usefulness of trientine and actively solicited the industry for a sponsor of the new drug. Again, Merck Sharp and Dohme agreed to develop the experimental drug, even though the potential market is approximately 100 people. Katie received trientine (Cuprid®) and her symptoms vanished; she was able to finish high school and graduated with honors from Harvard University.[3]

ORPHAN DRUG HISTORY

The story of the struggle for the Orphan Drug Act is testimony to all that is right and much that is wrong in America. It is encouraging, it is distasteful; it is a story of greed and of heroism. . . .[4]

Abbey S. Meyers

The 1960s

The word "orphan" first appeared in medical literature in reference to the use of adult drugs in infants and children. A combination of the repercussions of the Kefauver-Harris amendments to the Food, Drug, and Cosmetic Act and concerns about the testing of drugs in infants and children resulted in a situation where few drugs were tested in these patients–the children were described in 1968 as *therapeutic orphans*.[5] (See Chapter 4 for an explanation of these laws.)

The 1970s

Throughout the 1970s, activities associated with the research and development of orphan drugs were scattered and unorganized. According to Karch, in a book written prior to the Orphan Drug Act, "The orphan drug issue is too complex and too important to be simplified in black and white. Many elements contribute to the problem, and no single component carries all the blame. . . ."[6]

Because of the lack of funding to facilitate drug discovery and usage, life-saving drugs often remained in the research laboratory rather than in the hands of the patients. A survey conducted by the federal government in 1981 showed that of the 134 identified orphan drugs, only 34 were marketed.[7]

Individual researchers worked diligently and faced virtually insurmountable barriers when developing orphan drugs for use in afflicted patients. Carnitine is an example of a drug that, although known in the 1970s, was found to have additional therapeutic properties. Through a lucky twist in his research, Stephen DeFelice, MD realized that carnitine, a naturally-occurring enzyme found in the heart and other body organs, can help infants with severe neuromuscular abnormalities caused by carnitine deficiency. However, because the drug was not a new substance (thus, not patentable) and the costs of advancing this type of drug were substantial, most pharmaceutical manufacturers were not interested in testing the drug's activity further or developing the drug.

DeFelice tried several different tactics to expand the research efforts with carnitine, including arrangements with overseas manufacturers. The primary obstacles encountered in this process, however, were financial (costs of clinical trials), a lackluster performance of the drug in testing, and a shortage of support by entrepreneurs and established pharmaceutical manufacturers. Finally in 1978, he was able to convince Sigma-Tau Pharmaceuticals, an Italian pharmaceutical manufacturer, to fund the testing of the drug in the United States.[6] Today, two decades later, carnitine is a marketed orphan drug for a very rare disease–only a few hundred children are using it and annual sales are less than $5 million.

In the 1970s, DeFelice asked "Where will carnitine be in the 1980s? It will either be stirring the imagination of the medical world or be another false alarm in the world of hope." He further elucidates, "The message of the carnitine story, however, is not dependent on the fate of this drug. The message is more universal: we have quietly and effectively eliminated the environment necessary for creativity in medicine."[6]

It is important to note that there were some small-scale efforts by certain companies and organizations. Some pharmaceutical companies developed and provided "public service drugs" free of charge to individuals with specific conditions and limited financial resources. Several drug-development programs were instituted in the 1950s and 1960s to facilitate the development of cancer and epilepsy drugs because patients with these conditions desperately needed additional treatment options and commercial sponsors were not interested in developing them. The Centers for Disease Control in Atlanta also coordinated a program in which drugs were acquired from foreign manufacturers for use in American patients. Finally, a commission on drugs for rare diseases was established by the Pharmaceutical Manufacturers Association to alleviate some of the problems associated with orphan drugs. Unfortunately, none of these efforts addressed the "big picture" of the orphan drug issue– too many patients remained untreated without hope of effective drug therapy.

The 1980s

The event that initiated the solution of the orphan drug problem was a series of congressional hearings. Representative Henry Waxman of California was prompted to investigate this issue when the drug used by one of his constituents was confiscated by the U.S. Customs Service. The drug was pimozide, and the individual, Adam Seligman, suffered from Tourette's syndrome. At the hearing, consumers, including Seligman and Abbey Meyers, the current executive director of the largest voluntary organization for rare diseases in the United States, testified about the injustices of the existing state of affairs and the burdens associated with rare diseases.

Several meetings had been held between Representative Elizabeth Holtzman of New York, Melvin Van Woert, MD, a drug investigator, and patients with rare diseases. Through their group effort, an orphan drug bill was drafted and introduced into the House of Representatives. Unfortunately, the pharmaceutical industry, being both angry and embarrassed because they were portrayed as the "bad guy," did much to downplay the importance of orphan drugs and the need for legislation, and three years went by before the law was passed.

Luckily, one of the most forceful and memorable events in the history of the orphan drug issue occurred around the same time: the development of an episode of a popular television program, *Quincy*. In the show, which was broadcast in March 1981, the emotional story of a young man with Tourette's syndrome was described. The man had suffered with the disabling and embarrassing symptoms of this rare disease since childhood, only to realize that the drug that could alleviate his condition was not available in the United States. No U.S. pharmaceutical manufacturer would develop the drug for patient use because of the expense and doubtful financial returns.

The power of television cannot be understated. This personalized look at the orphan drug issue made many individuals, who were previously unaware of the existence and extent of the orphan drug problem, question the situation and demand legislative action to facilitate orphan drug development and distribution.

Of course, Dr. Quincy cannot take all of the credit for bringing the orphan drug issue into the limelight. Several drug investigators, patient advocate groups, and health-care professionals realized the inequity of the orphan drug situation and lobbied in Washington, DC for changes. National publicity on Tourette's syndrome and a letter-writing campaign organized by a coalition of voluntary disease organizations played a key role in bringing the orphan drug issue to the forefront of Congress. The letters described the need to develop incentives to entice pharmaceutical manufacturers into researching and marketing drugs of little commercial value.

To boost public awareness and support of the orphan drug problem, organizations of volunteers (primarily patients and consumers) formed the National Organization for Rare Disorders. After an additional episode on *Quincy* about myoclonus and orphan drugs, full-page newspaper advertisements, and the threat of veto by President Reagan at the last minute, this assembly of ordinary American citizens was successful in convincing Congress and the President to pass the Orphan Drug Act in 1983–just seven hours before the bill's deadline.[5,8]

> We look back on this adventure with a great sense of accomplishment and relief. It was an opportunity for patients with rare diseases to empower themselves. I doubt if we would have such an effective and cohesive group if we had not faced opposition at every turn. . . . We saw ourselves as an underserved minority, and we gained a sense of cohesiveness by focusing on our sameness rather than our differences. . . . We asked only for hope–hope that research would find an answer. But when we realized that our answers would not be manufactured because they were not profitable enough, all hope was lost. We united to regain that hope. And after the Orphan Drug Act became law we realized that we had served many purposes beyond the legislative victory.[4]
>
> *Abbey S. Meyers*

TODAY'S ORPHAN DRUGS

Because of the Orphan Drug Act, the status of the orphan drug issue has improved significantly. Now, patients afflicted with a rare

disease do not need to wait for the approval process to be complete–
often, they can acquire the drug while it is still experimental.[9]

Pharmaceutical manufacturers and researchers are more dedicated and determined to support the development of orphan drugs.
The number of orphan drugs that have been approved under the
provisions of the Act is considerably higher than the number of
agents available in 1981.[6] Many of these medications have alleviated crippling symptoms and saved the lives of many patients
with rare diseases.

Some Examples

Adagen®

Taking advantage of the provisions of the Orphan Drug Act, a
small pharmaceutical manufacturer has developed an experimental
drug called PEG-ADA (Adagen®, Enzon) that restores the immune
systems of children with severe combined immunodeficiency syndrome.[10]

> Our 7-year-old daughter, Allison, had been ill almost from
> birth. Kids get sick often, we knew that. . . . Allison was
> different. When she got a cold, she frequently developed
> pneumonia. We could bank on her getting sick every new
> season. . . . Doctors didn't seem to know what was wrong. . . .
> Her lung function was 80% below normal. She was in extreme
> danger and [had to] be kept indoors. Any infection would be
> life-threatening. . . .[10]

Severe combined immunodeficiency syndrome is an inherited
disorder of the immune system that makes children vulnerable to
common infections like chicken pox and measles. In some patients,
the disorder is caused by a deficiency of a specific enzyme called
adenosine deaminase, or ADA. PEG-ADA serves to replace this
enzyme and allows children to go to school, play with friends, and
live normal, active lives. In 1989, Allison became the seventh child
to receive PEG-ADA to restore her immune system. Her lungs are
clear and she can now attend school and visit friends without the
fear of infection.

Ceredase®

Another orphan drug, alglucerase (Ceredase®, Genzyme Corporation), is used to control the symptoms and reverse the disease process of Type I Gaucher's (pronounced "go-shays") disease. Gaucher's disease is an inherited disorder affecting 15,000 to 20,000 persons in the United States, mostly people of Eastern European Jewish ancestry. It is caused by an accumulation of fat in the body and its symptoms include fatigue, bone joint pain, anemia, and bone destruction. This condition can also be fatal.

> Laura . . . was born with a severe form of Gaucher's disease. Her first symptoms were anemia, daily nose bleeds, and chronic exhaustion. Then she developed an enlarged abdomen as her spleen and liver filled with fat-choked cells. "The worst was getting teased," Laura admitted, "Kids would ask [if I were] pregnant. . . ." She also suffered intense bone pain that would force her to lie in bed for days at a time.[11]

Alglucerase is an injectable form of the missing enzyme, b-glucocerebrosidase. Approved by the FDA in 1991, it was the first prescription drug available to treat Gaucher's disease. To attest to the serious need for therapy for this rare disease, the FDA demanded only one ten-month trial to evaluate the drug and only 24 patients were needed to participate in the trial.[12]

Because the symptoms of Gaucher's disease are very similar to those of other conditions, it is difficult to detect and diagnose correctly. However, when the disease is properly diagnosed and treated with alglucerase, it can be well controlled and patients' quality of life can be dramatically improved.

ORPHAN DRUG BARRIERS

Although there have been several success stories like those described, much time and effort, patient suffering, and deaths have occurred while waiting for action, such as the passage of the Orphan Drug Act. Even today, with the law in place, many patients continue to suffer without treatment or pay frustrating amounts of money for effective therapy.

What were some of the specific barriers that forced the development of the 1983 Orphan Drug Act and why should we be familiar with them? It seems that many of the current debates surrounding orphan drug development and marketing are similar to those experienced in the 1970s and early 1980s. Reviewing these barriers will make it easier to understand the current issues and foster construction of intelligent solutions.

The Bottom Line

As discussed earlier, the primary reason for disinterest in the commercial development and marketing of orphan drugs was a lack of financial incentives. Pharmaceutical manufacturers, as members of one of the most consistently lucrative industries in the United States, logically spend the majority of their time, energy, and resources on the development of drugs for diseases and conditions that affect large groups of patients. By marketing pharmaceutical products to treat hypertension or high cholesterol, for example, manufacturers are able to recoup all of the costs associated with the drug's research and development.

Orphan drugs, like carnitine, which had been discovered but not marketed, were quite difficult to research during the 1980s. The information available about orphan diseases was limited, including data regarding etiology (cause) and symptoms, and only a small number of patients were available on whom to conduct research. Furthermore, there was a lack of interest on the part of the FDA to provide funding for orphan drug research, thus making it difficult for academic investigators to develop orphan drugs. Pharmaceutical companies needed to be identified and recruited–similar to Merck Sharp and Dohme and trientine, the drug for Wilson's disease–to bring orphan drugs to market. Because most pharmaceutical companies were not interested in orphan drug research and sponsorship, this process was both frustrating and costly.

The expenses associated with prescription-drug research and development can be astronomical. According to the Pharmaceutical Manufacturers Association (PMA), the average time and cost to take a typical drug from the laboratory to the pharmacy shelf in

1991 was 12 years and $231 million dollars.[13] Thus, in the early 1980s, even if an orphan drug was successfully developed and approved by the FDA, the manufacturer and sponsor had a very slim chance of recovering any of the research and development costs and an even slimmer chance of generating a profit, because a limited amount of patients actually needed the product.

The Drug-Approval Maze

As alluded to above, the standard drug-approval process is quite costly and requires considerable time and effort to jump through necessary "hoops." As the agency responsible for the approval of safe and effective prescription drugs, the FDA must ensure that strict guidelines and specifications are met by pharmaceutical manufacturers requesting approval for nationwide distribution of prescription drugs. (See Chapters 4 and 5.)

The U.S. drug-approval process is the result of the realization that without standardized and comprehensive drug-evaluation procedures, harmful drugs might be marketed and cause significant damage. Most people remember or are familiar with the experience of pregnant women receiving thalidomide in the 1960s. This drug was banned worldwide after the medical community realized that it caused profound birth defects.

When trying to initiate orphan drugs into the traditional drug-approval process, pharmaceutical manufacturers found it difficult to meet requirements, especially those regarding clinical trials. When a drug is being considered for approval, the FDA reviews investigational trials of the drug in both healthy and ill patients. These patient groups need to be of a significant number in order for the FDA to make a well-informed judgment. Because the patient populations for many rare diseases are quite small, patient requirements were often difficult or impossible for investigators to meet, causing most orphan drugs to remain in the laboratory rather than on the market.

Adverse Event Accountability

Because orphan drugs are tested using a relatively small number of patients prior to approval, adverse events and drug toxicity are less likely to be documented than when testing standard prescription drugs in large patient groups. For example, if an adverse event, such as seizures, occurs in one out of 1,000 people, and only 200 people received the orphan drug during preapproval testing, it is probable that none of the people experienced a seizure. Thus, researchers would have no reason to suspect seizures as a potential adverse event. It is possible that this adverse event would not be seen until years after the drug's approval. Clearly, orphan drug sponsors potentially face significant liability concerns.

Patent Policies

The most important barrier to orphan drug development involves the nature of the substances that treat orphan diseases and the patent laws governing these substances. Drugs that are already known or on the market (i.e., aspirin or digoxin), those with previously expired patents, natural substances, and shelf chemicals are not patentable. For example, because carnitine, the orphan drug that replaces the enzyme that helps the body burn fat, is a naturally-occurring substance, it cannot be patented–any company can manufacture and sell the product without risk of lawsuit or infringement liability. Of course, pharmaceutical manufacturers will not take on the arduous task of researching and testing an orphan drug if, at a later time, another company can manufacture the product and sell it without expending any research and development costs.

Drugs that are developed using biotechnology, such as erythropoietin and human growth hormone, are not patentable because they are substances that exist in nature. Biotechnology processes simply permit the duplication of a naturally-occurring substance into amounts that can be sold commercially. This problem becomes even more important if the medical community realizes that an unpatentable orphan drug can effectively treat a common condition in addition to the rare disease for which it was originally developed. The following scenario provides a hypothetical example:

> Bio-X manufactures a recently-approved orphan drug called growth enzyme (GE). This drug has been approved for use in the treatment of children with an extremely rare enzyme defi-

ciency that stunts their growth. If, however, GE is found to be useful in promoting growth in children of small stature, a condition that affects *more* than 200,000 children in the United States, and this use is approved by the FDA, a competitor can copy the drug, slightly alter the chemical structure and manufacture their version of GE for this new use (or indication). Now, competition exists: two versions of GE are on the market. Bio-X still needs to recover the costs of research and development, but because the "copy-cat" company, Bio-X's competitor, charges a considerably lower price, it might be unable to do so. Being cost-conscious, patients with either condition will purchase the lower-priced product. Thus, assuming that the market for the drug remains relatively small, the competitor can experience sales opportunities that rightfully belong to Bio-X.

MORE BARRIERS

Prior to the Orphan Drug Act, orphan drugs' questionable profitability, existing patent laws, and the traditional drug-approval process were the principal barriers that limited the research, development, and marketing of orphan drugs. Without the ability to circumvent stringent patent requirements, as well as the lack of profit incentives, pharmaceutical manufacturers were not motivated to address the needs of patients afflicted with orphan diseases.

Today, new issues face pharmaceutical manufacturers, legislators, health-care professionals, and patients. As most people are aware, the costs of health care and medication have increased dramatically in the last decade. Patients' ability to pay for extended and complicated medical care is quite limited. Furthermore, insurance companies are often ineffective in managing the costs associated with chronic illness.

Patients with orphan diseases are in the same predicament. They are average Americans with average incomes who receive no supplements or benefits because of their rare conditions. Many orphan drugs, even if approved under the Orphan Drug Act, continue to be expensive and difficult to access. Finally, there remains an insufficient amount of rare disease and orphan drug information for patients, families, and health-care professionals. So, even if the drug-approval and patent systems were flawless, many patients would still not receive the therapies they need.

THE CATCH-22 OF ORPHAN DRUGS

On the basis of these examples, one can see why pharmaceutical manufacturers have been reluctant to initiate research into orphan drugs in the 1970s and early 1980s. Without promises of profit, or at least recovery of costs, there was little potential for financial gain. At the same time, however, it is easy to understand the value of orphan drugs to patients and the need for maintaining research and development efforts. The following chapters will clarify the provisions of the 1983 Orphan Drug Act, describe its success, and highlight the issues that continue to hinder researchers and patients.

NOTES

1. Abbey S. Meyers, "The Consumer's Role in Development of Orphan Drugs," in *Cooperative Approaches in Research and Development of Orphan Drugs* (New York, NY: Alan R. Liss, 1985):51-52.

2. Report of the National Commission on Orphan Drugs, U.S. Department of Health and Human Services, Office of the Assistant Secretary for Health (1989):1-2.

3. Egon Weck, "Medicine's Orphans: Drugs for Rare Diseases," *FDA Consumer* 2 (1988):12.

4. Abbey S. Meyers, "Working Toward Passage of the Orphan Drug Act: An Example of Determination," *American Medical Writers Association Journal* 3 (Number 1, 1988):3.

5. H.C. Shirkey, "Therapeutic Orphans," *Journal of Pediatrics* 72 (1968):119-120.

6. Fred E. Karch, ed., *Orphan Drugs* (New York, NY: Marcel Dekker, 1982):8.

7. Carolyn H. Asbury, *Orphan Drugs: Medical versus Market Value* (Lexington, MA: D.C. Heath, 1985).

8. Melvin H. Van Woert, "Introduction," in *Cooperative Approaches in Research and Development of Orphan Drugs* (New York, NY: Alan R. Liss, 1985):5-6.

9. Stephen E. Lawton, "Controversy Under the Orphan Drug Act: Is Resolution on the Way?" *Food Drug Cosmetic Law Journal* 46 (1991):327.

10. Aaron E. Ashcraft, "A Plea for 'Orphan Drugs'," *Newsweek* (30 October 1989):12.

11. Larry Thompson, "One Family's Struggle with Gaucher's Disease," *Washington Post Health* (25 June 1985).

12. Anonymous, "Ceredase: A Triumph Over Gaucher's Disease," *Medical Advertising News* (23 May 1991).

13. C. Vance Gordon and Dale E. Wierenga, "The Drug Development and Approval Process," *Orphan Drugs in Development* (1991):19.

Chapter 7

The Impact of the Orphan Drug Act

During the first five years of the 1980s, Congress debated, enacted, and perfected an orphan drug law. During the rest of the decade and continuing into the 1990s, significant discord over implementation of the law [exists] within the Food and Drug Administration (FDA) and on Capitol Hill.[1]

Stephen Lawton

THE ORPHAN DRUG ACT

In 1983, after years of deliberation, the Orphan Drug Act (Public Law [PL] 97-414) was passed to minimize the barriers associated with developing and marketing orphan drugs. The legislation, which amended the Federal Food, Drug and Cosmetic Act, was designed to prompt research and advancement of drugs with little commercial value, like PEG-ADA, through the establishment of financial incentives for pharmaceutical manufacturers and information sources for researchers and patients.

The Provisions

What changes were mandated by the Orphan Drug Act? In addition to providing incentives to make it easier for pharmaceutical manufacturers to research orphan drugs, the 1983 Act expanded the definition and criteria for orphan drugs. (Remember that rare or orphan diseases are those that affect less than 200,000 people in the United States, and that orphan drugs are medications developed to treat rare diseases.) The category of orphan drugs was expanded to include several other types of medications.

Orphan Drug Criteria

One category included in the list of potential orphan drugs was drugs already on the market. For example, if propranolol (Inderal®, Wyeth-Ayerst), a drug currently available to treat high blood pressure, is found to effectively manage the symptoms of Lou Gehrig's disease, it would receive orphan drug status and its sponsor, either the company that originally marketed the drug or another company, would enjoy all of the privileges associated with this status.

Additionally, if a drug is developed for a disease that affects *more than* 200,000 people, but its sponsor demonstrates that there is *no reasonable expectation* that the costs of its research will be recovered from sales in the United States, the drug can receive orphan drug status. This is the only criterion that is conditional–it depends on proof that costs will not be recovered. This proof includes (1) estimated costs for developing and distributing the drugs, and (2) estimated U.S. sales on which the sponsor has concluded development and distribution costs will not be recovered, either during the drug's remaining patent life or, if unpatentable, during the period of exclusive marketing allowed by the Orphan Drug Act.[2]

After defining the restrictions of the terms "rare disease" and "orphan drug," the Orphan Drug Act established four major provisions to help sponsors and researchers overcome the barriers associated with orphan drug development (Table 7.1).

Market Exclusivity

According to the Orphan Drug Act, a seven-year period of **marketing exclusivity** is provided for orphan drugs. This means that the FDA is prohibited from approving the same orphan drug for the same rare disease or condition. This exclusivity begins on the date that the orphan drug is approved and applies *only* to the therapeutic use for which the drug is designated. This provision does not bar the approval of the same drug for another disease or condition (rare or common), nor does it prohibit the approval of another drug for the

TABLE 7.1. Incentives Provided to Sponsors by the 1983 Orphan Drug Act

1. Exclusive marketing rights for seven years after approval of the orphan drug.

2. Tax credits (up to 50%) for clinical testing of orphan drugs.

3. Grants and contracts to support clinical and preclinical orphan drug research.

4. Flexibility and assistance in regulatory processes.

Adapted from Lawrence C. Weaver, "What You Should Know About Orphan Drugs," *Wellcome Trends in Pharmacy* (1991):4.

same rare disease (Table 7.2).[3] Combined with the seven-year market-exclusivity advantage is the additional caveat that this exclusivity is independent of the drug's patent status. To understand this benefit, it is necessary to understand market-exclusivity characteristics of standard or "non-orphan" prescription drugs.

Prescription drugs receive 17-year patent protection through the U.S. Patent Office. This means that from the day the patent is issued, the drug cannot be manufactured or sold by any other name or by any company for 17 years. However, the patent is usually issued during the time that the drug is being researched, so that the time spent completing the research and obtaining approval is deducted from the 17 years. By the time a prescription drug reaches the market, it often has less than 17 years protection. The patent-protection period might be decreased to eight or nine years, for example. After these years have passed, the **brand-name drug** goes "off-patent" and generic drug manufacturers can develop the same drug and sell it, usually for significantly lower prices. This competition limits the potential revenue that can be generated by the brand-name product's manufacturer. Orphan drugs, whether patented or not, always receive seven years of marketing exclusivity from *the day the drug is approved*–not from the day the patent is issued or the day research begins.

TABLE 7.2. Approval of Other Agents After Specific Orphan Drug Designation

IF THE INDICATION OF THE NEW DRUG IS:	AND NEW DRUG IS CHEMICALLY:	IS IT CONSIDERED AN ORPHAN DRUG ACCORDING TO THE ORPHAN DRUG ACT?
different (can be rare or common disease)	same as existing orphan drug	yes
same (rare)	new	yes
same (rare)	same as existing orphan drug	no

Tax Credits on Research Costs

A tax credit equal to half of the costs of conducting human clinical trials is provided to orphan drug manufacturers. This means that at the end of a tax-year, a company researching an orphan drug at a cost of $100,000 can subtract $50,000 from the amount of taxes owed to the federal government. One can see the benefit associated with this provision: it is possible that a pharmaceutical company that is dedicated to the research of orphan drugs can significantly minimize its tax liability.

Unfortunately, this incentive does not incorporate the ability of the sponsoring company to carry forward any losses from year to year–a problem for small pharmaceutical manufacturers that experience a financial loss. These companies pay no taxes if they experience a financial loss. According to the Act, however, in future years in which the company experiences a profit (financial gain)–and a tax liability–it is *not* able to reap the benefits of the prior years' tax credits.

Protocol Assistance

The third provision of the Orphan Drug Act requires that, upon request, the FDA must provide orphan drug sponsors (manufacturers and researchers) with written protocol recommendations regarding orphan drug approval. This service facilitates drug development because sponsors are able to ensure compliance with orphan drug legislation and FDA drug-approval requirements.

This provision is also important because, depending on the drug and the rare disease, the requirements for clinical testing and drug approval can vary. Although drug safety and efficacy must be demonstrated, there is considerable flexibility in the number and design of the trials needed. This service is coordinated by the FDA's Office of Orphan Products Development, a group organized in accordance with the stipulations of the 1983 Act.

Accelerated Approval

Finally, because of the Orphan Drug Act, the FDA drug-approval process is accelerated for orphan drugs. These drugs often receive compassionate or treatment investigational new drug (IND) status prior to marketing approval. This means that the FDA can allow open drug study protocols (or arrangements) under which physicians can request an orphan drug for patient use prior to the drug's approval, even if the patient is not participating in a clinical trial. The provision's goal is to broaden and expedite orphan drug distribution to needy patients during testing and approval.

Amendments to the 1983 Orphan Drug Act

Addition of Numeric Threshold to Definition of Rare Disease

To clarify the definition of "rare disease or condition" in the 1983 Orphan Drug Act, a numeric prevalence threshold was added in 1984. As described, this definition includes diseases or conditions that affect less than 200,000 persons in the United States. It also includes a disease or condition that affects more than 200,000 persons in the U.S., but that has no useful drug treatment because research and development costs cannot be recovered from U.S. sales.

Timing of Applications for Orphan Drug Approval

A 1988 amendment to the Orphan Drug Act stipulated that the orphan drug application must be made *before* submitting an application for marketing approval (either a New Drug Application [NDA] or a Product License Application [PLA]). Prior to this amendment, requests for orphan drug status could be filed at any time before FDA approval. Thus, if two companies were in the process of acquiring approval for the same drug and one company submitted and received orphan drug status just *before* the second company received marketing approval, the second company's drug application would be void (and their time and effort would be wasted). An example will be described in Chapter 8 that shows the potential controversies that still exist regarding this type of situation.

THE ORPHAN DRUG ACT SCOREBOARD: VICTORIES

Over 485 orphan drug designations have been granted by the FDA and at least 64 of these drugs have been approved for marketing.[4,5] The year 1991 alone saw a record 189 orphan drugs in development, compared with 133 in 1989. The average approval time for these orphan drugs was ten to 11 months. These data can be contrasted to the fact that, prior to the enactment of the Act in 1983, only ten drugs had been developed for rare diseases in the preceding decade.[6]

Orphan drug research and development has been spurred by the ability of smaller pharmaceutical companies (known as "start-up" companies) to license (purchase) and develop potentially useful compounds from larger, research-intensive pharmaceutical manufacturers.[7] After the passage of the 1983 Act, large companies combed through their "drug libraries" to find compounds that had not been heavily investigated because of a lack of monetary value, but that might prove medically useful. Many of these compounds were then sold to start-up companies where they were researched for therapeutic properties.

If a licensed drug is indeed proven effective in treating a rare disease, the start-up company can market the product and receive substantial revenues (i.e., enough to make the research endeavor cost-effective). Because of higher overhead costs (i.e., more employees and capital expenditures) and tax liabilities, such research activities are *not* cost-effective for larger pharmaceutical firms.

The examples provided in Chapter 6 of PEG-ADA and alglucerase are just two life-saving orphan drugs that were developed by small pharmaceutical companies and whose approval was accelerated by the Orphan Drug Act. Other drugs, including colony stimulating factors for patients with blood disorders, interferons for the treatment of certain cancers, and AIDS-related drugs are currently awaiting approval and will positively affect the health of many patients with rare diseases (Figure 7.1).

THE ORPHAN DRUG ACT SCOREBOARD: FAILURES

On the basis of the explosion of orphan drug research activity, it is clear that the Orphan Drug Act has successfully fulfilled its purpose: to facilitate the development and marketing of drugs for patients with rare diseases. The Act has even been hailed as "perfect" by some FDA personnel. However, as we all know, nothing is perfect. There are several issues that the Orphan Drug Act has failed to address and that merit our attention.

To determine the extent of the problems associated with patient acquisition and financing of orphan drugs, the National Commission on Orphan Diseases (NCOD)–a group of government representatives, health-care professionals, researchers, and patient advocates–was created by Congress. In 1989, this group conducted a survey of 801 patients and 270 physicians and made some interesting conclusions.[8] The results of the survey are summarized in Table 7.3.

The Information Shortage

New treatments, research advances, clinical trials, available voluntary support groups, and the location of treatment centers are just a selection of the types of information that patients and health-care professionals need. According to NCOD survey data, there is a serious communication gap surrounding orphan drugs and rare diseases. Information, although essential to all participants in the health-care system, is not readily accessible.

For example, according to the survey, 42% of physicians require,

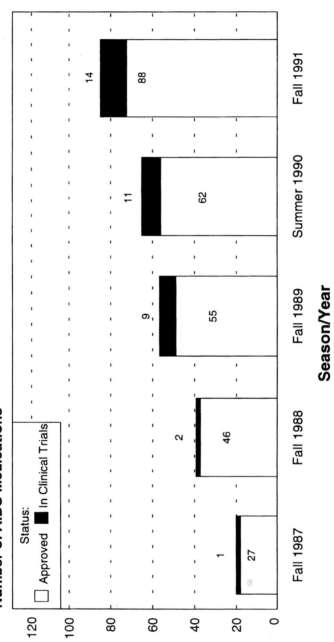

FIGURE 7.1. Drugs in Development: AIDS Medications

Number of AIDS Medications

Status:
Approved ☐   In Clinical Trials ■

Fall 1987: 1, 27
Fall 1988: 2, 46
Fall 1989: 9, 55
Summer 1990: 11, 62
Fall 1991: 14, 88

Season/Year

SOURCE: PMA AIDS Medicines in Development Survey

TABLE 7.3. Key Findings of NCOD Survey

Patients and Families

- have difficulty obtaining information about new treatments, research advances, appropriate voluntary support groups, and treatment centers for their disease;
- are willing to use investigational drugs but find it difficult to locate information on research projects;
- are prevented from working or attending school and are financially burdened by their disease.

Physicians

- need but are unable to find information about rare diseases for their patients;
- would prescribe an investigational drug for patients with life-threatening diseases;
- would be hesitant to use an investigational drug for which little information was available.

Investigators

- believe that it is harder to get funding for basic or clinical research on rare diseases than for common diseases;
- agree that lack of funds for research is the single greatest barrier to the discovery of treatments for rare diseases;
- admit that limited availability of patients for clinical studies is a major problem in orphan drug research.

Federal Agencies

- do not have special mechanisms to stimulate research on rare diseases.

Voluntary Organizations

- prepare and provide educational materials and programs for patients with rare diseases;
- maintain files and registries of patients, investigators or physicians, provide research grants or seed money to encourage scientists and physicians.

Adapted from Report of the National Commission on Orphan Diseases, 1989:1-2.

but are unable to find, printed information about orphan diseases that they can distribute to patients. In addition, over half have never prescribed an investigational drug product, although 27% of the 150 physicians who had not prescribed an investigational drug had *considered* prescribing such a product. Ninety-two percent of these physicians stated that they would prescribe an investigational drug for a patient with a life-threatening illness.

As a consequence of the information deficiency regarding orphan disease identification and treatment, many patients struggle with disabling and painful illnesses. Additionally, physicians are limited in their ability to diagnose and effectively treat patients. Other health-care professionals, including nurses and pharmacists, find it difficult to help patients cope with their disease.

As demonstrated by the NCOD survey, there is a significant need for disease and drug information for patients afflicted with rare diseases. A brief list of information sources has been compiled in Appendix B, Table B.2. The organizations listed have developed databases, informative publications and materials, plus networks of health-care professionals, patients, and researchers throughout the United States, in an effort to improve knowledge and treatment of rare diseases, and facilitate research and development of orphan drugs.

Treatment Price Tags

When questioned about orphan drug costs, 42% of the patients surveyed reported that their illnesses prevent them from working or attending school, and 43% stated that their illnesses constitute an extreme financial burden for their families. For example, patients with Gaucher's disease, the rare condition for which alglucerase has been approved, need life-long treatment of bimonthly injections costing $275,000 to $550,000 per year.[9] For patients with AIDS-related pneumonia, the annual cost of pentamidine is approximately $8,000. The financial burden of these drugs is often absorbed by other consumers. Medical insurance companies increase rates for all insured persons to cover the high costs of increasingly complex and expensive medical treatments, including orphan drugs, while rising Medicaid and Medicare burdens are paid by taxpayers.

Medical Insurance: For the Healthy Only?

Under the current health-care system, many patients cannot afford orphan drug costs. Even patients insured by respectable medical insurance companies struggle. Although this state of affairs is not a direct result of the Orphan Drug Act, it is an issue that affects all patients with rare diseases. Because the information regarding the prevalence, incidence, health-care needs, and medication-use needs of patients with rare diseases is not readily available, as well as because of the high costs, most insurance companies will not pay for orphan drug treatment. Patients, especially those with chronic rare diseases, are often denied insurance, lose their insurance, or are faced with doubled or tripled premiums after their diagnosis is made. These actions result in a system where only healthy people are insured. Rare-disease patients and volunteer agencies are dedicated to the idea of a national health-care system in which access to medical care is equal for those with rare diseases.[10]

Rare Disease Identification

Judy, a young mother and writer, contracted a virus in September of 1988. Although the symptoms were severe, they were of a short duration and passed. In October, however, her toes and fingers began feeling numb and her strength decreased. She finally arranged to see her family doctor in December and was promptly admitted to the hospital for a series of neurologic tests. After several days and visits from well-known neurologists, Judy's doctors told her she had Guillain-Barre syndrome, a rare but reversible viral illness that destroys the nerves. By spring, Judy had not gotten better; she felt worse. Upon contacting her family doctor again, she was referred to another specialist. After more tests and consultation with other experts around the country, the specialist concluded that Judy did *not* have Guillain-Barre, but an even more uncommon disease, chronic inflammatory demyelinating polyneuropathy. Four years later, after receiving appropriate medication, Judy is now healthy, strong, and thankful that she was finally able to obtain an accurate diagnosis.[11]

Because orphan diseases are so uncommon, patients with these afflictions often wait *two to five years* before a correct diagnosis is made.[12] Many physicians do not recognize the symptoms and characteristics of orphan diseases due to the limited amount of patients from whom information can be garnered. Even if the orphan disease is appropriately diagnosed, physicians lack knowledge of drugs that can treat the rare disease.

* * *

Written by a woman with a rare disease, the following narrative summarizes the frustrations and challenges that are still encountered by patients with rare diseases.

How to Know You Have a Rare Disorder

You know you have a rare disorder when the doctor triumphantly delivers the diagnosis, for this pronouncement has an immediate and peculiar effect on the doctor's speech. Thereafter, he/she replies to every probing question, "We just don't know." This phenomenon is accompanied by recurrent episodes of shoulder shrugging and intermittent scratching of the head.

You know you have a rare disorder when your spouse acquires the characteristics of a mole, one with an affinity for musty library stacks and an appetite for obscure information.

You know you have a rare disorder when your family and friends ask the third time for lessons in the spelling and pronouncing of your disease.

You know you have a rare disorder when ten doctors crowd into your hospital room, eager to examine the specimen.

You know you have a rare disorder when you consider handing out xeroxed copies of your medical history, rather than repeating it one more time.

You know you have a rare disorder when your interest in research grants exceed your enthusiasm for the Super Bowl.

You know you have a rare disorder when your name appears in the *Guinness Book of World Records* under longest time ever waited for a diagnosis.

You know you have a rare disorder when you map out a "Campaign to Educate All Doctors in America" concerning your disease. Ten down! Only 100,000 to go.

You know you have a rare disorder when you discover NORD and find countless others who have been through all this, too.

© *Barbara Seaman, 1990, Lawrence, Kansas.*
Reprinted with permission.

THE WINDS OF CHANGE–THE 1990s

The basic dilemmas posed by orphan drugs are the same as those posed by other new but expensive medical technologies being developed and introduced at a time of unprecedented escalations in health-care costs. . . . The public cannot afford to ignore questions of which patients should receive the benefits of these advances, who should decide, and who should pay for them.[2]

Carolyn Asbury

The Orphan Drug Act, although extremely successful in hastening the development and provision of necessary medications for patients with rare diseases, was written in the early 1980s. At this time, two of the most profound changes in the health and medical care of U.S. citizens had not yet altered our nation.

These two changes are the exploding number of patients with AIDS and the growth of biotechnology companies. AIDS was barely understood in the early 1980s and affected only a small number of people. No drugs were available to treat the disease or conditions related to it, such as *Pneumocystis carinii* pneumonia and Kaposi's sarcoma, a form of cancer. In addition, although small start-up biotechnology firms existed, they were mostly laboratories with a handful of researchers and chemists. Few biotechnology products had been manufactured. Furthermore, because they were so new, the ability of innovative biotechnology products to help patients was considered questionable at best.

However, these two changes have significantly changed our health-care system. Currently, there are over one million individuals infected with HIV.[12] And, since 1982, 14 biopharmaceuticals have been developed and approved by the FDA for conditions ranging from diabetes to chronic anemia associated with end-stage kidney disease.[13] The high prices of these new therapies, the need for prompt action in the AIDS crisis, and the subsequent struggle of biopharmaceutical drug manufacturers to win in the race to the orphan drug designation "finish line" have severely altered the status of the orphan drug issue.

MONOPOLY PRICING PRACTICES

When Congress adopted the [Orphan Drug] Act, it recognized that there was a possibility that the Act might be too inclusive; that is, it might give exclusivity to drugs that would have been developed without the incentives of the law. The result is an unnecessary monopoly and higher prices to consumers.[14]

Rep. Waxman, opening statement,
1990 Orphan Drug Act hearings.

In 1990, as a response to the shortcomings of the Act, as well as abuses of the Act by some pharmaceutical manufacturers, the Orphan Drug Act Amendments of 1990 (H.R. 4638) were submitted to Congress by Representative Henry Waxman and Senator Howard Metzenbaum. The bill was designed to return the focus of the Act back to its original intent: to provide incentives to pharmaceutical manufacturers likely to experience financial loss due to limited sales of an orphan drug and substantial research and development expenses.

Shared exclusivity was a primary component of the proposed amendments. This provision would allow companies that could prove simultaneous development of the same orphan drug, using a three-part test, to compete on the U.S. market. The amendments applied the shared-exclusivity provision retroactively. Thus, the exclusivity of orphan drugs *currently* on the market could be challenged by manufacturers who had researched the same drug. This change was welcomed by patients with rare diseases as well as advocate groups, such as the National Organization for Rare Disorders (NORD), because it helped patients afford drugs that were once too expensive. Companies with orphan drugs on the market were dissatisfied with this provision because it introduced competition to the marketplace and could potentially decrease their drug's sales.

The second provision of the 1990 amendments authorized revocation of orphan drug designation if it was determined that the patient population affected by a particular rare disease had grown to over 200,000 people by the end of the seven-year market exclusivity period. This amendment was also retroactive (i.e., it affects past occurrences). For sponsors of orphan drugs for AIDS patients, the orphan drug designation would be forfeited and new AIDS drugs would not receive orphan drug designation.

The third recommendation of the Orphan Drug Act Amendments of 1990 required the establishment of the Central Office for Rare Diseases, an agency to be housed in the Assistant Secretary of Health's office. This agency was designed to include researchers, rare-disease patients, and health-industry representatives. It would report federal government actions regarding orphan disease issues to Congress on an annual basis.[15]

After a series of compromises, the amendments were unanimously passed in the House of Representatives and the Senate with the accolades of patients and health-care professionals. However, in December 1990, President Bush shocked Capitol Hill by vetoing the law and forcing relevant and consequential issues to remain unaddressed. According to a statement signed by Mr. Bush, he was "concerned . . . that individuals with rare diseases may suffer because of changes that this bill would make in the incentives to develop new drug treatment."[10] The reasons submitted by Bush's Administration for his veto included:

1. *Competitiveness:* If the amendments were passed, incentives to develop orphan drugs would be considerably reduced, resulting in a decrease in orphan drug research and availability.
2. *Constitutionality:* Because the retroactive feature of the

shared-exclusivity provision potentially violates a clause of the fifth amendment to the Constitution, the provisions were not feasible.

3. *Office of Orphan Drugs:* The Department of Health and Human Services realized that the Central Office for Rare Diseases, the office created by the amendment, could be construed as taking authority away from the FDA–an insupportable flaw.[1]

Since the end of 1990 and throughout 1991 and 1992, other amendments have been proposed and are currently awaiting decisions:

Windfall Profit Tax

In October 1991, Representative Fortney (Pete) Stark introduced the orphan windfall profits tax bill (H.R. 3551). He proposed that orphan drug manufacturers should be able to recoup research and development costs associated with the orphan drug, as well as 25% of these costs in annual profits. This allows the manufacturer to gain substantial revenues from the orphan drug development process and, hence, serve as an incentive to develop orphan drugs. Patient groups like NORD are against this tax, however, because it requires government audits of the targeted companies' financial records, which companies are likely to avoid by minimizing orphan drug research. According to Abbey Meyers, this regulatory action would "truly destroy the Orphan Drug Act."[16]

Intellectual-Property Protection for Biopharmaceuticals

Although not proposed in the House of Representatives or the Senate, the protection of biotechnology drugs and biologics by an intellectual-property designation would minimize risks associated with research and development of such drugs. Like a patent, this designation would prohibit other pharmaceutical manufacturers from copying and modifying a biopharmaceutical and receiving FDA approval. Intellectual-property designation would be an alternative to the Orphan Drug Act for profitable products.

This proposal, among several others, was suggested by the NCOD after reviewing and evaluating the orphan drug situation in 1989. Other NCOD recommendations for amendment of the Orphan Drug Act included increasing the market exclusivity period of seven years, extending tax credits to all preclinical research activities, and extending patent protection afforded to one of the manufacturer's currently-marketed drugs for every orphan product developed and approved by the FDA.

Orphan Drug Sales Trigger

Another recent suggestion is a sales trigger on orphan drugs. If an orphan drug sponsor generates more than a specific dollar amount in cumulative sales before the seven-year exclusivity period terminates, the drug loses its marketing exclusivity and is treated like any other prescription drug. Thus, the originating sponsor recoups the orphan drug's research and development costs and other companies can submit and receive marketing approval to compete with the original product.

Patients would benefit from this provision because the orphan drug in question would conceivably be less expensive due to competition. According to Meyers, "[NORD] believe[s] that [this] option is the most reasonable because it does not punish manufacturers of orphan drugs and would not require companies to open their books to government auditors. Sales ceilings could simply be calculated by the number of prescriptions filled–data that are available from a variety of sources."[9]

The Pharmaceutical Manufacturers Association, however, is against this proposal. They believe the sales trigger will serve to further limit orphan drug development because the primary incentive provided by the Orphan Drug Act (exclusivity) is removed.[17] This particular incentive is especially important to manufacturers because of increasing research and development costs. It is estimated that ten years are required before *any* new drug recovers its research and development costs.[18] Actions to limit manufacturers' ability to recover orphan drug research costs might result in less research and a lower number of orphan drug approvals.

TODAY'S HEADLINES

Recent actions taken by the Senate Antitrust Subcommittee have advanced the belief that the sales trigger proposal is under serious consideration. In July 1991, Senator Metzenbaum began researching the extent of the abuses and shortcomings of the Orphan Drug Act in preparation for hearings held in 1992. He sent questionnaires to many pharmaceutical companies that were marketing highly profitable orphan drugs, and other companies that market potentially profitable orphan drugs.[19] The survey asked manufacturers to detail development and marketing costs for these agents, as well as estimate sales, list current prices, and determine annual patient costs. Certain details, such as the approximate number of patients using the product, the prevalence of "off-label" use of these products (i.e., use in patients with other diseases besides the rare disease for which the orphan drug was approved), and potential cost savings associated with the marketing of drugs currently prohibited by the Act, were also queried in the poll.[20]

Using the survey results, Senator Metzenbaum and Senator Nancy Kassebaum, an original sponsor of the 1983 law, jointly proposed a new orphan drug bill in November 1991 (S. 2060). According to Kassebaum, the measure "does not prevent the original sponsor of the drug from continuing to market that drug; it merely introduces the possibility of competition."[21,22] Specifically, the bill allows additional companies to seek and obtain permission to market their drugs if, at any time during the seven-year exclusivity period, the number of persons affected by the disease or condition exceeds 200,000. Additionally, if cumulative sales of the drug reach $200 million, exclusivity ends unless the sponsor can show that development costs exceeded that amount. Metzenbaum's survey showed that research and development costs for "blockbuster" orphan drugs were less than $55 million.[23]

One condition of the sales trigger proposal is that after an orphan drug's net sales exceed $150 million, other pharmaceutical manufacturers can begin submitting approval applications. This minimizes the delay in product approval after the $200 million target is met. Finally, the bill suggests the replacement of the FDA's Orphan Products Board by the Office of Orphan Products, which would consist of rare-disease agencies, researchers, and representatives of health-related companies to coordinate federal activities.[24]

Again, the proposed solution to the orphan drug problem has caused controversy. A representative of the PMA stated that "sales are not a reflection of profits because they do not take into account the cost of doing business. . . ." These costs include capital expenditures, manufacturing, marketing, and drug distribution, as well as the costs of researching drugs that fail to gain approval. Senator Orrin Hatch agrees that the Orphan Drug Act should not be amended. He suggests that the problems attributed to the law might reflect larger issues that should be addressed separately, such as biotechnology-product patents and patient access to health care.[24]

On the other side of the proverbial coin, NORD is convinced that the proposed measures would "strike a blow against escalating health care costs. . . . By leveling out the playing field, more true orphans [will be] developed."[25]

The truth of the matter is that both sides of this issue, like most other controversies, are relevant to the decision and must be considered when determining the scope of the Orphan Drug Act amendments. Although the health of the American people should be the prime consideration, the skyrocketing costs of drug research and development, and the potential impact of minimal research incentives are important factors to incorporate when making decisions. More data are needed to determine the truth of this conclusion regarding drug-development incentives. Additionally, it is valuable to develop contingency plans for unique situations or drugs. Thus, if a particular situation, like the unanticipated financial success of drugs like human growth hormone and pentamidine, occurs, the FDA would have a mechanism for managing the repercussions.

NOTES

1. Stephen E. Lawton, "Controversy Under the Orphan Drug Act: Is Resolution on the Way?" *Food Drug Cosmetic Law Journal* (1991):331.

2. Carolyn H. Asbury, *Orphan Drugs: Medical versus Market Value* (Lexington, MA: D.C. Heath, 1984):181-182.

3. Carolyn H. Asbury, "The Orphan Drug Act: The First 7 Years," *Journal of the American Medical Association* 265 (1991):893-897.

4. Gerald J. Mossinghoff, "189 Medicines in Testing for Rare Diseases," *Orphan Drugs in Development* (1992):1.

5. Abbey S. Meyers, "The U.S. Orphan Drug Act: Should the Law Cover Highly Profitable Drugs?" *World Pharmaceutical Standard Review* 1 (Number 9, 1991):25.

6. George S. Goldstein, "Refine the Orphan Drug Act, Don't Destroy It," *Medical Marketing and Media* 26 (1991):53.

7. Larry C. Weaver, "What You Need to Know about Orphan Drugs," *Wellcome Trends in Pharmacy* 13 (Number 6, 1991):5.

8. Jesse G. Thoene and Glenna M. Crooks, eds., *Report of the National Commission on Orphan Diseases* (Washington, DC: U.S. Department of Health and Human Services, February 1989):xiii-xviii.

9. Ernest Beutler, "Gaucher's Disease," *New England Journal of Medicine* 325 (Number 19, 1991):1358.

10. Anonymous, "Health Insurance Hearing," *Orphan Disease Update* 8 (Edition 9, 1990):1.

11. Judy O'Brien Goldman, "The Illness No One Could Explain," *Woman's Day* (15 October 1991):44-48.

12. Evan Ackiron, "Patents for Critical Pharmaceuticals: The AZT Case," *American Journal of Law & Medicine* 17 (Number 1, 1991):145-180.

13. Anonymous, *Pharmaceutical Manufacturers Association Annual Survey of Biotechnology Medicines in Development* (Washington DC: PMA, 1990).

14. Orphan Drug Act–Hearings Before the Subcommittee on Health and the Environment of the House Committee on Energy and Commerce, 101st Congress, 2nd session, serial no. 101-130 (1990).

15. Anonymous, "President Vetoes Orphan Drug Amendments," *Orphan Disease Update* 8 (Edition 9, 1990):1.

16. Anonymous, "Genzyme's Ceredase and Amgen's Neupogen Cited by NORD," *FDC Reports* (2 September 1991):T&G 2.

17. Thomas Copmann, Letter to the Editor of *Science* (18 April 1991).

18. Stephen J. Knoop and Daniel E. Worden, "The Pharmaceutical Drug Development Process: An Overview," *Drug Information Journal* 22 (1991):268.

19. Press Release by the Office of U.S. Senator Howard M. Metzenbaum of Ohio (16 July 1991):1.

20. Anonymous, "Orphan Drug Amendments in 102nd Congress: Senator Metzenbaum Initiates Foray into Orphan Drug Exclusivity Provisions with July 10 Questionnaires to Eight Firms," *FDC Reports* (15 July 1991):6.

21. Anonymous, "Kassebaum and Metzenbaum Introduce Orphan Drug Amendments," *PMA Newsletter* 33 (1991):1.

22. Nancy L. Kassebaum, Hearing transcript: "Introduction of Orphan Drug Amendments of 1991" (26 November 1991).

23. Anonymous, "R&D Expenses for all 'Blockbuster' Orphan Drug Products were Under $150 Million–Senator Metzenbaum Claims; Asserts Costs can 'Easily' be Recouped Under S 2060," *FDC Reports* (27 January 1992):9-10.

24. Anonymous, "Orphan Drug Amendments Aim to 'Fix a Law That Isn't Broken,' Senator Hatch Contends; He Predicts Labor Committee Will 'Soon' Hold Legislative Hearings," *FDC Reports* (27 January 1992):8.

25. Anonymous, "Orphan Drug Amendments Placing $200 Million Threshold on Cumulative Sales to End Market Exclusivity Introduced by Senators Kassebaum, Metzenbaum, Representative Studds," *FDC Reports* (2 December 1991):13.

Chapter 8

Current Orphan Drug Controversies and Proposed Solutions

Several changes in the health-care environment of the United States have prompted a new look at orphan drug regulations. Some of the most prominent catalysts include the progress in biotechnology, the marketing of biopharmaceuticals, confusion regarding certain provisions of the Orphan Drug Act–especially patent and market exclusivity regulations–and the AIDS crisis.

Because the issues described are interrelated, it is difficult to characterize their individual impact on the orphan drug situation. Gradually, like building blocks, these issues have transformed the health-care environment throughout the 1980s. Today, the orphan drug situation has been altered to the point where formal action is necessary. Equitable marketing conditions for orphan drug manufacturers and available life-saving orphan drugs for patients are two critical needs.

Unfortunately, the scope of formal action to solve orphan drug problems has been difficult to resolve. Many stakeholders have proposed and then thwarted potential solutions. In the meantime, the situation continues to worsen. At this time, we recognize that the future holds some type of change, but the nature and extent of the change remains unknown.

BIOTECHNOLOGY AND BIOPHARMACEUTICALS

The primary reason to consider amendment of current orphan drug laws is the advent of **biotechnology** and the marketing of biopharmaceuticals. **Biopharmaceuticals** are drugs produced using biotechnology–either **recombinant DNA processes** or **hybridoma technology**. These drug-development procedures, although not very complicated, are superior in their ability to produce life-saving medications. Biotechnology-derived drugs are now available to minimize symptoms and extend the life of patients with AIDS, reduce complications of chemotherapy for cancer patients, and effectively immunize individuals against hepatitis and influenza.

At least 15 biopharmaceutical agents are marketed in the United States and over 100 are in various stages of research, clinical trials, and development. Examples of orphan biopharmaceuticals approved in 1990 include interferon gamma-1b (Actimmune®, Genentech) for chronic granulomatosis disease, and CMV Immune Globulin (Massachusetts Public Health Laboratories) for cytomegalovirus infection associated with kidney transplants.

Unfortunately, there are several problems associated with the development and marketing of orphan biopharmaceuticals:

1. Some of these agents can be exceptionally expensive to research, produce, package, and administer. These costs are often passed on to patients with rare diseases.
2. Biopharmaceuticals that generate exceedingly high dollar sales can result in monopoly benefits for their manufacturers.
3. It is difficult to distinguish between some molecular entities that are produced using biotechnology, especially for the United States Patent Office.

All of these concerns have led to disruption and debate of the Orphan Drug Act by Congress and consumers.

Extraordinary Expenses

Although orphan drug cost was never expected to become a significant issue, several products are causing an uproar from both patients and consumer agencies. The price tags on several recently-approved orphan drugs are incredibly high. Some of these costs, as well as the uses of the orphan biopharmaceuticals, are listed in Table 8.1. These figures are determined on the basis of *annual* product usage. Remember that most rare diseases require ongoing therapy.

TABLE 8.1. 1991 Estimated Annual Sales of Selected Orphan Drugs

DRUG	1991 ANNUAL SALES (ESTIMATED)	INDICATION
erythropoietin–Epogen® (Amgen)	$375 million	dialysis-associated anemia in patients with end-stage renal failure
human growth hormone– Protropin® (Genentech)	$165 million	growth hormone deficiency
pentamidine–NebuPent® (Fujisawa)	$120 million	treatment of *pneumocystis carinii* pneumonia
alglucerase–Ceredase® (Genzyme)	$105 million	treatment of Gaucher's disease

SOURCE: National Organization of Rare Disorders (specific references available on request)

For the majority of orphan drugs, gross sales are less than $10 million per year. However, three orphan drugs reached annual sales of over $100 million in 1990 (pentamidine, erythropoietin, and human growth hormone). These drugs have been labeled *blockbusters*. For comparison, 1990 U.S. sales of terfenadine (Seldane®, Marion Merrell Dow Inc.), a popular antihistamine used in patients with allergies, was $102 million.

One of the most recent, and most expensive, orphan drugs is alglucerase (Ceredase®, Genzyme). This drug was described previously as a treatment for a fatal enzyme deficiency. The drug's cost is estimated at over $350,000 for the first year of treatment. For a person receiving 80% health-care coverage, the yearly cost of alglucerase therapy is still $35,000–more than an average worker's annual salary. The drug's dose (and thus cost) is tailored for each patient on the basis of patient weight.[1] According to Senator Howard Metzenbaum, who supports amendments to the Orphan Drug Act that would eliminate market exclusivity for drugs like these, pharmaceutical manufacturers of orphan drugs with expensive price tags are "charging outrageously high prices, because, with no competition, they know desperately ill people have nowhere else to turn."[1]

How will patients be able to use such expensive drugs? Who will pay? The government? Health-care institutions? Private organizations? As discussed earlier, insurance companies are reluctant to finance such treatments because of their high cost. Thus, patients are bearing the brunt of these costs. This pattern cannot continue without causing an increase in the number of patients who suffer or die because finances limit their ability to receive treatment.

The Monopoly Game

A situation in which a company possesses exclusive control over a particular market or segment of business is known as a monopoly. Most people are familiar with the control held by utility and railroad companies in the early twentieth century. This business practice was curtailed by the federal government when it realized that powerless consumers were being charged unjustly high prices.

With market exclusivity as granted by the Orphan Drug Act, it is possible that drug manufacturers can operate in a similar manner. Members of the industry know that, in many cases, high orphan drug prices will be paid by consumers with rare diseases simply because there are no alternatives.

With the introduction of expensive biopharmaceuticals, the threat of monopolies has come to the forefront–newspaper articles and television spots have decried the unfair costs of orphan biopharmaceuticals, including zidovudine for AIDS and erythropoietin for patients with kidney failure. Patients cannot afford high-priced products. They question why other companies cannot introduce another erythropoietin product so that the two can compete and lower prices. The answer to this question is found in the Orphan Drug Act. Market exclusivity, the major incentive allowed by the legislation to promote orphan drug development, prevents competition.

Is this situation fair to the pharmaceutical industry? Should more than one company be allowed to market the same orphan drug? What about orphan drugs that do not have the potential market of pentamidine and zidovudine? Competition in such markets would make the chance of cost recovery quite small. Furthermore, it is highly unlikely that many orphan drugs would be available at all if competition was permitted before their approval.

The Identity Crisis–Patenting Biopharmaceuticals

One consequence of simultaneous development of a product by several companies is the waste of limited, high-quality resources. The money and clinical resources required to ready a product for Food and Drug Administration (FDA) approval are doubled or tripled. This waste undoubtedly will be passed to the patient and public.[2]

Summary of Patent Law

Patents are analogous to a contract between the inventor and the public, as represented by the U.S. Patent Office. This contract is an exchange of promises. The government promises the inventor the right to exclude others from making, using, or selling the patented product for a limited time period, while the inventor promises the government a full, clearly written description of the invention. In the U.S., patent rights last for 17 years from the date granted. For drugs and medical devices, this period can be extended up to five years if there are delays in obtaining market approval from the FDA.[3]

There are specific criteria that an invention must meet for patenting by the U.S. Patent Office. The invention must be (1) useful, (2) novel, and (3) nonobvious. Pharmaceutical usefulness or **utility** is established when the results of standard drug-screening procedures can be interpreted by skilled scientists as showing utility or drug effectiveness. Clinical drug tests are not necessary, although they are helpful and desirable.

Novelty is interpreted as whether the invention is original or whether it has been used or patented before as part of "prior art." Inventions that are considered public knowledge are not patentable.

The requirement of an invention to be **nonobvious** is somewhat vague. According to patent law, an invention is not patentable if the differences between the subject matter (claims) of the invention and prior art are evident at the time the invention was made to a person of ordinary skill in the art. In other words, if an invention is an obvious solution to an existing problem, such as the "invention" of a system of a nail and a wrench to remove corks from wine bottles, it is not patentable.

Finally, before an invention can be patented, it must also be able to be clearly described in a written document, which is maintained by the Patent Office. This document provides instructions that enable any person adequately trained in the art to make and use the invention. This condition is known as the **enablement requirement**.

It is at this stage that many biotechnology products fail patentability tests. Often, biotechnology products cannot be adequately described in writing. Because the process is complex and the materials somewhat variable, a researcher using the instructions is often unable to manufacture the protein or microorganism without excessive experimentation. One way to minimize this complication is to provide an actual sample of the product, which is held at a national depository, such as the National Research Culture Collection. Researchers are then able to refer to the actual product, thus minimizing undue efforts.[3]

What Are Biopharmaceuticals?

Biopharmaceuticals–drugs produced using recombinant DNA or hybridoma techniques–are just one class of products developed using biotechnology. Because most biopharmaceuticals are developed using human genetic information, they are virtually identical to endogenous substances (found in the body), such as proteins and enzymes. The process of making biopharmaceuticals can be easily understood if it is viewed as a duplication method. A molecule or protein that produces a desired therapeutic effect is "photocopied" several million times to produce a volume large enough to use in patients. Like a photocopied document, the original and the duplicate look similar, function in the same manner, and are essentially interchangeable.

Although biotechnology generates life-saving drugs, controversies surrounding the development of identical substances have made approval and patient use quite complicated.[4] The first problem for biopharmaceuticals is patents. The Orphan Drug Act provides protection similar to patents for approved orphan drugs. But what if another product is different from the approved orphan drug in just one tiny way–an extra molecule or amino acid? Does the new product deserve another patent or is it the same drug? Which manufacturer should have patent protection–the one whose drug was approved first by the FDA or the one who developed the drug first (chronologically)? Is one drug simply a copy and modification of the other? Especially for some of the smaller biotechnology companies, the answers to these questions can mean the difference between market exclusivity with substantial sales and bankruptcy. Today, there are no answers; the U.S. Patent Office is still debating feasible solutions.[2]

Concerns About Simultaneous Research

The costs associated with redundancy of drug research are monumental. Is it not more feasible to pool knowledge so that the proverbial wheel is not reinvented several times over? Efficient resource use and research progress can save many more lives. Questions arise about whether companies researching the same drug should co-market the drug, or have their own brand-name product on the market.

A second issue concerns the benefits that are derived from biopharmaceuticals. Researchers, in their haste to obtain biopharmaceutical-product approval, are able to assess only the most obvious medical questions. Other potential but less-apparent uses of a biotechnology product (and the needs of the patients who can benefit from the biopharmaceutical) are often overlooked.

Illustrations of the Biopharmaceutical Controversy

Erythropoietin

Erythropoietin is a prime example of a biopharmaceutical surrounded by conflict. Derived by recombinant DNA technology, erythropoietin is an injectable medication that helps minimize one of the adverse effects of hemodialysis–anemia–in patients with severe renal failure. The drug stimulates red blood cell production (the cells that are lacking during anemia). Erythropoietin is valuable because, by minimizing anemia, it reduces the need for frequent blood transfusions, consequently decreasing costs.

Amgen, a California-based biotechnology company that researched and developed erythropoietin, received orphan drug status in June 1989. With this designation, and upon FDA approval, Amgen received seven-year exclusivity on the market–no other company can market erythropoietin until this time period has expired.

While Amgen was researching erythropoietin, however, so was a competitor, Genetics Institute. Genetics Institute also spent millions of dollars in developing and testing the use of erythropoietin, and received the first *patent* for the erythropoietin product (actually, for the process of erythropoietin separation from body fluids). Amgen, too, had a patent–for the discovery of the gene that produces erythropoietin.

In 1989, the fight over whether the two products were different enough to allow separate handling (according to patent laws) was taken to a Massachusetts court. The court found that, although the claims in each patent were valid, each company infringed on the other's patent. **Cross-licensing** of the two products was ordered. Upon appeal, however, Amgen was given marketing exclusivity for erythropoietin. The Genetics Institute patent was declared invalid, and their product was barred from the U.S. market. The Massachusetts decision was upheld in January 1992 when Genetics Institute attempted to appeal to the Supreme Court. As a result, Genetics Institute is allowed to market their product overseas only, giving Amgen sole marketing rights to erythropoietin in the United States.[5] It is estimated that, with monopoly control of the erythropoietin market, Amgen will see sales of approximately $400 million in 1992.[6]

HA-1A/E5

Another case that exemplifies the current debates that are raging in biotechnology arenas is that of two drugs, HA-1A and E5. In November 1991, a federal jury ruled that the two biopharmaceuticals, which are awaiting FDA approval, were essentially the same. HA-1A (Centoxin®), which is manufactured by Centocor Inc., and E5®, which is owned by Xoma Corporation, are monoclonal antibodies that treat patients with life-threatening gram-negative bacterial infections. These drugs work by inhibiting the ability of bacteria to release endotoxin, a poison that can cause death. Traditional antibiotics can kill bacteria, but they cannot prevent poisoning of the body by endotoxins that produce their lethal effects after the bacteria are eradicated.

According to the court, HA-1A infringed on E5's patent. Centocor had applied for a patent for HA-1A in 1983 and received it in 1991. Xoma received patent protection for E5 in 1990. To win the law suit, Xoma was able to prove to the court that E5 was the first monoclonal antibody researched as a treatment for gram-negative infection in *humans*. Centocor had researched HA-1A at that time, but only in *animals*. As of December 1991, Centocor was ordered to pay "equitable compensation" to Xoma as soon as HA-1A is marketed in the U.S. In the meantime, both companies are vying for first place in the race to receive FDA marketing approval.

Situations like these are not unusual or unexpected. According to the U.S. Patent Office, applications for patents are only evaluated on the basis of whether or not they represent a product that is unique from existing prior art,[7] not whether they infringe on other patents. Furthermore, because so many patent applications are processed through the Office, each one receives limited review. The issues described above are just a few of the concerns that will affect the development and marketing of biopharmaceuticals.

Solutions to the Biotechnology Debate

Many have suggested that the Orphan Drug Act should be amended to allow the co-marketing of biopharmaceuticals if it can be shown that two or more companies were developing the product independently at the same time. This amendment would eliminate the need to focus on patentability, yet continue to provide an incentive to biotechnology companies to continue rare-disease research. However, others argue that this advantage should be extended to any pharmaceutical company for any drug.

Because many current drugs will lose patent protection relatively soon, patent concerns are relatively unimportant to their manufacturers. For example, human growth hormone (Humatrope®, Eli Lilly & Company) loses marketing exclusivity in 1994. However,

the patentability issue will continue to affect future biotechnology-
derived drugs. Legislative action is necessary to minimize patent
problems and associated costs, as well as ensure that effective products are available for patients at reasonable prices.

THE AIDS CRISIS

According to the World Health Organization, between ten and 12
million people worldwide are infected with the AIDS virus. The
AIDS Action Council, a nonprofit advocacy group in Washington,
DC, has documented over 246,000 cases of AIDS in U.S. children,
adolescents, and adults. In a May 1992 report, the Council esti-
mated that there are over 1.5 million Americans infected with the
AIDS virus. Since 1981, over 130,000 Americans have died of
AIDS-related complications.[8]

Because of ways by which AIDS is spread and the prolonged
time before symptom development, it is a difficult disease to control
and prevent. As such, it is critical for the health-care community to
develop drugs and vaccines to combat HIV. Researchers worldwide
have dedicated massive amounts of time and resources to determine
the structure and nature of the virus, the infection's progression, and
possible treatment and prevention options, including medications
and vaccines. (See Table 8.2 and Figure 7.1.) As of January 1993,
16 medications have been approved for AIDS treatment.[8]

Research and development of AIDS drugs becomes more important as one realizes that time is of the essence–over one million
people are infected with HIV, and many are completely unaware.
Such individuals, therefore, can spread the virus unknowingly to
others and perpetuate the disease. Without intervention, the worldwide epidemic can only worsen.

What was the effect of the Orphan Drug Act on AIDS medication
approvals? Clearly, the record-breaking approval time for zidovudine
was a significant sign of the legislation's value for AIDS patients.
However, with the rise in the number of diagnosed cases of AIDS
beyond the Orphan Drug Act's 200,000 patient limit, it has been
proposed that AIDS medications should no longer benefit from orphan drug status. This change could have both positive and negative

TABLE 8.2. AIDS Medications in Development

Medications in Development	1987	1988	1989	1990	1991	1992
– approved medications	1	2	9	11	14	17
– medicines / vaccines	27	46	55	62	88	91
– companies developing medicines / vaccines	30	39	39	40	64	66
Results by Developmental Status	1987	1988	1989	1990	1991	1992
– phase I	15	13	22	18	28	26
– phase I/II	3	10	13	25	15	11
– phase II	2	12	11	7	22	23
– phase II/III	3	4	8	18	18	17
– phase III	2	6	6	14	16	15
– phase I/II/III	0	0	1	0	0	0
– application submitted	1	3	1	1	5	11
– in clinical trials	1	2	3	0	0	1
Results by Product Class	1987	1988	1989	1990	1991	1992
– antivirals	15	13	17	27	34	30
– cytokines	*	*	11	16	12	12
– immunomodulators	12	25	7	10	12	13
– anti-infectives	*	6	16	19	23	23
– vaccines	0	2	2	2	7	8
– others	*	*	2	3	8	9
Total Research Projects	**27**	**46**	**55**	**77**	**96**	**95**

SOURCE: *AIDS Medicines in Development*
Pharmaceutical Manufacturers Association, 1992 Survey Report

consequences. Because of the inability to receive exclusivity, two or more brands of new biotechnology-derived medications would be able to enter the marketplace and price competition is more likely. Furthermore, because the FDA places high priority on AIDS medications' approval, it is likely that new medications would continue to be approved in a timely fashion. One disadvantage of the loss of orphan drug status for pharmaceutical manufacturers would be the inability to obtain lengthened patent life and market exclusivity rights that characterize all orphan drugs.

Costly Medications

In response to the skyrocketing costs of AIDS therapies over the past several years, patients and consumer advocate groups have become outraged. Their complaints and court cases challenging zidovudine's patent compelled Burroughs Wellcome, the drug's manufacturer, to lower the drug's price from $10,000 to $2,200 a year.[9] However, this price reduction is an inadequate solution to the larger problem. Estimates of annual health-care expenditures for a patient with AIDS from diagnosis to death range from $25,000 to $60,000. Twenty percent of AIDS patients do not have insurance, a significant number are on Medicaid, and others are fighting minimal prescription-drug coverage and delays in application acceptance by insurers.

With the approval of didanosine (Videx®, Bristol-Myers Squibb) in October 1991, AIDS patients have another therapy alternative. (Note: Didanosine is not an orphan drug; Bristol-Myers Squibb relinquished orphan drug status upon approval by the FDA.) The wholesale price of a year's supply of didanosine is over $1,500. Using treatment investigational new drug (IND) regulations, the drug's manufacturer has provided didanosine to over 23,000 AIDS patients since September 1989 (even though the drug was not yet FDA approved).[10] Also, with didanosine's approval, the prices of AIDS medications are likely to decrease even further due to competition.

Time Constraints

Although pharmaceutical manufacturers have provided important AIDS medications to patients prior to approval and at increasingly lower prices, the need for more intense research and accelerated approval of AIDS medications and vaccines remains. The FDA has realized the magnitude of this problem and developed an abbreviated approval system for such drugs. Instead of submitting the usual New Drug Application (NDA), which all pharmaceutical manufacturers file during the last stage of product approval, this system requires a briefer document called the accelerated NDA, as described in Chapter 5.

Patent Monopoly vs. Patient Care

Although the drug-approval process for AIDS drugs has been strengthened through actions by the FDA, problems surrounding patent protection and market exclusivity for life-saving drugs like zidovudine remain. Burroughs Wellcome is the first company to face a decision that weighs the right of the corporation to receive compensation versus the public's right to life and health. According to the Supreme Court in 1858, "Whilst the remuneration of genius and useful ingenuity is a duty incumbent upon the public, the rights and welfare of the community must be fairly dealt with and effectively guarded. Consideration of individual emolument [benefit] can never be permitted to operate to the injury of these."[8]

Proponents of patent laws argue that without such laws, life-saving medications like zidovudine would never have been invented, and that the high price of the drug stimulates other pharmaceutical manufacturers to develop competing products. Patent law opponents cite the dire need for optimal patient care as soon as it is available, regardless of cost. They believe that waiting for competition to reduce prices is not ethical, especially when compared with the intangible patent system.[8]

On the basis of decisions to date, the federal court has taken the side of those who argue in favor of the patent law. Thus, for high-priced drugs that treat serious conditions, pharmaceutical manufacturers can enjoy both pricing protection and market exclusivity, either through the patent system or the Orphan Drug Act. For patients, this means that the costs of such drugs will be determined and regulated by the industry, with minimal influence by others, including the government and health-care community.

A proposed solution to this dilemma–which will affect future AIDS medications–is the granting of compulsory licenses to other pharmaceutical manufacturers.[8] As a result of such licenses, other versions of zidovudine, for example, can be marketed in the U.S. The patent holder of the original drug would be fully compensated for the loss in sales due to competition. This resolution is unfavorable because of the need for the federal government (or more exactly, taxpayers) to finance the use of such drugs in patients who were previously unable to pay for them. One could argue that if the government is subsidizing costs of AIDS drugs, it should subsidize the costs of other expensive medications. The licensing solution does, however, maintain the patent system's market-exclusivity incentives while providing greater patient access to life-saving AIDS drugs if patients can afford them. It also forces consumers to confront both the tangible and intangible costs of this uniquely fatal disease.

NOTES

1. Marian Uhlman, "Examining the Cost of Orphan Drugs," *Philadelphia Inquirer* (19 January 1992):D1.

2. Donald C. McLeod, "Biotechnology: Product Development and Evolving Patent Law," *DICP Annals of Pharmacotherapy* 23 (July/August 1989):606.

3. Burton Amernick, "Essentials of Patent Law," *Journal of the National Cancer Institute* 81 (Number 19, 4 October 1989):1450.

4. John H. Barton, "Patenting Life," *Scientific American* 264 (Number 3, March 1991):40-46.

5. Anonymous, "Business Roundup: The Final No," *Medical Advertising News* (January 1992):6.

6. Henry Gee, "Amgen Scores a Knockout," *Nature* 350 (14 March 1991):99.

7. Donna Shaw, "A Bruising Battle Over Two Lifesaving Drugs," *Philadelphia Inquirer* (3 November 1991):D2.

8. Anonymous, "AIDS Pipeline: Symptomatic Relief," *Medical Advertising News* (January 1992):30-31.

9. L. Thompson, "The High Cost of Rare Diseases," *Washington Post Health* (25 June 1991).

10. Anonymous, "On the Horizon: In and Out of the FDA," *Pharmacy Practice News* (November 1991).

Chapter 9

Why Do Consumers Evade the Traditional System?

It was 1985, and Mike's companion had AIDS. There were no drugs or other therapies to treat the disease, and his companion continued to get sicker. They heard through a Gay Men's Health Network that a number of experimental substances were being tested in California by a group of AIDS patients. Mike called them and found out that a large group of patients were indeed trying many different kinds of drugs, some that came from Europe, some that were new and unique. None of these drugs were being tested in the U.S at that time. This group of patients had decided to take matters into their own hands. With their friends and themselves dying, they planned an approach to study these new substances. They obtained or, in some cases, actually made the drugs themselves, distributed them to each sick person willing to try them, and evaluated each therapy. Upon hearing this, Mike became very excited and hopeful, and he asked for a one-month supply of two of the drugs to be mailed to him, so that his companion could join the study.

In 1987, Fred was experimenting with psychoactive substances, primarily with hopes of finding a drug that would increase his creativity, memory, and productivity as an artist. Because he did not use "hard" drugs, and the drugs he did use he took only on special occasions or for very specific reasons, he did not consider himself to be a drug abuser, but rather "an explorer of the mind." Fred knew an underground chemist who was making some of the designer drugs that were out on the street at that time. He asked the chemist if he knew of any legal chemical substances that improved creativity and memory. The chemist consulted some reference books of chemical structures and pharmacological properties. He discovered a substance that had been synthesized years ago but was never developed or approved for the pharmaceutical market. Upon consideration, the chemist decided to synthesize a small batch of this drug and let people like Fred try it. Many of the people who tried it thought that the drug had an effect of improving thinking and mental stamina. But after a few cases of toxic reactions, the Drug Enforcement Administration (DEA) discovered what was happening and the new drug was added to the controlled substances list, making it illegal to manufacture, distribute, or possess the substance.

What do these two cases have in common? Patients were searching for drugs with specific effects or benefits, but such substances were not currently available in the United States. Thus, these individuals searched until they discovered something that might prove worthwhile. The discovery is often a chemical substance that has not yet been synthesized and tested by a pharmaceutical company, or a drug that has not yet been researched fully and whose approval and marketing are pending.

SEARCHING FOR THE MAGIC BULLET

The right of nature . . . is the liberty each man [has] to use his own power . . . for the preservation of his own nature; that is to say, of his own life; and consequently, of doing any thing, which in his own judgment, and reason, he shall conceive to be the aptest means thereunto.

Thomas Hobbes, philosopher[1]

Many patients and consumers complain that it takes too long to discover, test, and approve new drugs for many illnesses, especially newly-discovered and life-threatening diseases. By the time a new drug is ready for market, or ready for clinical trials, many patients with the disease have died. Thus, for as long as there has been a formal drug-development and distribution system in the U.S., there have been ways of "getting around" the system in the hope of finding more effective and timely solutions for health problems. This evasion of the system might entail the procurement of drugs that already exist–drugs that are approved in other countries, but are not yet available in the U.S.–or the use of substances that have not been shown to have therapeutic value.

The inability of our contemporary drug-development system to find the miracle cure–the **magic bullet**–for our modern-day ills has frustrated, angered, and disheartened patients who wish to return to normal health. Patients with chronic and debilitating diseases, such as cancer, heart conditions, Alzheimer's disease, depression, and arthritis, know that real cures do not exist. While research and testing in some areas is progressing faster than ever, it is just not quick enough. The best that these patients can expect from medical interventions is an alleviation of symptoms and possibly a slowing of the disease progression to its inevitable end.

As you can easily imagine, especially when severe disability or death is imminent, people will do anything to achieve a miracle cure for themselves or their loved ones. Some patients engage in extreme approaches because the drug that they want is too expensive in the U.S. or because they do not want to go through the inconvenience (time and cost) of seeing a doctor for a prescription. Although people in such situations are resourceful at finding possible solutions, they also act less rationally. They can be careless at gathering, interpreting, and using information about unknown therapies, and often do not seek the advice of health professionals or others with relevant knowledge.

Historical Perspective

In the late 1970s, consumers recognized the seriousness of the plight of patients with rare diseases. By the mid-1980s, the AIDS epidemic increased recognition of patient needs to a state of understanding–many chronic diseases, whether newly-defined or not, could not be cured or treated with the same speed and effectiveness as common infections or nutritional deficiencies earlier in this century. The chance of finding cures for most new diseases is very small. It is likely that no single drug, or even a combination of drugs and other therapies, will successfully cure conditions like AIDS, arthritis, and Alzheimer's disease.

Patients search for effective therapies for their conditions using different strategies. Many patients search until they find a drug that they believe will be effective for their condition. The drug testing process usually consists of a one-time drug trial with one research subject: the patient, which is, in essence, self-experimentation. (See Chapter 3 for a discussion of this subject.) If the drug works, the patient will use it until he or she is cured or when symptoms are alleviated. If the drug does not produce benefits fairly quickly, then the search begins again for something else.

This haphazard, individual approach of self-experimentation has become more structured, rational, and scientific over the past decade. In organized groups, patients are beginning to design, initiate, and direct their own clinical drug trials. Often, the management of a clinical trial is solely in patients' hands. All activities are kept relatively secret, especially from the federal and state authorities. In other instances, patients lobby with pharmaceutical companies and the FDA to obtain "investigational drug" or "experimental" designations for new drugs. Under these designations, the drugs are available to patients through prescribers and researchers. Most often, however, patient groups petition and involve health professionals and biomedical researchers in patient-directed clinical trials.

Patients and advocacy groups also engage in the drug-discovery process on their own. For instance, during the early years of the AIDS epidemic, a variety of substances were identified by AIDS patient groups as potentially beneficial in preventing the growth of viruses or in enhancing the patient's immune system.[2] One such substance came from a type of cucumber tuber, or root, and it was called Compound Q.[3] When it was discovered that a laboratory experiment demonstrated that the substance killed HIV, the virus that causes AIDS, Project Inform, a San Francisco-based patient advocacy group, launched an underground three-month community-based clinical trial of Compound Q. At the time, no research or clinical trials were being conducted in the United States on Compound Q.

The study, which, although it was not authorized by the Food and

Drug Administration (FDA), was carefully designed by American physicians and English AIDS researchers. Fifty-one AIDS patients volunteered to participate in what was called a Phase I/II study by investigators. When the results became clear, the FDA acknowledged the validity of the trial and used it as the foundation for Compound Q research.[4] At the same time as the trial, many AIDS patients began to brew batches of Compound Q from a variety of plant materials. Unfortunately, none of the patients treated with either laboratory-derived or home-grown Compound Q were cured of AIDS.

WHY ARE PATIENTS SEARCHING
FOR THEIR OWN CURES?

Mary, a 50-year-old woman with breast cancer, has tried virtually every form of modern drug therapy and radiation without response. She recently read about an experimental treatment that has shown success in Mexico. The drug is not available in the United States market, nor is it an investigational or experimental new drug. The drug is considered by the U.S. medical establishment to be a quack medicine. As such, Mary cannot try the drug, even through enrollment in a clinical trial. Her only option, if she wishes to use the new drug therapy, is to go to Mexico. With high hopes, she and her husband plan a brief trip to Mexico City. The first morning after they arrive, they visit a clinic and see a physician who writes a prescription for the drug. It is filled while they wait. Mary brings the new drug therapy home with her believing that it will cure her cancer.

People have been engaging in self-care with a variety of therapies to deal with their health problems long before scientific medicine, health-care technology, and organized drug development existed.[5] Mary's story was real throughout the 1960s and 1970s, when patients went to Mexico searching for laetrile and other presumed cancer cures. The search for effective medicines in foreign countries still continues today. If the government and pharmaceutical industry are perceived by consumers as moving too slowly in their search for cures, then they will take matters into their own hands.

Unlike cases discussed earlier, Mary's situation involves a known drug treatment that exists somewhere other than the U.S. In many ways, this represents a more frustrating situation. It is *not* a case of total uncertainty about what might prove useful in treatment because the discovery process has already occurred. Patients simply cannot gain access to the result of that discovery.

Both of these situations show that the compliant patient is a part of the past. Patients are rejecting the paternalistic approach and emphasis on risk that the traditional health-care system promotes. These patients and their advocates "reject the view that the vulnerable and easily exploited in society (such as terminally-ill people) need protection from the risks of participation in experimental protocols. From their perspective, experimentation is not a burden but a form of treatment that should be available to all patients. . . ."[6]

There has been a request to rescind or change the section of the Kefauver-Harris amendments of 1962 affecting drug approval. According to the amendments, the FDA has 180 days to review a new drug application (NDA). In reality, however, the average review period is approximately three years, and it has changed little in the past 30 years despite changes to the drug-approval process. The lack of improvement has been attributed to the FDA's interpretation of its consumer-protection mandate.[7] "Unfortunately, it's not always clear what "safe" and "effective" mean. How safe must a drug be to avoid being dangerous? Does it have to be safe for all population groups? . . . The lack of concrete answers to these questions reveals that it is impossible to ensure complete safety and eliminate all danger related to drug development and marketing."[7]

At demonstrations regarding AIDS drug research outside the FDA headquarters in the late 1980s, some protesters wore signs that said, "I Got the Placebo." To them, this meant that they had received a death sentence. This issue has been described as a battle between those who are not ill and who have time to discover new drugs, and those who have very little time left and need effective medications quickly. Some researchers have addressed patients' needs by advertising "All subjects receive treatment–no placebos," when recruiting clinical drug trial participants!

Patients and their families and friends have become frustrated and, in some instances, have totally divorced themselves from the traditional drug-development and approval processes. Are patients willing to sacrifice experimental efficacy research and assume greater risks by using unproven therapies? Should the FDA approve drugs with minimal information and let patients and physicians decide if greater health risks are acceptable? What are the ramifications of such actions on the overall stability of the health-care system?

Using laetrile as an example, it is important to understand the other side of this issue. Neither controlled nor observational studies were conducted on laetrile's value as cancer therapy. As such, no one could dispute the drug's effectiveness, and cancer patients were very optimistic.[8] At the same time, laetrile marketers were portraying existing (FDA-approved) chemotherapy as overly harmful. As a result, patients who were considering traditional therapy became fearful. Some of these individuals might have died because of their false hope in an ineffective treatment and their fear of proven medicines.

Thus, drug safety and effectiveness standards are not useless notions of an overly-protective government. These standards protect patients from dishonest merchants and dangerous chemicals of questionable medicinal value.[8] (Just imagine a society in which the medicines sold in pharmacies were never tested!) It seems reasonable that patients, even those who are seriously ill, would not use a dangerous substance that had no recognized benefits. It is for these reasons that the drug-approval process is strictly regulated and drug-use trends are constantly monitored.

Who Deserves Attention Most? Another Perspective

What about patients with life-threatening diseases other than AIDS? Similar arguments against the traditional drug-approval system have been proposed by people with cancer, Alzheimer's disease, and other serious diseases. While the FDA, scientists, and health-care professionals believe that certain diseases are not serious, patients with those diseases often have a very different perspective on the matter.[9]

The FDA criterion for emergency or fast-track investigational new drugs (INDs) is that they will only be used for patients with diseases that are "immediately life-threatening," meaning "a reasonable likelihood that death will occur in a matter of months or in which premature death is likely without early treatment."[1] This definition is not as simple and straightforward as it appears. Many patients with cardiovascular disease, cancer, diabetes, and other serious, chronic illnesses might fit that criterion, but the development and approval of beneficial drugs for them is not speedy. Many patients believe that their lives are at stake to the same degree as AIDS patients or anyone else who is seriously ill.

To summarize, current drug-regulation processes are viewed by many patients and consumers as:

1. relying heavily on the standard of "sound science,"
2. assuming that being a research subject is a burden that should be distributed equally among all patients with the disease who might possibly participate in a clinical trial,
3. making a trade-off of medical advances in return for discoveries that are monitored and controlled,
4. taking an adversarial posture toward pharmaceutical companies, instead of a collaborative one.

PATIENT-DIRECTED STUDIES
AND OTHER ALTERNATIVES TO DRUG TESTING

Patients, support groups, and organized advocates have found a number of alternatives to traditional clinical drug testing. At one end of the spectrum is the individual search for and self-experimentation with any substance that might prove beneficial. Notions about which substances might produce desired effects can come from several sources: scientific papers, reference books on drug chemistry, mass-market tabloids, and underground newspapers. Some "drug discoverers" have even used information on pharmaceutical patents to synthesize their compounds. Patents for new chemical entities provide detailed information on the chemical-synthesis process, yields or amounts of drug produced at each step, extraction methods, and other useful scientific data. Other individuals have returned to the earth to search for cures among herbs and plant material.

Clinical Drug Trials for AIDS

At the other end of the spectrum, individual patients have asked for and received greater access to information about ongoing clinical trials from federal agencies. FDA-controlled hotlines for obtaining information about clinical trial enrollment has begun with the AIDS Clinical Trials Information Service (1-800-TRIALS-A). (See Appendix B.) This service provides information on every privately-sponsored experimental AIDS and AIDS-related treatment that is undergoing effectiveness testing in FDA-sanctioned trials. This service provides information on the drug being tested, the purpose of the study, which studies are still enrolling patients, locations where studies are taking place, eligibility requirements and exclusion criteria, and names and telephone numbers of contact persons.

Another fascinating approach is being developed by clinical scientists with interest from the FDA: the **N-of-1 clinical trial**.[10,11,12] While traditional clinical trials enroll hundreds or thousands of patients, N-of-1 drug experiments focus on just one patient. Using this approach, the amount of time and number of patients needed to assess the effectiveness of a drug can be reduced significantly. Some proponents have suggested that the information collected through a sufficient number of separate N-of-1 trials could produce data that would represent, in a way, one large-scale clinical trial.

Psychedelic Drugs

An interesting example of a nonprofit membership organization devoted to assisting the drug-development process is the Multidisciplinary Association for Psychedelic Studies (MAPS). Because our society and the U.S. government hold very negative views of psychedelic drugs and marijuana, they fail to recognize that these substances might offer a variety of therapeutic benefits. Due to the prevalence of drug abuse, the 1980s "War on Drugs," a lack of funding support, and in some cases, prohibition by law, very little research is performed on psychedelic substances.

A great deal of research in the U.S. in the 1950s and 1960s, and current research in Europe, has shown that some psychedelic substances, such as lysergic acid diethylamide (LSD) and methylene-dioxy-methamphetamine (MDMA) are useful in psychotherapy and psychiatric care, the treatment of alcoholism and other chemical dependencies, and in alleviating chronic pain in some terminally-ill patients. Marijuana has been shown to be useful in treating a number of medical conditions, such as glaucoma, nausea and vomiting from cancer chemotherapy, and asthma. Unfortunately for these patients, however, public perception regarding the recreational use of marijuana and other psychedelics has prevented researchers from studying their full therapeutic potential.

It is for reasons like this that MAPS was founded. MAPS assists legitimate scientists in designing protocols, securing approval and funding, conducting studies, and reporting results in the area of psychedelic-drug research. This organization has developed a protocol for the combination use of MDMA and psychotherapy in end-stage cancer patients that is currently awaiting FDA approval. They have also funded pilot studies on the safety and toxicity of these substances. In all instances, MAPS has been the initiator or facilitator, but they have left the actual experimentation to well-known scientists. They have also organized and sponsored scientific conferences and training programs for scientists. Finally, MAPS serves as an educational organization and information-exchange clearinghouse for health-care professionals and patients.

UNDERGROUND DRUG DEVELOPMENT

Smart Drugs

Besides therapies for AIDS, cancer, Alzheimer's disease, and other serious conditions, *healthy* consumers who want to improve their physical or mental performance are also searching for unapproved or hard-to-get substances. The recent explosion of interest in **smart drugs** is an excellent example. Publications and promotional materials have suggested that smart drugs not only improve memory, but they also "increase libido in humans and [are] powerful and non-toxic antidepressant[s]."[13]

These publications include remarkable reader-submitted stories of memory enhancement, increased creativity and productivity, and other drug benefits. Advertisements for smart drugs in *Mondo 2000* suggest that readers "kick start [their] consciousness." Other stimulating advertisements and headlines include "Grow your own Extra IQ," "Where Virtual Reality meets Think Drinks–the New Mood Food," "Turn on to Lucid Dreaming," and "Shape Your Mind."[13,14] In San Francisco, enterprising smart-drug users have created restaurants in which smart pills and drinks are sold. Captivating names, including Smart Lounge, Nutrient Cafe, and Smart Bar, are advertised on the outside of these establishments to entice potential customers. Interestingly, many computer buffs are regular users of smart drugs–they imagine their brains as hardware that can be expanded with the addition of memory.

Publications like *Nootropic News* and *Mondo 2000,* reveal their disdain for the FDA and the U.S. drug-development system by informing readers that the FDA has a desire to "minimize choice," and that they [the editors] are not responsible for "overseas compliance with their own country's restrictions." Proponents of memory-enhancing drugs claim that American scientists and physicians have not read European literature that supports the drugs' ability to enhance memory. "The FDA only evaluates drugs that work on specific diseases. . . . The FDA doesn't see improving performance, the quality of life, or conceptual abilities as a legitimate target for drug approval."[15,16]

While some smart drugs do have pharmacological activity and can provide some users with specific drug effects, one must also wonder how many or how much of the effects that are experienced are really a result of the placebo phenomenon. (See Chapter 3.) The purity and safety of illegal smart drugs is also questionable. For example, an imported shipment of smart drugs was seized by the FDA in January 1992, and many pills were found to vary considerably from their labeled strength.

It is important for consumers to understand that the FDA is in the process of evaluating the safety and effectiveness of several medications for use in Alzheimer's disease, including those currently known as smart drugs. Until the results of clinical trials are available, however, smart drug use poses both short- and long-term risks to one's health.

Investigational Medications and Counterfeit Drugs

Many patients do not want to wait for a clinical trial of a new, potentially life-saving investigational drug. Such patients, including people with AIDS, have turned to alternative sources of investigational medications, both illegal and legal. Illegal manufacturers and distributors of investigational chemicals can be dangerous, not only because of legal repercussions, but because of the likelihood of receiving counterfeit or adulterated products. However, some illegal distributors of investigational drugs have been very instrumental in providing needed medications to people with life-threatening conditions. For example, organized buying groups purchase bulk quantities of investigational medications from underground or overseas distributors and provide them to AIDS patients in the U.S.

Counterfeit drugs are designed to resemble brand-name prescription medications, and appear to be available everywhere in the world.[17] At first, many products that can be purchased overseas or through underground distributors do not appear to be imitations—their labeling and packaging closely resemble the real drug. In other instances, the products are obvious copies with poor markings and packaging. It is for reasons like these that consumers should be cautious when considering alternate sources of drugs, and using medicines without health-care professional supervision. The safety and effectiveness of counterfeit drugs can be much different than the safety and effectiveness of FDA-approved medications.

THE FUTURE OF DRUG DEVELOPMENT

Some critics of the existing drug-development system believe that challenges to this system will result in radical changes in the near future.[9] They suggest that the focus of drug development will shift to a patient- or consumer-rights orientation and that the FDA will have less control over prescription-drug distribution. Additionally, changes in regulatory policies, even if directed at one category of drugs or diseases (i.e., life-threatening conditions), will be expanded almost immediately to include many other clinical conditions. The control and operation of clinical trials will shift from investigators at large research hospitals to physicians from all backgrounds and institutions, and the dominance of the randomized-controlled clinical trial will weaken.

Other people have called for less radical approaches, such as restructuring of the present drug-approval process. Targeted and rational amendments of the drug-development system are currently occurring. (See Chapter 5.) However, because evaluations of current amendments will be needed before additional changes are made, substantial changes of the drug-approval process will occur slowly.

In the interim, many patients and consumer-based drug research and distribution organizations are not willing to wait for such assessments. Regardless of the nature of the changes to the drug-development system, the need for timely information on the part of health-care professionals and drug consumers is critical for appropriate counseling and decision-making. To help patients and health-care professionals understand how and why alternative drug sources are used, the next chapter uncovers the rationale and mechanisms of illegal drug distribution and drug importation.

NOTES

1. Thomas Hobbes, *Leviathan* (New York, NY: Hafner, 1926).

2. Anonymous, "Many AIDS Patients Using Unapproved Drugs," *American Medical News* 22 (December 1989):19.

3. Dennis Wyss, "The Underground Test of Compound Q," *TIME Magazine* (9 October 1989):18,21.

4. Naomi Pfeiffer, "Compound Q Goes Above Ground," *AIDS Patient Care* (February 1992):11-14.

5. L.S. Levin and E.L. Idler, *The Hidden Health Care System: Mediating Structures and Medicine* (Cambridge MA: Ballinger, 1981).

6. David J. Rothman and Harold Edgar, "AIDS, Activism, and Ethics," *Hospital Practice* (15 July 1991):135-42.

7. Jill Wechsler, "Reassessing Risk: The Key to Faster Drug Approvals," *Pharmaceutical Executive* (September 1991):16-19.

8. Robert J. Temple, "Access, Science, and Regulation," *Drug Information Journal* 25 (1991):8.

9. Harold Edgar and David J. Rothman, "New Rules for New Drugs: The Challenge of AIDS to the Regulatory Process," *Millbank Quarterly* 68 (Supplement 1, 1990):111-142.

10. Gordon Guyatt, et al., "A Clinician's Guide for Conducting Randomized Trials in Individual Patients," *Canadian Medical Association Journal* 139 (1988):497-503.

11. Gordon Guyatt, et al., "The N-of-1 Randomized Controlled Trial: Clinical Usefulness–Our Three-Year Experience," *Annals of Internal Medicine* 112 (1990):293-299.

12. Eric Larson, "N-of-1 Clinical Trials–A Technique for Improving Medical Therapeutics," *Western Journal of Medicine* 152 (1990):52-56.

13. John Morgenthaler, "Smart Drugs Update," *Mondo 2000* 5 (1991):36-37.

14. Jude Milhorn, "Smarter Drugs," *Mondo 2000* 6 (1992):38.

15. Interlab (British smart-drug manufacturer). Letter to Editor, *Mondo 2000* 6 (1992):39.

16. Stephen Rae, "Smart Drugs: Just Say Know," *Elle* (May 1992):108-112.

17. Anonymous, "Bad Medicine," *Pharmacy Update* 1 (Number 16, 12 November 1990):6-7.

Chapter 10

Nontraditional and "Underground" Drug Discovery and Distribution Systems

George has Alzheimer's disease, and before his memory and ability to function deteriorate too far, he begins searching for any therapy that might slow the progress of his disease. Although very few beneficial treatments exist in the United States, several drugs are available overseas for Alzheimer's disease. One whole category of drugs, called **nootropics**, have been synthesized, tested, approved, and marketed in Europe, and seem to enhance the efficiency of the brain's functioning. To obtain these drugs, George asks his sister to purchase several different nootropic drug products for him on her next trip to Europe.

Situations like the one described above happen regularly, not only for Alzheimer's patients, but also for AIDS patients and others for whom adequate treatments are not yet available in this country. Many patients want to use particular drug products, but find that the drugs are not approved in the United States.

The stories in Chapter 9 about Mike, Fred, and Mary and their search for specific drugs are also relevant here. However, George's case presents a special problem. While the FDA allows people like Mary to travel to another country, seek professional care, and return with her own personal, but limited, supply of a medication not approved in the U.S., it is illegal for someone to purchase medicines for George in a foreign country.

Availability and accessibility are the main reasons that people turn to foreign suppliers of prescription drugs. A lack of availability of a particular drug product means that the drug itself cannot be provided by pharmaceutical manufacturers to legitimate dispensers, or that it cannot be provided by dispensers to the general public. The primary reasons for unavailability of a drug product are listed in Table 10.1.

Lack of accessibility to a drug product means that the drug is available, but the individual patient or consumer cannot obtain it. Three main reasons for problems of accessibility are: (1) cost of the drug product (and whether the patient is covered to some extent by insurance); (2) fear, distrust, or dissatisfaction with the traditional health-care delivery system; and (3) geographical distance from the dispenser or supplier of the drug. When patients and consumers do not have access to medicines, or when medicines they want are not available, they will consider a nontraditional approach to obtaining those medicines.

SEARCHING FOR DRUGS FROM NONTRADITIONAL SOURCES

Patients, especially those with seriously debilitating or life-threatening diseases, have focused their concern and anger regarding drug accessibility primarily at two groups, the FDA and the pharmaceutical industry. As discussed in Chapter 9, the FDA is viewed by many people as an agency whose major function has been to slow progress in the development of new treatments. Patients and consumers conclude that the FDA has become overly

---

TABLE 10.1. Reasons Why a Prescription Drug Might be Unavailable to U.S. Consumers

- the drug has not been investigated or developed by a U.S.-based company

- the drug has not been approved by the FDA for medical use in the U.S.

- the drug has been removed from the U.S. marketplace

- the drug's use has been limited to specific conditions or certain types of patients, but not for others

- the drug is usually available but some problem in its production or distribution has made it temporarily unavailable

protective of society as a whole at the great expense of individual patients who are dying. In addition, like most government agencies, the FDA is too large and bureaucratic to change in significant ways any time soon. Pharmaceutical companies, as shown in previous chapters, are viewed by many consumers as having no social consciousness, or as profit-hungry with the sole purpose of pushing drugs on an unsuspecting public.

Mass media, books, pamphlets, newsletters, organized patient support groups, and consumer advocates have been developed and organized to promote unproven or unapproved drug therapies to patients. They suggest that patients can buy drugs from supply houses, show them how to find drugs overseas, and even provide sample forms required by U.S. Customs, lists of suppliers, and catalogues from those suppliers with drug costs and shipping charges.[1] In a situation where a decision to use a drug has been made, but that drug is unavailable or inaccessible, nontraditional approaches become attractive. Alternative sources of drug supply and distribution networks for delivering drugs to users are outlined below.

DRUG SUPPLY AND DISTRIBUTION NETWORKS

The traditional American pharmaceutical delivery system is described from two different perspectives in Figures 10.1 and 10.2. The system basically consists of the location of drug manufacture, storage and distribution, and acquisition by consumers. Drug product transfer to and from the legitimate distribution system takes place at the manufacturer, wholesaler, and consumer levels. First, we will consider sources of drug supply, and then discuss drug-distribution networks.

The Flow of Drugs in Society

The work of epidemiologists has been useful in describing supply sources and drug flow in society. The basic epidemiological approach is relatively simple. A classic example of the value of the epidemiologic approach involves malaria and its transmission to

FIGURE 10.1. Sources of Supply and the Flow of Legal and Illegal Drug Products in the U.S.

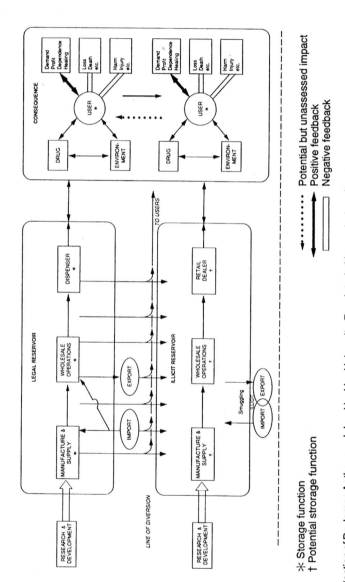

Collection of Dr. James Anthonoy, Johns Hopkins University. Reprinted with permission of Lexington Books, an imprint of Macmillan, Inc. from SOCIETY AND MEDICATION by John P. Morgan and Doreen V. Kagan. Copyright 1983 by Lexington Books.

FIGURE 10.2. Diversion and Counterfeiting of Legitimate Prescription Drugs

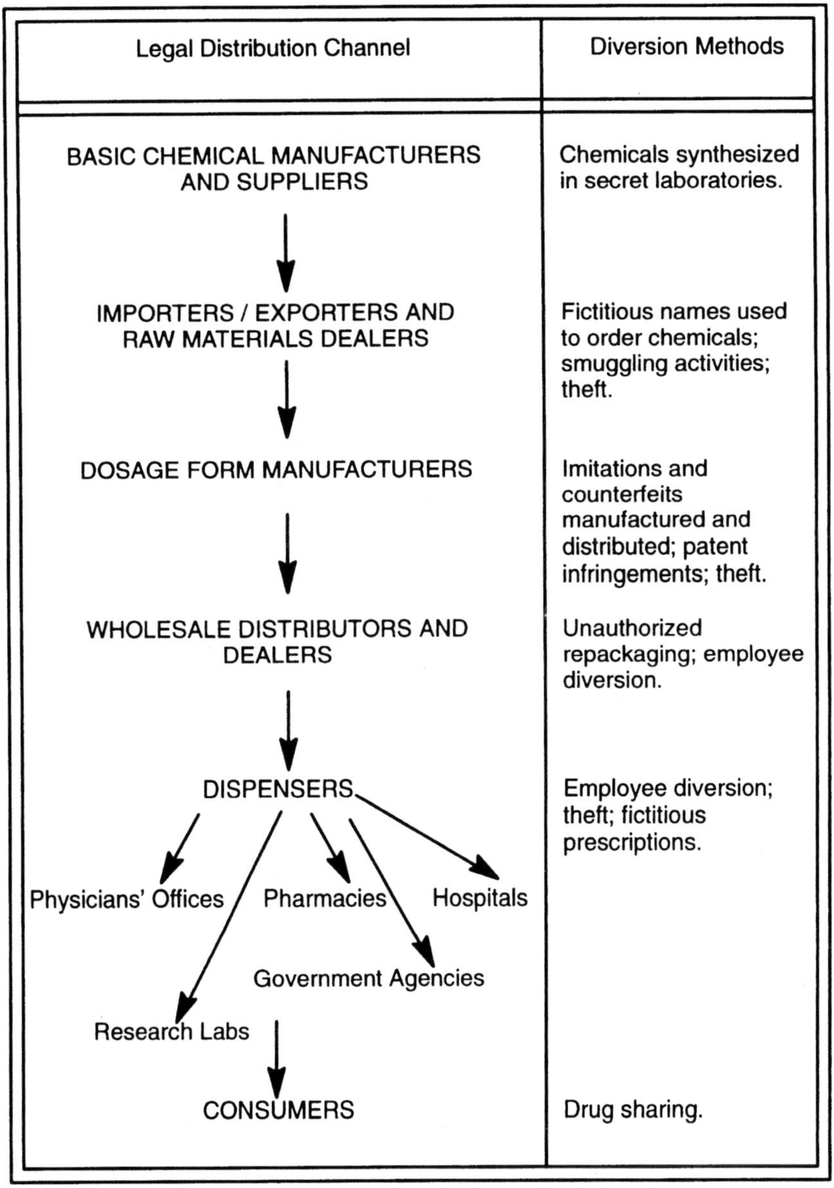

Legal Distribution Channel	Diversion Methods
BASIC CHEMICAL MANUFACTURERS AND SUPPLIERS	Chemicals synthesized in secret laboratories.
↓	
IMPORTERS / EXPORTERS AND RAW MATERIALS DEALERS	Fictitious names used to order chemicals; smuggling activities; theft.
↓	
DOSAGE FORM MANUFACTURERS	Imitations and counterfeits manufactured and distributed; patent infringements; theft.
↓	
WHOLESALE DISTRIBUTORS AND DEALERS	Unauthorized repackaging; employee diversion.
↓	
DISPENSERS	Employee diversion; theft; fictitious prescriptions.
Physicians' Offices Pharmacies Hospitals	
Government Agencies	
Research Labs	
↓	
CONSUMERS	Drug sharing.

Modified from M. Krieg, 1967.

humans. The organism that causes malaria lives for part of its life cycle in standing water. Mosquitos acquire the organism from the water and pass it on to the main host, humans. The organism is the causative agent of the disease, or the **contagion**. It exists in **reservoirs** (water and human beings), and is transmitted from one reservoir, its source, to another. This transmission, or spread of the disease, is done by a **vector** (animals or people who carry the causative agent), in this case a mosquito, or a **vehicle** (an inanimate object that carries the contagion). Once the contagion and its reservoirs are identified, and the mode of transmission to other reservoirs, such as people, is traced, preventive measures can be developed and implemented to reduce further disease outbreaks, to limit its spread through the population, and to prevent the disease from occurring in the future.

The work of Dr. James Anthony, an epidemiologist at Johns Hopkins University, has shown how drugs move through legal and illegal channels, and the consequences for consumers (Figure 10.1). From his perspective, drugs that cause problems can be viewed as contagions, or causative agents, that reside in reservoirs, or places where they are stored and can be obtained.[2] These drug contagions then move through vectors or vehicles to the ultimate user. Dr. Anthony suggests that reservoirs (sources of supply) of drug products exist for both legal and illegal drugs, and that drugs actually can move between legal and illegal reservoirs.

Another perspective looks at drug-distribution channels and tries to identify specific physical places where products can be removed from the traditional flow of drugs (Figure 10.2). This view was first described by Margaret Krieg in the 1960s, when issues of drug diversion, importation, and counterfeiting were being discussed.[3] In her 1967 investigation, Krieg discovered large-scale trafficking of bogus and bootleg pharmaceuticals. It seemed that the traditional pharmaceutical delivery system was providing contaminated, misbranded, counterfeited, resold samples, pirated, or adulterated drug products.

Krieg's view of the legitimate drug-distribution system starts with raw chemical suppliers. Suppliers provide these materials to pharmaceutical manufacturers, who prepare products in finished dosage forms. These products are shipped to wholesalers, who then distribute them to retailers. Various retailers, or drug dispensers, provide the drug products directly to patients and consumers. Krieg noted various points in the legitimate distribution network where drugs can be diverted or where counterfeit drugs can be introduced. The amazing consideration is that her model was developed in the 1960s, and it is fully accurate and relevant to our situation in the 1990s!

Another related perspective is provided by people who work in the chemical-dependency field. These health-care professionals see the diversion of certain drugs at the other end of the continuum–after drug users have obtained the drugs illegally and when they are having problems and seeking help. This research has focused more on psychotropic medications, such as amphetamines and barbiturates in the early 1970s, and recently, tranquilizers.[4] Their research goal was to identify the routes by which certain drugs reach the black market from the traditional drug-distribution system (Figure 10.3).

As you can see, diversion of legitimate drugs occurs from two key sources, the producers, packagers, and dispensers of medicines; and individual patients. The more common routes of drug diversion involves packagers, especially outside the country. Large amounts of drugs produced in the U.S. are shipped outside the country for repackaging and distribution. However, some of those drugs can find their way back into the U.S. through various export or smuggling operations. This has been the case with many recent incidents involving legitimately-made pharmaceuticals.

The Role of Multi-Tier Drug Prices

Drug diversion from the legitimate pharmaceutical delivery system is made easier by differential or multi-tier pricing requirements for pharmaceutical products. (See Figure 10.4.) Differential pricing of pharmaceuticals is a concern that has plagued pharmacists for years, especially those in independent, community stores.

One major link in the country-to-country and wholesaler-to-wholesaler journey of diverted drugs is nonprofit institutions, mostly hospitals and nursing homes. Certain institutions purchase pharmaceuticals at greatly reduced costs, but beyond their needs. They then divert excess drugs to wholesalers at a great profit. Opportunities

FIGURE 10.3. Routes by Which Legitimate Drug Products Reach the Black Market

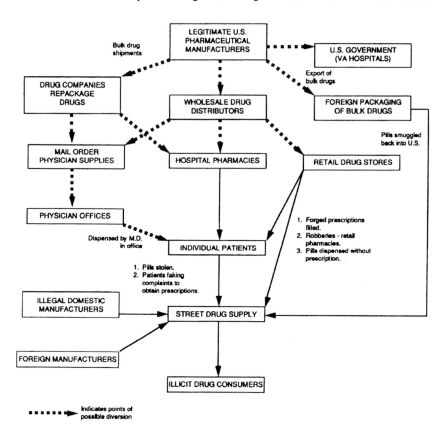

for successful and profitable drug-diversion schemes are enhanced by the wide variation in prescription-drug pricing policies at the manufacturer, wholesale, and various retail levels.

A scam controlled by criminals was uncovered in 1992, but the method for diverting drugs was similar to that used in the early 1980s and even the 1960s.[5] In this case, prescription drugs were purchased by nursing home organizations at a deep discount (sometimes as much as 90%) from pharmaceutical manufacturers. In reality, the nursing homes were illegitimate–they did not really exist. The purchased drugs were resold to pharmaceutical wholesal-

FIGURE 10.4. Drug Diversion from Pharmacy Distribution Systems

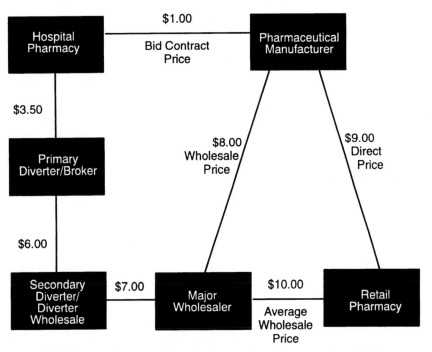

SOURCE: Senate Subcommittee on Oversight and Investigation, 1985.

ers in a different part of the country (who were accomplices with the criminals, in this case). The wholesalers then sold the drugs at regular wholesale prices to unsuspecting retail pharmacies, where the drugs were dispensed to patients.

Different prices for various "dispensers" of these pharmaceutical products was important in realizing a profit in this scam. (Refer to Figure 10.4.) According to Richard Allen, the director of the Georgia Drugs and Narcotics Agency, "If there was no price differential, there would not be this problem. As long as companies keep giving different prices to different people, you are going to have these diversions. There is too much profit in it."[8]

One attempt to deal with differential pricing of legitimate pharmaceuticals was passage of the Prescription Drug Marketing Act in 1984. This legislation was designed to expose inequities and illegal activities created by discriminatory pricing. For instance, it prohibits health-care providers who service long-term care facilities (i.e., nursing homes) from reselling the drugs and other products they purchase at great discounts from manufacturers.

Another piece of legislation, the Omnibus Budget Reconciliation Act (OBRA), was passed in 1990. It includes a best-price provision that requires drug manufacturers to negotiate with state Medicaid programs to provide drugs at the lowest price. In return, Medicaid reimburses pharmacies for all of the manufacturer's products. While OBRA '90 has lowered Medicaid drug expenses, some pharmaceutical manufacturers have raised drug prices to non-Medicaid purchasers.

Other improvements to minimize drug diversion include pharmaceutical profession and state boards of pharmacy involvement in monitoring and controlling the flow of pharmaceutical products in the legitimate drug-distribution system. The differential or discriminatory pricing schemes that contribute to drug diversion are currently being evaluated by pharmacy organizations and Congress.[6]

In summary, drug products can come from many nontraditional supply sources. They can be legitimate products that have been diverted from the traditional drug-distribution system, or they can be illegitimately produced by unauthorized manufacturers. Legitimately-produced pharmaceuticals (such as samples from a physician's office) can also be diverted from the traditional distribution system, or, like George's Alzheimer's disease medications, imported from foreign mail-order supply houses (Table 10.2).

DRUG DIVERSION AND NONTRADITIONAL DRUG DISTRIBUTION

A number of congressional investigations over the past decade have uncovered loopholes in the traditional drug-distribution system. The drug-distribution system is unable to prevent the introduction of substandard, ineffective, or counterfeit pharmaceuticals. Investigations concluded that "American consumers cannot purchase prescription drugs with the certainty that the products are safe and effective."[7]

TABLE 10.2. Nontraditional Sources of Diverted Drugs

ORIGINAL SOURCE IS LEGITIMATE	ORIGINAL SOURCE IS ILLEGITIMATE
patients with prescriptions	people with forged prescriptions
physicians' offices	illegal manufacture (domestic or foreign) and smuggling
pharmacies	robberies of drug-distribution locations (pharmacies)
mail-order pharmaceutical supply houses	legitimate foreign manufacturers distributing drugs not approved in the U.S.

Health-Care Professional Involvement

Physicians who prescribe drugs inappropriately, and pharmacists who dispense drugs illegally or divert them, contribute to the problem of drug diversion. Research suggests that diversion of drugs from pharmacies is *not* a common activity, and it represents a small percentage of the total amount of drugs that might be available through a nontraditional source.[3] A major news report or two might have appeared over the past few years describing a drug-diverting pharmacist, but these events and stories are rare.

Physicians, mostly those who are poor prescribers, might be responsible for creating an unauthorized source of supply. Some physicians, just like some pharmacists and nurses, act unprofessionally. Others, however, do not intend to act unprofessionally and certainly do not plan to divert drugs, but their poor monitoring of problem patients leads to diversion. As noted in Figure 10.3, physicians can be fooled into prescribing drugs for patients who fabricate complaints. This has become more of a concern in recent years with the advent of direct-to-consumer advertising and the growth of consumer consciousness and the patient rights movement. In each case, patients are seeing physicians already knowing what they want in the way of a drug, or even demanding it as they walk into the doctor's office.[8]

The Most Common Culprits–Patients

Illegitimate distribution of legitimately-produced pharmaceuticals is primarily conducted by patients. Many people have prescriptions and receive their drugs legally from the traditional distribution system. However, they share drugs with relatives, friends, and coworkers. This is the most common way of obtaining a drug without a prescription.[3] Informal referral systems (e.g., relatives, friends, co-workers, neighbors who interact and communicate among themselves about disease and therapies) are an excellent example of social networks. Through these networks, ideas and information (either good or bad, correct or incorrect) about disease and therapies, and even actual drug products, are exchanged and disseminated.

When we think of nontraditional drug distribution, we tend to think of grossly illegal activities operating on a large scale by unscrupulous people. We also consider "street drugs" and think that most illegal activities involve the illicit manufacture of dangerous "drugs of abuse." Illegal users of psychotropic drugs actually represent a small percentage of total illegal users of pharmaceuticals. Most people "on the street" tend to use and misuse alcohol, marijuana, cocaine, opiates (such as heroin), and other nonpharmaceutical substances. If they use a psychotropic drug, it is usually not a drug diverted from a legitimate supplier. Rather, they obtained it from a source well outside traditional systems, such as an illegal manufacturing operation.

Patients must remember that possession and use of a prescription drug in the U.S. requires a valid prescription from a physician or designated prescriber. If you borrow a few pain pills or tranquilizers from your spouse's or friend's prescription, you are considered to be an illegitimate user, and in fact, you are breaking the law. This activity occurs much more often than we realize. Just think about the last time you borrowed or used someone else's prescription medication, even if it was taking a few penicillin tablets left over from your son's or daughter's recent bout with an infection.

PRESCRIPTION DRUG IMPORTATION

At last! The proven, affordable treatment you need is easy to come by . . . and as close as your mail box! Now you can obtain medications of guaranteed quality inexpensively, legally, and hassle-free.

cover of *How to Buy Almost Any Drug Legally
Without a Prescription*

Prescription drug importation has recently received a lot of attention. Drug importation has stirred up hope, controversy, and anger among government agencies, the health-care community, and patients. The ability to import and use drugs that are either unapproved in the United States or much less expensive overseas is an exciting opportunity for patients suffering from AIDS, rare diseases, or chronic illnesses that require the continual purchase of medications. However, much of the information presented in books and articles that make claims like the above is *false* and *misleading*. To understand what patients can and cannot do, and the implications for health-care professionals, especially physicians, it is important to separate the myth from the truth regarding government policies and patients' rights.

Why Import Drugs?

Ed is losing his hair, and is concerned about it. He visited his physician and received a prescription for a drug that prevents hair loss and restores hair growth with continued use. Ed must use this drug for the rest of his life if he wants to prevent further hair loss. After using this drug for about six months, Ed is quite pleased with the results. However, the treatment is very costly. Because his insurance company does not recognize hair loss as a disease, they will not reimburse any portion of his medication bill. Upon seeing information about a "pharmaceutical company" based on a Caribbean island that mails prescription drug products to the U.S., Ed obtains a price catalogue. He is shocked to see that a three-month supply of his drug is only one-quarter of the price that he currently pays. Ed decides to take charge of his therapy and orders a six-month supply.

People like Ed are not unique. American drug consumers have been going to Canada or Mexico for years to obtain certain drug products. More recently, consumers have discovered mail-order drug supply houses that are located just off-shore of the U.S. or in European countries. During a recent visit to Tijuana, one of the authors (MM) found a copy of *Baja Visitor* magazine, a tourist publication, to contain not only listings of attractions and sight-seeing trips, but a number of advertisements for Mexican pharmacies. These pharmacies sell antibiotics, minoxidil (for hair loss), anti-aging drugs, and many other medicines that are available only with a prescription in the United States. The ability to purchase these products without a prescription was a prominent promotional message in these advertisements. The San Diego *Union-Tribune* covered the recent Food and Drug Administration (FDA) attention to illegal importation of prescription medications from foreign sources. The FDA estimated that "youth" or anti-aging drugs alone represent a $2 billion black-market operation annually.[10]

Besides Mexico, Canada serves as a primary source of foreign drugs, as well as FDA-approved, but costly, agents. Terfenadine (Seldane®, Marion Merrell Dow) is an example of a drug for which many consumers travel to Canada. In Canada, terfenadine, codeine, and other medications, are available over-the-counter (without a prescription). Patients can even have such medications mailed to them from Canada to their homes. According to an FDA official, "There is a substantial black market, where a patient will call the [Canadian] pharmacy, order a drug, pay with a credit card over the phone, and then have the drug mailed to him in the U.S."[11] If caught by U.S. customs, the U.S. postal service, or the FDA, imported medications can be confiscated, but charges are rarely brought against the person who purchased them.[1]

As discussed earlier, the primary reason for patients to even consider importing drugs from other countries is the availability of different, and possibly effective, medications. Because drug-approval requirements in most foreign countries are much less strict than those of the FDA, drugs that are either investigational or not approved in the U.S. *are* approved and available in other countries. For patients with AIDS, cancer, rare diseases, and other life-threatening conditions, the opportunity to use such medications is one that cannot be ignored.

The other highly-promoted reason to consider foreign sources of medications is lower prices. According to the book by James Johnson, ". . . a[n] [imported] drug is cheaper . . . By ordering from abroad, you can save money on most of your current prescription medications."[8] InterPharm, a drug wholesaler based in Nassau, Bahamas, promotes the availability of "30% to 60% [savings] over U.S. [drug] prices,"[12] using direct mailings to consumers as well as print advertisements in newspapers and magazines.

There are several concerns associated with the ability of patients to acquire drugs overseas. Sidney Wolfe, MD and other consumer advocates are concerned that patients' ability to use unapproved medications might bias clinical trials in the U.S. because of patient self-experimentation. Physicians are worried that their names will be used by patients to acquire and use foreign drugs. Most physicians are not aware of the characteristics, efficacy, and adverse effects of foreign drugs or how to monitor patients who are taking them. Doctors who sanction a patient's use of an unapproved drug can also be liable for any patient harm, similar to liability resulting from their writing a dangerous prescription.

The FDA Drug-Importation Policy

The FDA permits Americans to order foreign pharmaceuticals for personal use, but there are strict guidelines as to how this activity can occur. First and foremost, imported medications must be products that *are not* approved or available in the U.S., and must be imported for *personal use*, not for cost savings, selling, or other commercialization. Thus, imported drugs can be neither marketed nor used in clinical trials, nor available through treatment investigational new drug (IND) regulations (which are in place for most AIDS and orphan drugs under investigation). Only small supplies of foreign drugs can be imported–less than a three-month supply–and the patient must name a physician who manages his or her treatment. Furthermore, the drugs cannot be fraudulent or present an unreasonable health risk (Table 10.3).[13]

According to an FDA document describing the drug-importation policy, the FDA has permitted importation of certain drugs, given the stipulations described above, for years with the purpose of "allow[ing] people to import through their personal baggage small quantities of medicines they may have been treated with while

TABLE 10.3. Characteristics of Drugs Allowed for Importation into the United States
• not available or approved in the U.S.
• use supported and supervised by a physician
• for personal use only
• three-month supply or less
• not fraudulent or dangerous
• drug use/ importation is not commercialized

traveling abroad, and [giving] individuals with serious conditions the ability to import through the mail personal-use quantities of unapproved drugs that they feel might be helpful in treating their conditions."[1] According to the FDA document, this policy has gained greater interest in recent years because of the plight of AIDS patients, as well as patients with life-threatening diseases, who are interested in acquiring foreign drugs in order to alleviate the symptoms of the deadly disease.

The drug-importation policy is significant in many ways. Consumers can shop for their therapies worldwide (mostly through the mail), and can make their own decisions whether or not the risks of engaging in these activities are outweighed by potential therapeutic benefits. Americans "now have a world of pharmaceuticals from which to choose, albeit at their own risk."[14]

Reactions

According to the FDA, the illegal drug-importation schemes described in Johnson's book are illegal, inaccurate, and incomplete. The book "seriously misrepresents the government's importation policy for unapproved drugs," and does not discuss the fact that importation is only allowed for drugs *not* approved in the U.S.[15] According to the FDA, import alerts have been issued to automatically detain imported products that appear to violate the personal import policy.[2]

Other major concerns addressed by the FDA in response to Johnson's book are the health risks associated with unsupervised use of imported medications. These drugs are not familiar to U.S. physicians and health-care professionals, and only minimal information is provided regarding proper use. Furthermore, it is likely that consumers who use foreign drugs without consent from a physician or other health-care professional are violating state and local laws.[14]

Foreign Pharmaceutical Manufacturers– An Example of FDA Action

On January 30, 1992, in response to letters from concerned pharmacy organizations and consumers, the FDA declared an import alert (a ban on products and increased surveillance at U.S. borders) on medications promoted by InterPharm; Interlab of London; Northam Medication Service International of Nassau; Inhome Services of Delemont, Switzerland; International Pharmacy of Nassau; International Products of Hanover, Germany; and Azteca Trio International of Zona Rio Tijuana, Mexico. According to the FDA, some of the products sold by these organizations are counterfeit copies of U.S. products.[16]

AIDS Buying Clubs and Guerrilla Clinics

Another significant issue relating to the importation of prescription drugs is the organization of buyers' clubs. These clubs are nonprofit groups that import drugs–usually, but not always, AIDS medications that are unapproved in the U.S.–for a reasonably low cost. Buyers' clubs are generally viewed as medication distributors for AIDS patients, and have not been interfered with by the FDA in deference to the seriousness of the disease.[17]

Several concerns with buyers' clubs have arisen, however. The first pertains to the acquisition and merchandising of AIDS medications to patients other than those served by the club. In other words, these organizations might be recompounding the drugs, repackaging them for sale, and then selling the medications at a profit, thereby becoming commercial organizations and violating the importation law. To determine if this is true, the FDA has conducted inspections of clubs' records to assure a "one-to-one" relationship between the amount of drug imported and the amount of drug provided to the patient.[16]

Guerrilla clinics are staffed voluntarily by health-care professionals who are dissatisfied with the lack of responsiveness of the traditional health-care system. These clinics manufacture and distribute AIDS medications, and monitor HIV-infected patients for signs of efficacy and toxicity.[18] According to a newsletter published by Persons With AIDS (PWA), a New York-based advocacy group, "There would be no guerrilla clinics if the government would take a leadership role in developing AIDS drugs and setting treatment guidelines. Desperate people feel they have no choice." PWA also organizes a buyers' club for over 5,000 AIDS patients.[19]

The U.S. pharmaceutical industry has responded to the growing number of buying groups and clinics. Because some drugs that are imported by AIDS buying groups are also approved in the U.S., they compete with American-manufactured medications, making members of the pharmaceutical industry indignant. United States companies have resorted to giving away AIDS medications to convince Americans to use them instead of drugs acquired by buying groups.

Patient Education Activities

At the other end of the spectrum are groups and organizations that provide information about pharmaceutical products, but are *not* involved in the actual buying and selling of drugs. One example of this approach are the various AIDS support groups and their activities, which have been described before.

Another example are newsletters for individuals interested in certain types of drugs. For instance, *Nootropic News* provides information for the "advancement of human knowledge."[20] In essence, it is a newsletter about smart drugs, substances that can improve memory, thinking abilities, and other mental activities. Research on these drugs is aimed at finding solutions for Alzheimer's disease, certain traumas that damage the brain, and other problems of brain functioning. *Nootropic News* is a good example of the many consumer-oriented drug information sources of this type that are available. Its editor and publisher clearly state throughout the newsletter that they "only report the facts represented in the scientific literature, and in no way advise anyone to obtain or use these agents."[9] Their editorial policy, and that of most other similar newsletters and informational sources of this type, is "that individuals should have the right to decide for themselves what they put into their body, but we recognize the coercive powers of the U.S. Government to prevent us from doing this and we intend always to work within the law."[19]

Some of those so-called coercive powers are valuable in preventing a variety of medication problems and drug-use disasters and protecting patients and society. However, some of the FDA's powers can limit or prevent individual patients from obtaining potentially-useful therapies. The organizations that provide drug-importation information, such as that in *Nootropic News*, believe that they are doing a service to the general public. As you can see, it comes down to a fine line between the rights of individuals to make decisions for themselves versus the right of society to protect its members (most of whom are patients at one time or another).

PROBLEMS RESULTING FROM NONTRADITIONAL DRUG DISTRIBUTION

Many problems can result when patients or consumers obtain drugs from nontraditional sources of supply and unapproved distribution networks. These problems can arise even if the drug product itself was produced originally by a legitimate pharmaceutical company. These problems include drug products of questionable effectiveness; drug products of unknown quality, content, and strength; deception in the buying and selling of drugs; adverse reactions to substances, especially those for which information is lacking or the real ingredient(s) is (are) unknown; and interference with other therapies the patient might be taking.

Opportunities for Deception

Several foreign drug-distribution companies, including Inter-Pharm, and several individuals, like James Johnson, have exaggerated the appropriateness of purchasing and experimenting with unapproved drugs, especially when purchased at suspiciously low prices. Most would agree that the promotion of illegal actions like these is unfair and injurious to patients and the U.S. drug-approval and health-care systems.

The importation of counterfeit drugs, especially products claiming to be manufactured by U.S. companies, presents a real problem. A 1984 survey of 25 pharmaceutical manufacturers found that 36% of them had experienced serious counterfeiting problems abroad in the previous five years.[6] In 1985, the U.S. Customs Service and the FDA began a joint effort to examine counterfeit products and trace them to the original manufacturer. A potency analysis was also performed by an analytical laboratory to determine whether the counterfeit products contained an active ingredient. Although counterfeit products are a concern, drugs diverted from legitimate sources remain a more significant problem for law enforcement agencies than illegal drug trafficking.[21]

Disrupted Patient Therapy and Risks of Drug Use

Patients who use drugs without the knowledge of a health-care provider, especially their pharmacist or physician, increase their risks for certain problems, both with the imported or illegal drug and with other drugs they are currently using. Depending on the source of supply for new drugs, these problems can result from contaminants, questionable drug potency, and unknown ingredients.

One example of risky drug products is nutritional supplements and vitamins. The FDA is currently concerned about the promotion of vitamins as medical treatments. FDA regulations prohibit vitamin and other dietary-supplement manufacturers from stating unproven health claims and from selling these products as medicines.[22] In a recent disaster, a batch of the amino-acid supplement, L-tryptophan, which is promoted as an over-the-counter stress reducer and insomnia treatment in the U.S., was contaminated with chemical by-products in the manufacturing process. Use of L-tryptophan resulted in over 1,500 cases of a blood disorder and 38 deaths.

An FDA task force is studying the L-tryptophan tragedy and is likely to recommend the regulation of amino acids and certain other nutrients as drugs. (These agents have been termed "nutraceuticals" by the health-care community.) Manufacturers of such products will need to submit scientific data from clinical trials and prove safety and effectiveness before marketing nutraceuticals in the U.S.[22]

If a medication is a good one, regardless of its source, patients still run risks when using it. If the drug has not been used before, there is a risk of adverse reactions to the drug or other ingredients in the tablet, capsule, or liquid preparation. Remember the sulfanilamide disaster in 1937 (Chapter 1)? The drug was good, but the solvent in which it was dissolved was lethal to humans. Patients also increase the chance of having the drug interact with other drugs that they are currently using, which can disrupt therapy.

Words of Caution

Drug distributors, manufacturers, and buying groups take widely different approaches to issues of consumer rights and legality. Some organizations are engaged in illegal activities, and consumers should be doubly aware of them. Not only are they providing drug products illegally, but the quality of those drug products is highly suspect. Other organizations are facilitating the drug-distribution process for certain patients who are allowed to import drugs into the U.S. What the patients are doing, if they are following FDA guidelines, is correct and legal. The products they receive are manufactured by reputable companies, and they are usually of high quality. Price lists are available simply by writing or making a telephone call. It is important to note, however, that there are no mechanisms for monitoring quality in such distribution networks.

For health-care professionals, it is important to remember that patients might believe they have very good reasons for going to nontraditional sources of drug products. Often, patients do not understand why the system is designed as it is, and how it protects them from ineffective and dangerous drugs. Patients also might not know or understand the possible dangers of obtaining and using drug products that have not been evaluated using appropriate quality control procedures. The information presented above should help to elucidate some of these dangers and make patients aware of all aspects of the issue.

Before acting upon the information presented in books, magazines, or through friends, it is important for patients to talk with a health-care professional and to learn about the companies and drugs in which they are interested. As mentioned earlier, importing drugs can be illegal if the strict rules are not followed. Although the risks and benefits of such activity can be difficult to weigh, all aspects should be considered before making a decision.

IMPROVING THE DRUG-DISTRIBUTION SYSTEM

A recent survey of over 1,000 Americans found that nearly 80% believed that a person should have the choice of using promising therapy for treating incurable illness, even if the drug is not approved by the FDA. Interestingly, while 79% believe that patients with fatal and incurable disease should have the power to decide whether to take an experimental drug, 88% said they would still want freedom of choice even if the drug had serious but reversible adverse effects.[23]

To minimize the problems associated with drug diversion, prescribers, dispensers, and other public health professionals need to educate patients about the dangers of "going around" the system. To that end, the last chapter presents and discusses ways of empowering consumers and health-care professionals with information.

NOTES

1. Brad Stone, "Book on Importing Drugs is Misleading and Could Cause Harm," *FDA Talk Paper* (9 January 1991).

2. James C. Anthony, "The Regulation of Dangerous Psychoactive Drugs," in *Society and Medications: Conflicting Signals for Prescribers and Patients*, eds. J.P. Morgan and D.V. Kagan (Lexington, MA: D.C. Heath, 1983):163-180.

3. Margaret Krieg, *Black Market Medicine* (Englewood Cliffs, NJ: Prentice-Hall, 1967).

4. D.E. Smith and D.R. Wesson, "Legitimate and Illegitimate Distribution of Amphetamines and Barbiturates," *Journal of Psychedelic Drugs* 5 (1972):177-181.

5. Anonymous, "Drug Diversion in Kansas City," *NARD Journal* 114 (Number 2, February 1992):44-47.

6. Anonymous, "APhA Works to Fend Off Discriminatory Pricing," *Pharmacy Today* 31 (Number 8, 1992):1,6.

7. Anonymous, "Drug Diversion: Congressional Report," *American Pharmacy* 25 (September 1985):56-60.

8. Lisa A. Ruby and Michael Montagne, "Direct-to-Consumer Advertising: A Case Study of the Rogaine® Campaign," *Journal of Pharmaceutical Marketing and Management* 6 (Number 2, 1991):21-32.

9. James H. Johnson, *How to Buy Almost Any Drug Without a Prescription* (New York, NY: Avon, 1990):xi.

10. Philip J. LaVelle, "U.S. Targets 'Youth' Drugs Shipped Here," *San Diego Union* (17 March 1991):A-1,A-9.

11. Jean McCann, "Patients Hop the Border to Shop for IBD Drugs," *Drug Topics* 136 (Number 3, 3 February 1992):15.

12. Advertisement for InterPharm, Inc. Nassau, Bahamas, found in *World War II* (September 1991).

13. Jeff Jellin, ed., "Regulatory Loopholes," *Pharmacist's Letter* 7 (Number 2, February 1991):11.

14. Denise Grady and Doug M. Podolsky, "Mail-Order Drugs From Abroad," *American Health*, (December 1988):11-12.

15. Anonymous, "Drug Book Misinterprets Government Policy," *Pharmacy Update* (15 April 1991):3.

16. Anonymous, "FDA Import Alert," *FDC Reports* (3 February 1992):T&G 15.

17. Anonymous, "FDA Will Inspect 'Buyers' Clubs' for Unapproved AIDS Drugs," *FDC Reports* (30 September 1991):T&G 2.

18. Naomi Pfeiffer, "Compound Q Goes Above Ground," *AIDS Patient Care* (February 1992):11-14.

19. Gregg Laskowski, "Notes from the Underground," *American Druggist* 205 (6 June 1992):28-35.

20. John Lesley, ed., "Legal Review," *Nootropic News* (April 1992):2,9,10.

21. Gene R. Haislip, "The Traffic Light in Licit Drugs," *Drug Enforcement* (Fall 1983):31-33.

22. Steven Findlay, "The Rules on Selling Vitamins," *U.S. News and World Report* (4 May 1992):70.

23. Anonymous, "Americans Want Option to Choose Unapproved Drugs," *Pharmacy Times* (April 1992):19.

Chapter 11

Empowering Consumers
and Health-Care Professionals

CONSUMERISM AND SELF-MEDICATION

Many people have a renewed interest in taking charge of their own health-care due to the pervasive "consumerism" movement in American society. This movement has been growing in the United States since the 1960s when groups like the March of Dimes sponsored medical research for polio vaccines. Today, patients and their loved ones are leading the crusade to influence drug research and distribution. Although they are not medical specialists or disease experts, they are not willing to sit back and wait for the established medical system to take action. For example, patient lobbyists are forcing redistribution of medical funds towards AIDS research, and Alzheimer's disease victims' family members have organized to expedite the approval of valuable foreign drugs.[1]

Activities like these are an expression of consumer consciousness, which usually evolves through three stages (Table 11.1). Expanding consumer consciousness–the desire to know more about what is going on and to have a say in it–is especially evident in health-care. Patients want more information about health and their disease or condition. They want personal control over their health and in making health-care decisions. They want to be "in charge" of staying healthy or getting better if they become ill.

While this is true, a recent survey found that most patients do not consider themselves "consumers." They lack the motivation to practice consumer behaviors, such as seeking information, exercising independent judgment, and applying cost-sensitivity principles when purchasing medical services or products.[2] It is important for

TABLE 11.1. Stages of the Consumer Movement in the U.S.

STAGE	DESCRIPTION
1	The producer of a good or the provider of a service (pharmaceutical manufacturer and health-care system) controls all aspects of the interaction or exchange with a consumer (patient).
2	The consumer (patient) begins to question the way things are done and asks for more information.
3	The consumer (patient) has equal input into the interaction or decision-making process, and often controls it.

consumers to realize that medical and health-care services, including those provided by hospitals, physicians, and pharmacists, are subject to the same evaluation as dry-cleaning, home repair, and other such services.

Although the stakes are higher when treating health conditions, the criteria for "good" services are the same and should be applied to health-care situations to ensure that consumers are receiving optimal care. There is no reason why a consumer should be uncomfortable or unhappy with health-care services. It is likely that, as consumers become more aware of the advantages and disadvantages of the current health-care system, they will be more willing to "shop" for the best services or care and to cease relations with less-than-optimal health-care professionals or organizations.

The Self-Care Movement

A major part of the consumerism trend is the development of the self-care movement. For a variety of reasons, including a distrust of the existing system and a need to control costs, more people want to engage in self-diagnosis when they experience symptoms and believe that they are ill. They also want to direct the use of treatment(s), including the choice to use nontraditional approaches, such as herbal remedies or chiropractors, that exist outside organized traditional health-care systems. A study reported in the *New England Journal of Medicine* determined that, in 1990, Americans made an estimated 425 million visits to providers of unconventional therapy, and spent approximately $14 million. To compare, in the same year, Americans made 388 million visits to primary care physicians. Thus, the frequency of unconventional therapy use is higher than expected, and is an important consideration for physicians and other health-care professionals.[3]

Self-care practice has both positive and negative repercussions. While consumer involvement and control is commendable, in the real world of medication use, humans often are not rational in making decisions to use pharmacologically-active substances. While self-care and self-medication are beneficial in many situations, most patients will make such decisions and act without the assistance or supervision of a pharmacist, physician, or other health professional. Consumers, especially those involved in self-care and self-treatment practices, are usually not aware of all possible treatment options when developing a therapeutic plan. At the same time, one can argue that health professionals, who are dominated by the scientific approach to medicine, are not optimal decision makers either. They often do not know about, or make their patients aware of, alternative healing models (i.e., holistic medicine) and other types of treatment, such as non-drug therapies (i.e., diet modification), which can be less expensive and equally efficacious.

SOURCES OF QUALITY DRUG INFORMATION FOR PATIENTS AND CONSUMERS

High-quality health-education programs for consumers, and initiatives that teach health-care professionals methods of effective communication are fundamental needs of the current health-care system. Consumers need to understand health and illness behaviors (i.e., the reasons why they act as they do when they are ill, and optimal ways to receive the best possible health-care) and how medications are developed and used for specific diseases. This information is helpful not only for patients to understand physician decisions, but to make intelligent decisions on their own regarding health-care.

In response to the consumerism movement and the desire for useful drug and disease information, several organizations and support groups have published effective and practical information sources. Compendia, brochures, booklets, videos, radio shows, television appearances, presentations, and other media are available for patients, all of which discuss various health concerns and treatment alternatives. To help consumers evaluate these materials and programs, the Consumer Health Information Source has provided a comprehensive criteria list (Table 11.2).

The United States Pharmacopeial Convention

The United States Pharmacopeial Convention (USP) is one of our country's best sources of objective, high-quality information. The USP was established in 1820 as a private, voluntary, nonprofit organization to establish official standards for the analytical testing of drug products, such as strength, quality, purity, packaging, and labeling. These standards are published regularly as the *United States Pharmacopeia* and the *National Formulary*.

In the late 1970s, the USP decided to establish official standards for drug information. Their mission is to develop and maintain a clinically relevant, consensus-based, continually-updated, easy-to-use drug information database for both health professionals and patients. The result is the annual publication *USP-Dispensing Information* (*USP-DI*). Their publications for consumers include *About Your Medicines*, *About Your High Blood Pressure Medicines* (published by Consumer Reports Books), and patient education leaflets (package inserts) for individual drugs. These leaflets are available from many pharmacists.

National Council on Patient Information and Education

Established in 1982, the National Council on Patient Information and Education (NCPIE) is a nonprofit coalition of organizations that is committed to improving communication between health-care

TABLE 11.2. Criteria Used to Evaluate the Quality of Drug Information

CRITERION	DESCRIPTION
• Qualifications of Author(s)	academic credentials, institutional affiliation, previous publications
• Content	significance, accuracy, balance, documentation, authority, timeliness
• Readability	quality of writing, style
• Ease of Use	clear organization, indexes, table of contents
• Pathways to Further Information	bibliographies, reading lists, referral sources, resource organizations
• Physical Quality	size of type, clarity of print, aesthetic appeal, binding, durability
• Consumer Orientation	usefulness in making intelligent decisions concerning an individual's health and use of health-care services; appropriateness for lay use; supportive rather than threatening tone and style
• Appropriateness of Intended Audiences	targeted toward cultural and ethnic groups (i.e., African Americans, elderly, children, Hispanics)

professionals and patients about prescription medications. The group's goals are to better prepare patients to work with health-care providers, to help patients take medications safely and effectively, to increase consumer awareness of the right and the need to know about prescription medications, and to increase professional awareness of the need to give more and improved information about drug therapy to patients.

The Public Citizen Health Research Group

The Public Citizen Health Research Group (PCHRG), based in Washington, DC, was founded by Ralph Nader, a well-known consumer advocate, and is currently led by Sidney Wolfe. PCHRG has published a number of books and pamphlets on ineffective medications and problematic drug-taking behaviors.[4,5] Additionally, Wolfe speaks for many consumers as a lobbyist and advocate in health-related matters.

Consumer Union

A number of health- and medication-related books and materials are provided by Consumer Union.[6,7] Consumer Union publishes *Consumer Reports*, a monthly magazine of test reports, product ratings, and buying guidance. The publication also includes information on medical and drug products and services. Consumer Union's charter is to "provide consumers with information and counsel on consumer goods and services, give information and assistance on all matters relating to expenditures of family income, and initiate and cooperate with individual and group efforts seeking to create and maintain decent living standards."[6] They do not accept advertisements or engage in any commercial activities so that they can ensure objectivity in product comparisons.

Additional Information Sources

In a critical review of available reference and resources of drug information, a panel of health professionals judged that one book was superior to others.[8] The book is titled *The Complete Drug Reference*,[9] which is a detailed version of the information presented in *About Your Medicines*, prepared by the United States Pharmacopeial Convention and published by Consumer Reports Books. *The Complete Drug Reference*, however, is also expensive and somewhat technical. Other useful drug-information books include *The Essential Guide to Prescription Drugs*,[10] *The Pill Book*,[11] and *Worst Pills, Best Pills*.[4] To help consumers learn more about drugs and diseases, a complete list of information sources is provided in Appendix B.[12,13,14]

Guidelines for Choosing Pharmacists and Physicians

One of the most important information resources that consumers have is a knowledgeable and cooperative health-care professional.

When it comes to the safe and rational use of drugs, the best health-care professional to consult is the pharmacist. Pharmacists are the most accessible of all health-care professionals, as well as the best educated regarding drug benefits and risks. The average pharmacist has studied for five or six years, primarily in basic sciences (i.e., chemistry, biology) and pharmacy-specific courses, such as pharmacology (the science of drug action), pharmaceutics (the science of drug dissolution, absorption, metabolism, and elimination), and pharmacotherapeutics (the appropriate use of drugs in specific diseases). Pharmacy students also work directly with patients in hospitals, clinics, nursing homes, and community pharmacies. Finally, to become licensed, a pharmacy student must work for up to 300 hours with a practicing pharmacist and pass a detailed written exam. By the time a pharmacist is licensed, the drug information that he or she possesses far outweighs any other health-care professional. Because they are so valuable, pharmacists should be chosen with great care (Table 11.3). The suggestions in Table 11.3 can also be applied when choosing a physician, dentist, or other health professional.[15]

Consumers should remember that the pharmacist is a drug expert, as well as a check and balance for medical mistakes and physician malpractice. As such, a pharmacist should not be selected on the basis of price or convenience, alone. Because of lower overhead costs and a decreased number of employees, a convenient and inexpensive pharmacy might not provide the information and auditing services that consumers should demand.[16]

A current trend in community pharmacy management is the development of consumer- and patient-directed services. Drug monitoring, one-on-one counseling, smoking cessation programs, high blood pressure screening and monitoring, and health education classes are just a handful of such services. Consumers' desire for a convenient and friendly source of health and drug information, as well as the need for pharmacists to generate revenue from other sources besides drug products, have motivated this positive trend. What this trend signifies for patients is an opportunity to develop a long-term relationship with a knowledgeable health-care professional, as well as to improve the quality of their health and medical care.

TABLE 11.3. How to Choose a Health-Care Professional

Ask the following questions of each health-care professional being evaluated:

• Does the pharmacist double-check each prescription to ensure that errors are not made? Are computer programs used to check for drug interactions?

• Are your concerns and interests more important than those of your physician? Or, does the pharmacist comply with physician directions, regardless of whether they are in your best interest?

• What professional services does he or she offer?
    (i.e., drug information counseling, drug monitoring, health-care suggestions and monitoring, consultation with your physician)

• Does the pharmacy keep complete patient records?
    (i.e., do records include all the drugs that you currently use, including over-the-counter products? Are allergy, smoking status, age, and other factors included and considered?)

• How does the pharmacist use patient records to ensure the best care for you, the patient?

• Does he or she have a reputation for honesty and fairness? Is he or she well-liked in the community? How satisfied are other patients with the pharmacist and his or her services?

• Does the pharmacist have a personality and style that makes you comfortable?

• Is the pharmacist willing to answer your questions about your disease(s), drugs, and health concerns? Does he or she provide written information that is useful and understandable? Do time constraints inhibit his or her ability to talk with you about your health-care questions?

• Will the pharmacist help you determine which treatment alternative (i.e., generic versus brand-name drugs) is the least expensive, if cost is a concern?

• Is he or she accessible by phone and in person?

• Is the pharmacy neat and well-organized? Are employees neatly dressed and friendly?

• Is the merchandise in the pharmacy appropriate and reliable (i.e., not a questionable or quack remedy)? Are products in-date (i.e., not expired or stale)?

EVALUATING ADVERTISEMENTS FOR PRESCRIPTION AND NONPRESCRIPTION DRUGS

The Value of Educated Consumers

Advertising messages for all types of products and services are often both appealing and convincing. Short punchy sentences and catchy tunes are used to generate interest and consumer recall of the product or service. The primary goal of the savvy advertiser is to generate a feeling in the reader of an unfulfilled need and to provide an alternative to satisfy that need. In most instances, when selling cars, clothes, or vacations, this marketing tactic is effective and innocuous. The dangers associated with misinterpretation of the message or the provision of incomplete information are minimal. However, when reading or listening to advertisements for either prescription or nonprescription drugs, the consumer must be careful to understand the whole message and to develop rational expectations of the advertised drug product.

Many people have seen or read advertisements for the prescription drug, minoxidil (Rogaine®, Upjohn). The minoxidil advertisements describe the availability of a new treatment alternative for men and women experiencing hair loss, and advise the audience to see a doctor or to call a toll-free phone number for additional information. Success rates and the testimony of users is provided, as well as information about adverse effects and potential risks associated with use of the product. It is easy to imagine how the news of this novel drug might excite consumers and motivate them to learn more about the product and whether it is a viable option for them. It is also easy to imagine a consumer seeing the advertisement and going to his or her physician to demand a prescription for the drug, regardless of the appropriateness of this choice in terms of the patient's health.[17]

This dilemma is not specific to minoxidil. Messages regarding any drug product that are provided in direct advertisements to consumers can be misconstrued. The advertiser (the pharmaceutical manufacturer) must decide whether the message that is to be advertised is of value to the general public, worthy of direct communication, fairly balanced, scientifically accurate, and whether consumers will be subject to minimal misunderstanding and false expectations.

Consumers, too, must make educated decisions when considering an advertisement for a drug product. It is important to understand *all* of the information presented. All drugs have both benefits and risks, and every drug is not necessarily appropriate for every patient. For example, minoxidil, the hair loss treatment, is most effective in young men who have only recently noticed hair loss and should *not* be used in people with high blood pressure and other types of cardiovascular disease. In addition, the drug must be applied to the scalp faithfully every day for up to *four months* before any hair growth is seen. Without knowing this information, many patients begin using this product, are disappointed with the lack of immediate results and discontinue treatment before the four months have passed. By knowing all of the facts—on any drug—consumers can not only avoid frustration with medications, they can become more effective health-care decision makers.

The Role of Health-Care Professionals

Often, a consumer who sees or reads a prescription or nonprescription drug advertisement, and who is interested in the product, will discuss the drug with a health-care professional: a physician, pharmacist, or nurse. As such, health-care providers must be aware of the messages that consumers are receiving and learn to prevent misinterpretation or false expectations by providing complete and understandable product information. Such information includes details about the product, its efficacy, its adverse effects, and the types of patients that will benefit from its use. It is important for health-care professionals to listen to consumers' needs and to provide objective and complete information in a way that consumers will understand and remember.

To help both consumers and health-care professionals evaluate advertisements for prescription drugs, Millstein describes ten characteristics of prescription-drug advertising that should be evaluated (Table 11.4).[18] In some cases, information to answer many of these questions can be inaccessible or difficult to interpret. The advice and guidance of a health professional, particularly a pharmacist, can assist consumers in better understanding the true message of drug advertisements.

TABLE 11.4. Key Questions to Consider when Evaluating Nonprescription- and Prescription-Drug Advertisements

Does the advertisement:

1. Extend or distort the claims for usefulness beyond those approved in the final product labeling?

2. Contain quotes from a source that improperly implies such quotes are typical of statements that would be made on the basis of greater general experience with the drug?

3. Make claims on the basis of poor quality research favorable to the product and not on contrary evidence from much better research?

4. Feature a seemingly favorable quotation out of context, while omitting unfavorable data from the same source?

5. Contain quotes from one authoritative source while failing to quote from other experts who differ, resulting in an imbalance of viewpoints?

6. Feature information from sources that report no adverse effects, but fail to report from others that do?

7. Contain information previously valid but rendered obsolete or false by more recent research?

8. Refer to published data as authoritative when it is not unqualifiedly so?

9. Feature seemingly favorable data from some source, but omits negative data from that same source?

10. Contain statements suggesting fewer contraindications, warnings, and other safety or effectiveness issues than competing products, when in fact the use and cautionary information is quite similar?

Source: L. Millstein, *Encyclopedia of Pharmaceutical Technology* 1988.

ASSISTANCE AND GUIDANCE FOR HEALTH PROFESSIONALS

The decision to seek help for health problems rests with the consumer. It is most important that consumers do not make health decisions, or select and use specific treatments without any information, advice, or guidance from health professionals. There are some basic guidelines that each health professional who is consulted should discuss with current and prospective self-medicators (Table 11.5). Guidance and accurate information are essential for the improvement of consumer self-medication behaviors. In practice, each person who wishes to self-medicate should be assessed and monitored to the same degree as prescription-drug takers. This includes taking a drug history, managing their medication use, and providing consumers with drug education programs.

Improving Consumer Understanding of Drug Discoveries

A study of media accounts of prescription-drug use has demonstrated several trends that should make health-care professionals cautious when discussing drug information with patients. The study found that 34% of media stories report the effects (usually negative) of currently-marketed prescription drugs, 24% report about new drugs and their uses, and 20% describe concerns about pricing and the economics of prescription-drug development.[19] About one-

---

TABLE 11.5. Guidelines for Discussions with Self-Medicating Consumers

The health-care professional should:

1. Help the consumer identify as clearly as possible the problem (e.g., symptom, state, condition, illness prevention) and how to go about treating it.

2. Provide drug information and tell the consumer to carefully read the labels of products he or she wishes to use in self-medication.

3. Counsel consumers about the potential dangers (e.g., side effects, adverse reactions, contraindications, effects from long-term use, and possibilities of misdiagnosis) of the medications they wish to use in self-treatment.

4. Inform consumers to self-medicate for only a short period of time; most drug products intended for self-medication are meant only for symptomatic relief; they should not be used for extended periods.

5. Advise consumers to beware of promotional campaigns, media reports, and the general advice of people who are not trained and who do not have personal experience in health-care; ensure that they know your quality as a source of information.

quarter of all media reports were events, such as press conferences, held to describe a new-drug discovery. It is critical for consumers to realize that great discoveries and major breakthroughs are rare events, and stories of such occurrences should be viewed with caution. Some guidelines for consumers when reading or watching media reports of events in health-care are provided in Table 11.6.[20]

Empowering Consumers with Knowledge and Skills

The key to active consumer involvement in health-care is *empowerment*. Consumers need to be advocates for themselves, and to enlist knowledgeable professionals and other influential individuals who can act as advocates for them in the health-care arena. Instructions for both consumers and health-care professionals are provided in Tables 11.7 and 11.8.

THE INFLUENTIAL HEALTH-CARE CONSUMER

Like other major decisions, health-care choices must be made by the most important individual in the health-care team–the patient. Physicians, nurses, pharmacists, and other health-care professionals are a support structure to ensure, restore, and promote patient wellness. Consumers or patients who are dissatisfied with their health-care professionals should be willing to question these individuals

---

TABLE 11.6. Guidelines to Interpreting Media Reports of Medical Breakthroughs and Drug Use Problems

- Check the source of the news report, both the original source of the story and the news service that carried it.

- News reports about "cures" for many chronic diseases or completely successful treatment of most life-threatening diseases are probably false. Very few drugs exist that actually cure a patient totally and permanently (antibiotics and certain injectable drugs are the wonderful exceptions).

- Determine what the true research results were, especially given the number of patients involved, the duration of the study, and what kinds of treatments were employed.

- Consult with a health professional about the report you have read and ask for his or her interpretation.

TABLE 11.7. Guidelines for Consumers as Advocates for Themselves

- Do not be afraid to ask questions and get understandable answers.

- Educate yourself about your diseases and the types of therapies that are available to treat them. Use your local library to find the books listed in this chapter and Appendix B.

- Become aware of high-quality resources for health and drug information, advice, and guidance.

- Collect objective and relevant drug information, and keep it handy for easy reference.

- Complain about things that dissatisfy you with your medical care, including costs. Your health-care professional is responsible to help you improve your health cost-effectively.

- Get a second opinion and do not begin prescribed treatment(s) if you are confused, uncertain, or feel pressured.

- Choose your health-care professionals well.

- Support efforts that make necessary changes in the health-care system.

---

for complete information, and if necessary, make changes in this support structure (i.e., find another pharmacist or physician). Supporting legislative efforts to improve the health-care system is also an important activity for consumers and health-care professionals who want to achieve equitable and high-quality medical care.

Remember, the process of becoming or staying well is not a passive process, it is an active one. Consumers and patients need to actively search for information and synthesize it to make good health-care decisions. While health-care professionals are often the source of this information, physicians and pharmacists cannot presume to understand each patient's perspective and thus, cannot make optimal decisions for the patient. At the same time, health-care professionals must realize that consumers might not comprehend terminology, medical procedures, and the consequences of particular decisions and health-care options. Supportive guidance and clear explanations by health professionals encourage optimal health-care decision making by patients and the team effort that patients desire.

TABLE 11.8. Guidelines for Health-Care Professionals as Patient Advocates

- Treat patients as individuals, with a specific knowledge base, and particular concerns, fears, and experiences.

- Be aware of individual patient needs (i.e., information, empathy, additional explanation).

- Share knowledge of patients with other professionals in the health-care team.

- Provide professional services at reasonable costs.

- Ensure that patients can obtain and properly use safe and effective medications, therapies, and devices when needed.

- Do not forget patients after their immediate needs or questions have been answered. Follow up to ensure appropriate medical care.

- Give special care and assistance to patients of diminished autonomy and to those who are disenfranchised.

NOTES

1. Dick Thompson, "Your Money or Their Lives," *TIME Magazine* (12 October 1992):66-67.

2. D. Lupton, C. Donaldson, and P. Lloyd, "Caveat Emptor or Blissful Ignorance? Patients and the Consumerist Ethos," *Social Science & Medicine* 33 (1991):559-568.

3. David M. Eisenberg, Ronald C. Kessler, Cindy Foster, et al., "Unconventional Medicine in the United States," *New England Journal of Medicine* 328 (1992):246-252.

4. Sidney Wolfe, *Worst Pills, Best Pills: An Older Adult's Guide to Avoiding Drug-Induced Death and Illness* (New York, NY: Pantheon, 1988).

5. Public Citizens Health Research Group, *Over-the-Counter Pills That Don't Work* (Washington, DC: Public Citizens Health Research Group, 1983).

6. Editors of Consumer Reports Books, *Health Quackery: Consumer Union's Report of False Health Claims, Worthless Remedies, and Unproved Therapies* (New York, NY: Rinehart & Winston, 1980).

7. Editors of Consumer Reports Books, *The New Medicine Show* (Yonkers, NY: Consumer Reports, 1989).

8. Steven Findlay and Sarah Burke, "Best Books," *U.S. News and World Report* (20 May 1991).

9. U.S. Pharmacopeial Convention, *The Complete Drug Reference* (New York, NY: Consumer Reports Books, 1991).

10. James W. Long, *The Essential Guide to Prescription Drugs* (New York, NY: Harper Collins, 1991).

11. Anonymous, *The Pill Book* (New York, NY: Bantam Books, 1990).

12. Boston Women's Health Book Collective, *The New Our Bodies, Ourselves* (New York, NY: Simon & Schuster, 1992).

13. Stephen J. Williams and Sandra Guerra, *Health-care Services in the 1990s: A Consumer's Guide* (New York, NY: Pantheon, 1988).

14. Harold Cornacchia, *Consumer Health: A Guide to Intelligent Decisions*, fourth edition (St. Louis, MO: Mosby, 1989).

15. Food and Drug Administration, "How to Talk to (and Listen to) Your Pharmacist," *FDA Consumer* 14 (April 1980):15-18.

16. Herb Denenberg, "How to Choose a Pharmacist," *Pennsylvania Pharmacist* (January 1990):7.

17. Lisa Ruby Basara, "Direct-to-Consumer Advertising: Today's Issues and Tomorrow's Outlook," *Journal of Drug Issues* 22 (Number 2, 1992):317-330.

18. Lloyd G. Millstein, "Advertising and Promotion of Prescription Drug Products," in *Encyclopedia of Pharmaceutical Technology*, volume 1, eds. J. Swarbrick and J.C. Boylan (New York, NY: Marcel Dekker, 1988):147-187.

19. Charles Winick, "Reporting Drug Truth in the Media," in *Society and Medications: Conflicting Signals for Prescribers and Patients*, eds. J.P. Morgan and D.V. Kagan (Lexington, MA: D.C. Heath, 1983):221-231.

20. Ralph C. Heussner, Jr. and Marla E. Salmon, *Warning: The Media May be Hazardous to Your Health. A Consumer's Guide to Medical News and Advertising* (Kansas City, MO: Andrews & McMeel, 1987).

Appendix A

Glossary of Acronyms and Terms

ACRONYMS

AIDS:	acquired immunodeficiency syndrome
ADR:	adverse drug reaction
AMA:	American Medical Association
APhA:	American Pharmaceutical Association
AZT:	azothymidine (also known as zidovudine or Retrovir®)
CANDAR:	computer-assisted NDA review
CBER:	Center for Biologic Evaluation and Research
CDER:	Center for Drug Evaluation and Research
ddI:	didanosine (also known as Videx®)
DEA:	Drug Enforcement Agency
DNA:	deoxyribonucleic acid
DQRS:	Drug Quality Reporting System
FDA:	Food and Drug Administration
FTC:	Federal Trade Commission
HIV:	human immunodeficiency virus
IND:	investigational new drug
IRB:	institutional review board
LSD:	lysergic acid diethylamide
MAPS:	Multidisciplinary Association for Psychedelic Studies
MDMA:	methylene-dioxy-methamphetamine
NCOD:	National Commission on Orphan Diseases
NDA:	new drug application
NORD:	National Organization for Rare Disorders
OBRA:	Omnibus Budget Reconciliation Act
OTC:	over the counter (nonprescription)
PCHRG:	Public Citizens Health Research Group

PDR: Physicians' Desk Reference
PLA: product license application
PMA: Pharmaceutical Manufacturers Association
PWA: Persons With AIDS
USP: United States Pharmacopeia
VNR: video news release

TERMS

abbreviated NDA: A new drug application for a generic drug. The drug's sponsor must demonstrate equivalence to the brand-name drug as well as adherence to appropriate manufacturing practices. Safety and efficacy measures are not necessary.

accelerated NDA: A new drug application for a drug that might have the potential to cure or treat a serious, life-threatening illness. The regulatory review process for drugs with accelerated NDAs is shortened to give patients the opportunity to use the drug as quickly as possible.

adulterated: Impure or contaminated. This term is used in the Food, Drug, and Cosmetic Act of 1908. According to the law, drugs sold in the United States cannot be adulterated or misbranded.

advertising: Marketing activity that effectively communicates information to encourage directly or indirectly the purchase of goods or services. Also an unofficial term in regulatory literature that is applied generally to all forms of drug promotion.

adverse drug reaction: A drug effect that is negative or unfavorable to the patient's health (i.e., anemia) potentially making discontinuation of the drug necessary. This term is different from "side effect"; side effects are unfavorable (i.e., headache) but do not affect a patient's health or condition negatively. This differentiation is relative and depends on the patient and his or her disease or condition.

antisera: Sera (plasma) that contains antibodies against particular organisms. Antisera can be used to treat or prevent infections.

approvable letter: Letter from the FDA to a drug's sponsor indicating that the drug-approval process is almost complete. The sponsor must respond to the FDA in ten days or less.

biologic: Any virus, therapeutic serum, toxin, antitoxin, vaccine, blood, blood component or derivative, allergenic product, or analogous product applicable to the prevention, treatment, or cure of human disease or injury.

biopharmaceuticals: Drugs produced using biotechnology; either recombinant DNA or hybridoma processes.

biotechnology: The collective processes used to produce biopharmaceuticals.

blinding mechanism: The process of ensuring that everyone involved in the drug trial is unaware of who is receiving the experimental drug and who is receiving a traditional drug treatment, or a placebo, throughout the duration of the study. In experimental studies, a lack of knowledge about which patients are receiving the treatment being studied can be limited to just the patients (single-blind), both patients and clinicians (double-blind), or patients, clinicians, and the scientific evaluators (triple-blind).

brand-name drug: A drug for which the sponsor has patent protection in the United States. Also known as a proprietary drug.

clinical inquiry: A simple, non-experimental method of determining a drug's safety and efficacy on the basis of observations in a group of patients. No control group is used.

clinical trial: Testing of a new drug in healthy or sick humans to determine the drug's safety and/or efficacy.

contagion: Causative agent of a disease (i.e., bacteria, virus).

control group: This group of patients receives a different type of treatment, either a traditional one (already approved and used in therapy) or no treatment (they receive a placebo) in a clinical trial.

controlled clinical trial: A clinical trial in which some patients (control group) receive either traditional treatment or placebo and other patients (treatment group) receive the drug under study. The use of a control group provides a meaningful yardstick against which to measure the value of the new drug.

cross-licensing: The marketing and distribution of a product by two different manufacturers; can be a remedy to disputes over patent protection and marketing exclusivity rights.

drug: Natural or synthetic substances that are effective in the prevention, treatment, or cure of human disease or injury.

efficacy: A drug's ability to effectively treat or reduce the symptoms of a disease or condition.

enablement requirement: A condition required by the U.S. Patent Office regarding patented inventions. A document must be submitted by the inventor that enables any person adequately trained in the art to make and use the invention.

empirical approach: The treatment of disease using first-hand observation and experimentation in individual patients. This medical practice was common prior to the 1900s.

experimental group: This group of patients receives the new drug that is under investigation in a clinical trial.

experimental study: A research method in which one group of subjects (experimental group) receives a new treatment (e.g., drug, device, surgery), and are compared with one or more control groups who receive different treatments. These groups are studied over the same time period using the same measurements of safety and effectiveness.

fair balance: A provision of the FDA regarding pharmaceutical promotion. Promotional activities must present an objective, complete, and balanced representation of the advantages (efficacy) and disadvantages (adverse drug reactions) of a pharmaceutical product.

generic drug: A drug for which the sponsor does not have patent protection in the United States. Several drug manufacturers can make and distribute the drug at any time. Applications to receive approval to market a generic drug are called abbreviated NDAs.

hybridoma technology: A process by which biopharmaceuticals are manufactured. It uses living organisms to replicate and produce a pharmaceutical product, such as monoclonal antibodies.

indication: The disease(s) or condition(s) for which a drug is approved by the FDA. For example, zidovudine's indication is "the alleviation of AIDS-related symptoms of patients with HIV."

informed-consent process: The process by which patients participating in a clinical trial are notified of the purpose, design, duration, benefits, confidentiality procedures, and voluntary nature of the trial. This process is mandatory for the conduct of clinical trials.

institutional review board: A group of physicians, pharmacists, researchers, and consumers that reviews clinical trial research plans and protects participating patients from unethical research practices.

investigational new drug: A new chemical entity for which human safety and effectiveness has not yet been demonstrated, but that does seem to be valuable on the basis of animal testing.

magic bullet theory: The belief that specific pills or medications are targeted to cure a specific disease or condition immediately.

marketing: The process of planning and executing the conception, pricing, promotion, and distribution of ideas, goods, and services to create exchanges that satisfy individual and organizational objectives.

marketing exclusivity: The ability of a drug's sponsor to promote and distribute a drug in the United States marketplace without competition, usually for a specified period of time. During this time period, the FDA is prohibited from approving the same drug for the same disease. For example, orphan drugs receive seven-year marketing exclusivity.

medicalization: The process of redefining or relabeling a personal or social problem as a medical condition, thus necessitating involvement in and control by the health-care system. It can be described as the substitution of medical care for conditions that were once non-medical in nature (i.e., alcoholism, hair loss).

misbranding: Incomplete or incorrect prescription drug labeling. This term is used in the Food, Drug, and Cosmetic Act of 1908. According to the law, drugs sold in the United States cannot be adulterated or misbranded.

molecular manipulation: The control and maneuver of the molecular structures of chemical substances to alter, and hopefully improve, their medicinal properties.

N-of-1 clinical trial: Drug experiment using one patient. Conceivably, such trials could, if done in a consistent and well-designed way, be collectively analyzed in a manner similar to one large-scale clinical trial. Such a method has been suggested in the evaluation of experimental AIDS medications.

new drug: A drug that is not marketed in the United States, but that might possess efficacy in the treatment of a particular condition. A new drug might or might not be a new molecular entity. To receive marketing approval, a new drug application must be filed with the FDA.

new drug application: A comprehensive document filed by a drug's sponsor to the FDA upon completion of safety and efficacy testing in animals. Preliminary findings are explained in an attempt to receive approval to continue research in human subjects.

new molecular entity: A substance that is different and unique in terms of its structure, physical characteristics, and potential medicinal benefit. Approximately 30 new molecular entities are approved by the FDA for marketing as pharmaceuticals in the United States each year.

nonobvious: An invention must be unique and different enough from the existing state of the art, or nonobvious, as evaluated by an individual of ordinary skill in the art, to qualify for a patent.

nonprescription drug: A medication for which a physician's prescription is not necessary for purchase and use. Also known as over-the-counter medications or OTCs.

nootropic: See "smart drug."

novelty: An invention that is original and not a part of the existing state of the art. This requirement is necessary for an invention to receive patent protection.

orphan disease: Specific rare diseases that traditionally have not had a sponsoring organization, supporting investigator, or agency dedicated to its research, prevention, or treatment.

orphan drug: A drug that appears or is proven effective in the treatment of a rare or orphan disease, but that is not usually profitable to its sponsor.

patent: A contract between an inventor and the U.S. Patent Office that gives the inventor the right to exclude others from making, using, or selling the product for a limited time period (usually 17 years) in exchange for a full description of the invention.

placebo: An inactive form of treatment, usually an inert sugar pill, received by patients in the control group. The use of a placebo provides the rationale for the control group to receive no (beneficial) treatment so that a good comparison can be made with the results of the experimental group.

placebo phenomenon: The occurrence of disease alleviation or cure upon ingestion of a placebo. In many cases, this phenomenon is attributed to the patient's psychological conviction that their disease can be cured by the use of a drug, regardless of its true efficacy. This phenomenon can confound and potentially minimize the value of controlled clinical trial results.

post-marketing surveillance: Also known as Phase IV clinical trials, these activities are designed to evaluate a recently-approved drug's safety and efficacy. Drug inspections and sampling, the completion of clinical trials in specialized populations (i.e., elderly, women), and drug quality monitoring are included.

prescription drug: A medication for which a physicians' prescription is necessary for purchase and use, and that is obtained only through a licensed pharmacy. Also known as ethical drugs.

promotion: The vehicle by which a product, its price, and distribution methods are coherently and persuasively described to consumers. This term encompasses advertising and related forms of information dissemination. Also a marketing term for the techniques used at the point of purchase to encourage buying, such as displays, coupons, and rebates.

randomization: The process of assigning individual patients to different treatment groups in such a way that each patient has an equal chance, independent of every other patient, of being selected for any particular group. The goal is to make all study groups as equal as possible at the beginning of the experiment. Also known as random assignment.

randomized controlled clinical trial: Clinical trial in which patients have an equal and independent chance of becoming a member of either the control or the treatment group.

rare disease: A disease that affects less than 200,000 people in the United States.

recombinant DNA process: A process by which biopharmaceuticals are manufactured. It uses human DNA and living organisms to replicate and produce a pharmaceutical product, such as human insulin.

regulatory review period: The time period between NDA submission to the FDA and the final decision regarding drug approval. According to law, this period cannot exceed 180 days, however, it can be extended if the FDA requests additional information from the sponsor.

reservoir: The source of a contagion; the place where a contagion resides.

shared exclusivity: The ability of two orphan drug sponsors to promote and distribute a drug in the United States marketplace without competition from any other drug manufacturers. Shared exclusivity is only mandated when both companies can prove that they developed an orphan drug simultaneously.

smart drug: Drugs that are promoted as possessing the ability to improve memory, creativity, and intelligence. Most smart drugs are not approved for use in the United States and are acquired illegally through foreign mail-order drug houses and underground drug-distribution mechanisms.

sponsor: The organization that submits drug documentation to the FDA for drug approval. May or may not be the drug's original manufacturer.

summary basis of approval: A document that summarizes the key findings and characteristics of a new drug, including safety and efficacy data, pharmacokinetics, and product labeling.

supplemental NDA: This request is submitted when the sponsor would like approval to market an existing drug with either a new indication or new labeling, or when manufacturing procedures have changed. This information is additional to the original NDA for the drug.

surrogate end point: Short-term evidence of a drug's effectiveness in the treatment of a serious, life-threatening illness. Surrogate endpoints are used to justify approval of such drugs and distribution to needy patients. Continuing study of safety and efficacy are necessary.

treatment IND: Promising new drug that might have value in treating desperately ill patients. As a result of legislation permitting the accelerated approval of such drugs, clinical trial design, adverse drug reaction reporting systems, and FDA/sponsor communications have improved and the time to approve such drugs has decreased.

utility: The ability of an invention to serve a useful purpose, as evaluated by individuals skilled in the arts. Utility is necessary for an invention to receive patent protection.

vector: Animal or person who carry a contagion (i.e., mosquitos can carry the organism that causes malaria).

vehicle: Inanimate object that carries a contagion (i.e., drug needles can carry the virus that causes AIDS).

Appendix B

Drug and Disease Information Directory

The purpose of this information directory is to provide consumers and health-care professionals with information sources in the following areas:

1. Clinical trials of new drugs
2. Orphan drugs and rare diseases
3. Volunteer health organizations
4. Drug and disease information

The reader is also referred to the chapters discussing each topic for additional references and information.

TABLE B.1. Clinical Trial Information Sources

ORGANIZATION	DATA AVAILABLE/ SERVICES	CONTACT
AIDS Clinical Trials Information Service	• informs patients and health-care professionals about FDA-sanctioned private clinical trials for experimental AIDS therapies • provides names of contact persons for information on clinical trials	phone: 800.TRIALS.A
FDA Office of Scientific Evaluation (OSE)	• handles inquiries and problems associated with Investigational New Drug (IND) applications and New Drug Applications (NDAs) • provides medical and scientific data on drug products	phone: 301.443.4320

TABLE B.2. Orphan Drug and Rare Disease Information Sources

ORGANIZATION	DATA AVAILABLE/ SERVICES	CONTACT
National Information Center for Orphan Drugs and Rare Diseases (NICODARD)	• organizes a database for scientific investigators, sponsored by the Office of Orphan Products Development of the FDA • provides an up-to-date list of designated orphan drugs and biologics	NICODARD P.O. Box 1133 Washington DC 20013 phone: 800.456.3505
National Organization for Rare Disorders (NORD)	• coalition of more than 100 voluntary health organizations and consumers • educates the public and health professionals about orphan diseases and drugs • provides a comprehensive rare-disease database with over 5,000 diseases • organizes drug-cost sharing programs for patients (supported in conjunction with pharmaceutical firms) • provides travel subsidies for patients (supported by grants from organizations and businesses) • provides grants and networks for researchers • publishes *Orphan Disease Update*, a quarterly newsletter for patients	Abbey Meyers Executive Director, NORD P.O. Box 8923 New Fairfield CT 06812 phone: 203.746.6518

ORGANIZATION	DATA AVAILABLE/ SERVICES	CONTACT
Office of Scientific Policy and Legislation of the National Institutes of Health	• scientific contact at the NIH • serves as mechanism of government technology transfer • reports the proceedings of the National Commission on Orphan Diseases	Stephen C. Groft, PharmD Office of Scientific Policy and Legislation National Institutes of Health Building 31, Room 4B-35 Bethesda MD 20892 phone: 301.496.1454 fax: 301.402.0280
Office of Orphan Products Development, Food and Drug Administration	• provides FDA assistance on orphan drug designation • provides protocol assistance for researchers • distributes orphan drug research grants • organizes orphan drug legislative action	Marlene E. Haffner, MD Director, Office of Orphan Products Development Food and Drug Administration Room 8-73, HF-35 Department of Health and Human Services Rockville MD 20892 phone: 301.443.4903 fax: 301.443.4916
Orphan Medical	• distributes orphan drugs directly to patients • licenses orphan drugs from pharmaceutical companies • promotes research and treatment programs for patients	Bert Spilker Executive Director Orphan Medical 13911 Ridgedale Drive Minnetonka, MN 55305 phone: 612.541.1868 ext. 594

TABLE B.2 (continued)

ORGANIZATION	DATA AVAILABLE/ SERVICES	CONTACT
Pharmaceutical Manufacturers Association Commission on Drugs for Rare Diseases	• provides financial assistance for development of orphan drugs • reports on conferences of orphan drug discovery, development, and distribution	Thomas L. Copmann, PhD Executive Director PMA Commission on Rare Diseases 1100 Fifteenth Street N.W. Washington DC 20005 phone: 202.835.3554 fax: 202.785.4834
Swedish Orphan AB Orphan Europe SARL Orphan Pharma USA	• organizes international distribution of orphan products • assists in bringing orphan products into the U.S. • organizes a rare-disease database for patients and researchers	Lawrence C. Weaver, PhD 7110 Riverview Terrace Minneapolis MN 55432-3045 phone: 612.574.1694 612.625.2136 fax: 612.624.2974

TABLE B.3. Volunteer Agency Information Sources

Several comprehensive resources are available regarding volunteer groups. One is published by Demos Publications Inc. in New York, and is titled *Voluntary Health Organization: A Guide to Patient Services* by Labe Scheinberg and Diana M. Schneider (1987). This publication provides names, addresses, phone numbers, and a listing of services offered by all United States volunteer health agencies. Another book is published by Oryx Press in Phoenix, Arizona. *Consumer Health Information Source Book* (third edition, 1990) is written by Alan M. Rees and Catharine Hoffman, and includes an address list of health-related organizations and a comprehensive list of educational publications, including books, that are provided by these organizations.

The table below provides a selective listing of these organizations for initial reference. Readers should refer to recent editions of the books described above for updated information.

DISEASE OR CONDITION	ORGANIZATION
AIDS	Gay Men's Health Crisis, Inc. New York NY National Hemophilia Foundation New York NY American Red Cross Washington DC
Alcoholism	Alcoholics Anonymous New York NY Al-Anon Family Group Headquarters, Inc. New York NY National Council on Alcoholism New York NY National Clearinghouse for Alcohol Information Rockville MD
Allergies	American Allergy Association Menlo Park CA Asthma and Allergy Foundation of America Washington DC American Celiac Society Jersey City NJ Food Sensitivity, Inc. Jersey City NJ Gluten Intolerance Group of North America Seattle WA
Alzheimer's Disease	Alzheimer's Disease and Related Disorders Association, Inc. Chicago IL
Amputation	National Amputation Foundation, Inc. Whitestone NY
Amyotrophic Lateral Sclerosis	The ALS Association Sherman Oaks CA Muscular Dystrophy Association New York NY
Arthritis	Arthritis Foundation Atlanta GA

TABLE B.3 (continued)

DISEASE OR CONDITION	ORGANIZATION
Asbestosis and Related Disorders	American Lung Association San Mateo CA
Asthma	Asthma and Allergy Foundation of America Washington DC National Foundation for Asthma, Inc. Tucson AZ American Lung Association San Mateo CA
Ataxia	National Ataxia Foundation Wayzata MN Muscular Dystrophy Association New York NY
Autism	National Society for Children and Adults with Autism Washington DC Autism Services Center Huntington WV
Birth Defects	March of Dimes Birth Defects Foundation White Plains NY National Association for the Craniofacially Handicapped Chattanooga TN American Cleft Palate Educational Foundation Pittsburgh PA
Blindness	National Federation for the Blind Baltimore MD American Council of the Blind Washington DC American Foundation for the Blind New York NY National Braille Association, Inc. Rochester NY National Braille Press Boston MA
Burn Injuries	Phoenix Society, Inc. Levittown PA
Cancer	American Cancer Society New York NY Candlelighters Childhood Cancer Foundation Washington DC Cancer Connection Kansas City MO Foundation for Dignity Philadelphia PA
Cerebral Palsy	United Cerebral Palsy Association, Inc. New York NY National Easter Seal Society Chicago IL March of Dimes Birth Defects Foundation White Plains NY National Association of Sports for Cerebral Palsy New York NY
Chronic Bronchitis	American Lung Association San Mateo CA

DISEASE OR CONDITION	ORGANIZATION
Crohn's Disease	National Foundation for Ileitis and Colitis, Inc. New York NY
Cystic Fibrosis	Cystic Fibrosis Foundation　Bethesda MD
Deafness	National Information Center on Deafness Washington DC American Society for Deaf Children Silver Spring MD Telecommunications for the Deaf, Inc. Silver Spring MD
Diabetes	American Diabetes Association, Inc.　Alexandria VA National Diabetes Information Clearinghouse Bethesda MD Juvenile Diabetes Foundation International New York NY
Down's Syndrome	National Down's Syndrome Congress　Park Ridge IL March of Dimes　White Plains NY
Drug Abuse	Narcotics Anonymous　Van Nuys CA Drugs Anonymous　New York NY Families Anonymous　Van Nuys CA PIL-ANON Family Program　New York NY
Dysautonomia	Dysautonomia Foundation　New York NY
Dyslexia	The Orton Dyslexia Society　Baltimore MD Foundation for Children with Learning Disabilities New York NY
Dystonia	Dystonia Medical Research Foundation Beverly Hills CA
Eating Disorders	American Anorexia/Bulimia Association, Inc. Teaneck NJ National Association of Anorexia Nervosa and Associated Diseases　Highland Park IL
Emphysema	American Lung Association　San Mateo CA
Endometriosis	Endometriosis Association, Inc.　Milwaukee WI
Epilepsy	Epilepsy Foundation of American　Landover MD
Gaucher's Disease	Gaucher's Disease Registry　Orange CA

TABLE B.3 (continued)

DISEASE OR CONDITION	ORGANIZATION
Geriatric Disorders	Gray Panthers Philadelphia PA Jewish Association for Services of the Aged New York NY
Growth Disorders	Little People of America, Inc. Owatonna MN Human Growth Foundation Bethesda MD
Guillain-Barre Syndrome	Guillain-Barre Syndrome National Foundation Akron OH Guillain-Barre Syndrome Support Group International Wynnewood PA
Head Injury	National Head Injury Foundation Framingham MA
Heart Disease	American Heart Association Dallas TX
Hemophilia	National Hemophilia Foundation New York NY American Red Cross Washington DC
Herpes	Herpes Resource Center Palo Alto CA American Social Health Association Palo Alto CA

Huntington's Disease	National Huntington's Disease Association, Inc.
	     New York NY
	Huntington's Disease Foundation of America
	     New York NY

Hypertension (High Blood Pressure)	American Heart Association Dallas TX National High Blood Pressure Education Program Bethesda MD
Incontinence	The Simon Foundation Wilmette IL HIP, Inc. Union SC
Infertility	Resolve, Inc. Belmont MA
Kidney Failure	National Kidney Foundation, Inc. New York NY Diabetic Renal Transplant Self Help Group Brooklyn NY
Learning Disabilities	Foundation for Children with Learning Disabilities New York NY HEALTH Resource Center Washington DC

Lupus Erythematosus	American Lupus Society Lupus Foundation of America, Inc. Arthritis Foundation	Torrance CA St. Louis MO Atlanta GA
Mental Illness	National Alliance for the Mentally Ill Recovery, Inc.	Arlington VA Chicago IL
Liver Disease	American Liver Foundation Children's Liver Foundation, Inc.	Cedar Grove NJ Maplewood NJ
Mental Retardation	Association for Children with Retarded Mental Development Association for Retarded Citizens Council for Exceptional Children Special Olympics	 New York NY Arlington TX Reston VA Washington DC
Migraine Headaches	National Headache Foundation	Chicago IL
Multiple Sclerosis	National Multiple Sclerosis Society Eastern Paralyzed Veterans Association	New York NY New York NY
Muscular Dystrophy	Muscular Dystrophy Association	New York NY
Myasthenia Gravis	Myasthenia Gravis Foundation Muscular Dystrophy Association	White Plains NY New York NY
Narcolepsy	American Narcolepsy Association	San Carlos CA
Neurofibromatosis	National Neurofibromatosis Foundation, Inc.	 New York NY
Obesity	Overeaters Anonymous, Inc.	Los Angeles CA
Paget's Disease	Paget's Disease Foundation, Inc.	New York NY
Parkinson's Disease	American Parkinson's Disease Foundation Parkinson's Disease Foundation Parkinson's Education Program–USA	 New York NY New York NY Newport Beach CA
Psoriasis	National Psoriasis Foundation Psoriasis Research Institute	Portland OR Stanford CA
Rare Diseases	National Organization for Rare Disorders (Table B.2) New Fairfield CT	
Reye's Syndrome	National Reye's Syndrome Foundation, Inc. Belmont MA	

TABLE B.3 (continued)

DISEASE OR CONDITION	ORGANIZATION
Scleroderma	United Scleroderma Foundation Watsonville CA Scleroderma Federation New York NY
Scoliosis	National Scoliosis Foundation, Inc. Belmont MA
Sickle Cell Disease	National Association for Sickle Cell Disease, Inc. Los Angeles CA
Spina Bifida	Spina Bifida Association of America Chicago IL March of Dimes White Plains NY
Spinal Cord Injury	Paralyzed Veterans of America Washington DC National Spinal Cord Injury Association Newton MA American Paralysis Association Short Hills NJ
Stroke	National Stroke Association Denver CO Stroke Clubs International Galveston TX American Heart Association Dallas TX
Stuttering	National Stuttering Project San Francisco CA
Sudden Infant Death Syndrome	National Sudden Infant Death Syndrome Foundation Landover MD The Compassionate Friends, Inc. Oak Brook IL
Tay-Sachs Disease	National Tay-Sachs & Allied Disease Association Cedarhurst NY
Tourette Syndrome	Tourette Syndrome Association Bayside NY
Wilson's Disease	Wilson's Disease Association Washington DC
Organizations dealing with Disability	Clearinghouse for the Handicapped Washington DC Disabled American Veterans Washington DC Goodwill Industries of America, Inc. Bethesda MD National Organization on Disability Washington DC National Handicapped Sports & Recreation Association Washington DC PRIDE Foundation Atlanta GA Scouting for the Handicapped Irving TX

TABLE B.4. Drug and Disease Information Sources

ORGANIZATION	DATA AVAILABLE/ SERVICES	CONTACT:
Food and Drug Administration (FDA) Consumer and Professional Relations Department	• provides drug information through the Bureau of Drugs • publishes the *FDA Drug Bulletin* and other publications • manages contracts and grants for drug use studies • provides mechanisms of communication with health-care professionals	Food and Drug Administration Department of Health and Human Services Rockville MD 20892 phone: 202.295.8012 To report drug-product defects (24-hour emergency number): 301.443.1240
FDA Office of Public Affairs (OPA)	• handles a broad range of inquiries from consumers • publishes *FDA Consumer* and other brochures • develops news releases and communications for mass media	For information on nutrients, drug additives, safety of consumer products: 301.443.3170 For weekly recorded consumer message: 301.443.4489
FDA Toll-free Phone Line for Health-Care Professionals	• provides a mechanism for health-care professionals to ask questions about the agency's policies on medical advertising, marketing, and promotion • allows health-care professionals to report information on potentially illegal promotional activities	phone: 800.238.7332 fax: 800.344.3332

TABLE B.4 (continued)

ORGANIZATION	DATA AVAILABLE/ SERVICES	CONTACT:
Multidisciplinary Association for Psychedelic Studies (MAPS)	• assists legitimate researchers in designing research protocols, securing approval and funding, conducting research studies, and reporting results in the area of psychedelic-drug research • organizes and sponsors conferences and training programs for scientists on the subject of the potential medicinal value of psychedelic drugs • serves as an educational organization and information-exchange clearinghouse for health-care professionals and patients	MAPS 1801 Tippah Avenue Charlotte NC 28205 phone: 704.358.9830

ORGANIZATION	DATA AVAILABLE/ SERVICES	CONTACT:
National Council on Patient Information and Education (NCPIE)	• conducts national education campaigns to improve communication about prescription medications, using television, radio, and print public service announcements • sponsors the only national observance to promote safe and effective use of medications • prepares major research reports describing medication misuse in the U.S. • designs and distributes resources (pamphlets, badges, posters) to support medication information and education activities	Robert M. Bachman Executive Director, NCPIE 666 11th Street, NW Suite 810 Washington DC 20001 phone: 202.347.6711

TABLE B.4 (continued)

ORGANIZATION	DATA AVAILABLE/ SERVICES	CONTACT:
National Pharmaceutical Council (NPC)	• organization of pharmaceutical manufacturers committed to maintaining high research, innovation, quality, and integrity standards • encourages communication between health-care policy leaders and the industry to examine mutual concerns and issues • publishes technical and scientific information for health-care professionals, consumers, and health program administrators • provides the opportunity for pharmacy students to learn about the industry through funded internships	NPC 1894 Preston White Drive Reston VA 22091 phone: 703.620.6390 fax: 703.476.0904

Pharmaceutical Manufacturers Association (PMA)	• organization of over 100 pharmaceutical companies that discover, develop, and produce prescription drugs and biologics • organizes and participates in coalition of consumers, industry groups, and health-care professionals to influence public policy • publishes several summary reports regarding drug development, and pharmaceutical industry, and relevant legislative developments	PMA 1100 Fifteenth Street Washington DC 20005 phone: 202.835.3463
United States Pharmacopeial Convention (USP)	• provides official standards for analytical testing of drug products, such as strength, quality, purity, packaging, and labeling • develops and maintains a clinically-relevant, consensus-based, continually-updated, easy-to-use drug information database for both health professionals and patients • publishes *USP-Dispensing Information (USP-DI)* and *Drug Information for the Consumer* • organizes a database of drug problem reports, health-care professionals can call with information or complete a reporting form	USP Convention 12601 Twinbrook Parkway Rockville MD 20852 phone: 301.881.0666 800.227.8772 To receive reporting forms or report drug problems: 800.638.6725

TABLE B.5. Recommended Reference Books for Consumers

About Your Medicines. Published by the United States Pharmacopeial Convention, Rockville, Maryland. The 1991 edition is available in paperback for approximately $5.95.

AARP Pharmacy Service Prescription Drug Handbook. Published by the American Association of Retired Persons (Scott Foresman), Glenview, Illinois. The 1988 edition is available for approximately $13.95.

The Complete Drug Reference. Published by the United States Pharmacopeial Convention and Consumer Reports Books, New York in 1991.

Consumer Health: A Guide to Intelligent Decisions, fourth edition. Written by Harold Cornacchia and published by Mosby, St. Louis, Missouri in 1989.

Drug Information for the Consumer. Published by the United States Pharmacopeial Convention, Rockville, Maryland. The 1991 edition is available for approximately $25.00.

The Essential Guide to Prescription Drugs. Written by James W. Long and published by Harper Collins, New York in 1991.

The PDR® Family Guide to Prescription Drugs. Released in 1993, this book is published by Medical Economics Data, and has a retail price of approximately $25.00.

Guide to Prescription and Over-the-counter Drugs. Published by the American Medical Association (Random House), New York. The 1988 edition is available for approximately $25.00.

Handbook of Nonprescription Drugs. Edited by Edward Feldman and published by the American Pharmaceutical Association, Washington, DC. The 1991 edition is available for approximately $75.00.

Health Care Services in the 1990s: A Consumer's Guide. Written by Stephen J. Williams and Sandra Guerra, and published by Pantheon, New York in 1988.

Health Quackery: Consumer Union's Report of False Health Claims, Worthless Remedies, and Unproved Therapies. Written by the Editors of Consumer Reports Books, and published by Rinehart & Winston, New York in 1980.

The New Medicine Show. Written by the Editors of Consumer Reports Books, Yonkers, New York in 1989.

The New Our Bodies, Ourselves. Written by Boston Women's Health Book Collective, and published by Simon and Schuster, New York. The 1992 edition is available for approximately $20.00.

Over-the-Counter Pills That Don't Work. Published by the Public Citizens Health Research Group, Washington, DC in 1983.

The Pill Book. Published by Bantam Books, New York in 1990.

Understanding Prescription Drugs. Written by Dorothy Smith and published by Pocket Books, New York. The 1986 book is available for approximately $4.50.

Worst Pills, Best Pills: An Older Adult's Guide to Avoiding Drug-Induced Death and Illness. Written by Sidney Wolfe, and published by Pantheon, New York in 1988.

Index

Page numbers followed by "f" or "t" indicate figures or tables.